"Anyone who has made golf a part of his or her life understands golf as more than a game. The love of golf and God's meaning in our lives makes The Way of an Eagle *identifiable reading, worth every moment."*

Gary V. Adams, the man who brought metalwoods to the game
and founder of Taylor Made Golf Company
and Founder Club Golf Company

"The Way of an Eagle *show us how great champions balance their lives through faith. It helps us understand what faith can mean in our lives, both on and off the course, with wonderful examples to help guide us."*

Jim Awtrey, CEO, PGA of America

"The Way of an Eagle *is a wonderful read for people who are looking for examples of how faith can impact their lives and performance. This is an inspirational and helpful book."*

Ken Blanchard, coauthor of *The One-Minute Manager*
and author of *We Are the Beloved*

"Fabulous reading for all those serious about their golf game and the direction of their lives."

Chaplain John Dolaghan (Ret.), national director,
Fellowship of Christian Athletes National Golf Ministry

"This is much more than another book about golf. In it, some of the game's finest practitioners share their insights into the faith that gives them peace—and the sport that gives them a forum for spreading that faith."

Larry Dorman, *New York Times*

"The qualities demonstrated by the players included in this book are the characteristics of great champions in sport and *in life. We invite you to read this book for insights into the beliefs and values that have made them great."*

Timothy W. Finchem, commissioner, PGA Tour

"If you love God, golf, and other golfers, this book is a must! I believe every golfer should have one. The Way of an Eagle *will encourage you in your faith and provide you with a tremendous tool for sharing your faith with other golfers."*

Ramsey Gilchrist, Senior PGA Tour Chapel

"To read The Way of an Eagle *is to share with these professional golfers the thrilling realization that Christianity is true. The stories of the Tour players found in this book are testimonies of faith and how that faith affects their lives."*

Bobby Grace, president, Bobby Grace Golf Design, Inc.,
makers of "The Fat Lady Swings" milled mallet

"Anyone who had watched an eagle soar will appreciate the subject of this book. . . . This treasure of testimony will be a blessing to all who read it."

Dr. Richard C. Halverson, U.S. Senate Chaplain (Ret.)

"The gamut of emotions, successes, and failures in a game of golf is a microcosmic parallel to the game of life—but when you walk the course with Jesus . . . well, check it out!"

Johnny Hart, creator of *B.C.* and *Wizard of Id* and honorary chairman of the B.C. Open

"This is a remarkable collection of stories from a remarkable group of men and women. By reading this book you will learn a lot about golf, but you will learn even more about life."

Charles S. Mechem Jr., commissioner, Ladies Professional Golf Association

"Life offers many rewards, but few match the privilege of watching firsthand the rigors of applying one's faith to the game of golf. Inside these pages are the insights of humble men and women who have learned how to soar like an eagle. . . . The Way of an Eagle *is a book that shares the secrets of soaring.*"

Larry E. Moody, executive director, Search Ministries PGA Tour Bible study

"Going through The Way of an Eagle *is like having a conversation with Reverend Billy Graham and the late Harvey Penick at the same time. This wonderful collection of bold statements of faith is worth reading—and rereading.*"

Dan Quayle, 44th vice president of the United States

"The Way of an Eagle *is an inspiring tale of how the world's greatest golfers live out their faith not only on the greens and fairways but in their daily lives. It will entertain and inspire not only golfers but all who read it.*"

Ralph E. Reed Jr., executive director, Christian Coalition

"The Way of an Eagle *is a touching and inspirational book on the importance of Christian faith in the lives of some of the world's greatest golfers. Here these top players tell us how they found their faith in God . . . and how their Christian commitment has helped them deal not only with the thrill of victory but also with the agony of defeat.*"

William E. Simon, former secretary of the treasury

"A Christian's life demands faith, commitment, and much discipline. A professional golfer's life requires purpose, dedication to goals, and lots of practice. How these two commitments interweave is a thrilling story told in each life in this book."

Mrs. Karsten Solheim, vice president, Karsten Manufacturing Corporation

"In a day when many stories about our sports heroes are so disturbing, The Way of an Eagle *introduces us to true champion of golf . . . and of life. . . . These personal stories from 'inside the ropes' will uplift and inspire you to pursue the only score that really matters in life—Jesus Christ.*"

J. Cris Stevens, Alternative Ministries, LPGA Tour Fellowship

THE WAY
· OF AN ·
EAGLE

ROBERT DARDEN
AND
P.J. RICHARDSON

THOMAS NELSON PUBLISHERS
Nashville • Atlanta • London • Vancouver

Dedication

Dedicated to my sister Danni Leigh Mayfield.

—Robert Darden

Dedicated to my loving and understanding wife, Billie,

to my sons, Terry and Michael,

and to Jerry and Nancy Slocum,

who unselfishly shared their love for the Lord with me.

—P.J. Richardson

Copyright © 1996 by Bob Darden and P. J. Richardson

All rights reserved. Written permission must be secured from the publisher to use or reproduce any part of this book, except for brief quotations in critical reviews or articles.

Published in Nashville, Tennessee, by Thomas Nelson, Inc., and distributed in Canada by Word Communications, Ltd., Richmond, British Columbia, and in the United Kingdom by Word (UK), Ltd., Milton Keynes, England.

Unless otherwise noted, Scripture quotations are from the NEW KING JAMES VERSION of the Bible. Copyright © 1979, 1980, 1982, 1990, 1994 Thomas Nelson, Inc., Publishers.

Scripture quotations noted TLB are from THE LIVING BIBLE (Wheaton, Illinois: Tyndale House Publishers, 1971) and are used by permission.

Library of Congress Cataloging-in-Publication Data

Darden, Bob. 1954-
    The way of an eagle / Bob Darden and P. J. Richardson
        p.   cm.
    ISBN 0-7852-7701-3
    1. Golfers—Biography.2. Christian biography.I. Richardson, P. J.II. Title.
GV964.A1D371996
796.352'092'2—dc20
[B]
                                                                                    95-33301
                                                                                    CIP

Printed in the United States of America

1 2 3 4 5 6 7 - 02 01 00 99 98 97 96

Contents

A Word from Byron Nelson. vi

A Word from Max Lucado. vii

Acknowledgments. viii

Wally Armstrong. 1

Paul Azinger. 7

Pat Bates. 15

Brad Bryant. 21

Barb Bunkowsky. 27

Bobby Clampett. 31

Jay Delsing. 39

Bob Estes. 45

Rick Fehr. 51

Jackie Gallagher-Smith. 59

Larry Gilbert. 65

Gary Hallberg. 69

Morris Hatalsky. 75

Joe Jimenez. 81

Steve Jones. 85

Patty Jordan. 91

Brian Kamm. 99

Al Kelley. 105

Betsy King. 109

Bernhard Langer. 115

Tom Lehman. 123

Steve Lowery. 131

Don Massengale. 137

Rik Massengale. 141

Dick Mast. 149

Larry Mize. 155

Barb Mucha. 161

Larry Nelson. 169

David Ogrin. 175

Don Pooley. 181

Larry Rinker. 187

Laurie Rinker-Graham. 193

Loren Roberts. 197

Ted Schulz. 203

Scott Simpson. 209

Paul Stankowski. 217

Suzanne Peta Strudwick. 225

Mike Sullivan. 231

Nancy Taylor. 237

Doug Tewell. 241

Stan Utley. 247

DeWitt Weaver. 253

Kermit Zarley. 259

A Word from Byron Nelson

I was very pleased to be asked to write the foreword for *The Way of an Eagle*. Over the past year, Peggy and I have attended several PGA, LPGA, and Senior Tour Bible studies, and it's inspiring to realize that so many of these fine young golfers, their spouses, and their caddies are focused on how to live the right way as much as they are on how to play winning golf.

In order for any of us to do that—to live the right way—it's certainly most important to study the Bible and do what it says. The Bible promises that we will be rewarded someday if we obey Christ's teaching. And the only way we can learn about His teaching is from the Bible.

I was very fortunate to be taught these things by my wonderful Christian parents. Not only because of how it has helped me live my life on this earth, but for the life I hope to have with God in heaven one day. We all know that our life on this earth is really very brief, but eternity is forever—and that heavenly destination is well worth striving for. If we can live properly, we have the assurance of spending eternity with those who have believed as we do.

I've tried very hard all my life to live in this way. And today my friends respect me more for the way I've lived than for the golf I've played, which makes me feel much better than having won any of those tournaments—including the eleven in a row!

The world of professional golf is not an easy one. There are many pressures, many distractions, and many ways to stray from the right path. That's why the stories of these Christian golfers are so encouraging and inspiring. I hope you'll enjoy reading them as you discover how studying the Bible and learning about Jesus has changed these men's and women's lives.

—Byron Nelson

A Word from Max Lucado

I love this book because it unites two of my favorite topics: faith and golf. My faith is much older and, hopefully, much stronger. I came to faith as a child, and I took up golf because my aging body refused to return to the basketball court.

They have much in common, these two friends. Both faith and golf demand time. Both faith and golf demand focus. Both lead you to beg for grace and shake a fist or two at heaven. Faith has its shares of bunkers, and golf has its share of prayers. And I'm still looking for a bumper sticker that reads: "God gave my life a mulligan."

Perhaps that's why I enjoy golf; it puts in eighteen holes what life puts in eighty years—ups and downs and a few good bounces.

And perhaps that's why I admire these golfers you are about to meet. They share the passions. In a game that demands it all, they have given first to a higher call. They aren't perfect, but they have found One who is. They are proud of their profession, but even prouder of their Lord.

To follow Christ as you walk the fairways and greens is no easy task. These golfers are faced with temptations and challenges few of us realize, but they will tell you that there is no person they would rather have in their foursome than the Nazarene carpenter. He may not keep every ball in play, but He does keep every soul in His hand. And you don't have to be a scratch golfer to be on His team.

So here is a salute to all you professionals who set the pace and sink the putts. We are proud of you. May you do the very best and give the glory to the One who made it possible.

And here is a salute to the rest of us who stand in the gallery. Though our games may suffer and our scores may sputter, we have one gift that surpasses it all: a tee-time in heaven. I'll see you there.

—Max Lucado

Acknowledgments

To the many touring professionals who gave so willingly of their time, their stories, and their golf tips.

To John Dolaghan, director of the National Golf Ministry of the Fellowship of Christian Athletes, and his dedicated staff.

To Dean Bouzeos and Tim Kilmer, associate directors.

To Ramsey Gilchrist and Cobby Ware of the Senior Tour Chapel.

To Jim Hiskey and Rob Tipton of *Links Letter.*

To Larry Moody of Search Ministries and the PGA Tour Bible Study Group.

To Cris Stevens of Alternative Ministries and the LPGA Tour Fellowship.

To Mary Darden, photographer, coordinator, and most excellent touring companion.

To the PGA Tour, Senior PGA Tour, and the LPGA Tour for their cooperation.

To the volunteers at the various PGA, Senior, and LPGA tournaments who always made us feel so welcome.

—Robert Darden and P.J. Richardson

Wally Armstrong

WALLY ARMSTRONG EXPLODED onto the PGA Tour in 1973, finishing just three strokes behind Gary Player in his first Masters, and ultimately finishing with a rookie record 280. Over the next eleven years, he played and led in a number of tournaments, finished among the top 80 in earnings six years running, and eventually earned a Lifetime Membership to the Tour.

But it was after Armstrong retired that he became a household name—and face. He parlayed a gift for teaching and gab into a successful second career as golf teacher and swingmeister. Armstrong's famed infomercial with Pat Sum-

Photo courtesy of *Gator Golf*

merall and Kenny Rogers, twenty-odd golf videos (with more than 500,000 units sold), imaginative use of teaching props, and a host of clinics, seminars, and magazine articles have made him instantly recognized even outside the golfing community.

And in the course of all of that frenzied activity, Armstrong has become an active, dynamic ambassador for his faith, with a ministry that reaches far beyond the United States.

During my senior year at the University of Florida, I was captain of the golf team and involved in all kinds of activities, including student government, fraternity activities, the lettermen's club, and the athletic council. That didn't leave me much free time, but there was one more club I wanted to attend—a club for Christian athletes on campus. I was interested in what they were doing and thought it could help me. That year, I attended a couple of their meetings, and they asked me if I would become an officer. That was fine with me—until I learned they had appointed me chaplain!

Thank goodness, at the next meeting we had a special speaker. His name was Ander Crenshaw, and he talked about a person named Jesus Christ and how he had an exciting relationship with Him. He said that as he got to know Jesus and talked with Him, a supernatural power began to act within him.

I had never heard of such a thing before. My only thoughts about God were that He would judge me after I lived my life. I hoped He would grade me on the curve. Like making the cut in a golf tournament where only the top half of the field continues to play after the first 36 holes, I thought if I did more good things than bad, I'd make the cut with God.

But Ander said that was not true. The only way God would accept a person is if he or she accepted His Son, Jesus Christ.

As Ander continued to share, I learned something about Jesus I had never before understood. Jesus came so that we might have eternal life. The Bible says, "For God so loved the world that He gave His only begotten Son, that whoever believes in Him should not perish but have everlasting life" (John 3:16).

Jesus also came to provide a way to know God on a personal level and experience a life with real meaning. Jesus said, "I have come that they may have life, and that they may have it more abundantly" (John 10:10).

Jesus also claimed to be God. He said, "He who has seen Me has seen the Father" (John 14:9). Numerous times men tried to stone Him to death because He claimed to be God. Jesus said, "I am the way, the truth, and the life. No one comes to the Father except through Me" (John 14:6). This clearly showed me that there is only one way to come to God.

From Ander's talk I learned that Christianity is not a "religion," like we think of other religions. It is a close friendship with Jesus Christ, who is God.

And Jesus is not like any other famous person of history. Napoleon was a great person, but he is dead. Buddha was a famous religious leader, but he, too, is dead. Jesus Christ is God, and He is alive today.

As Ander closed his talk, he told us a statement Christ made:

Behold, I stand at the door and knock. If anyone hears My voice and opens the door, I will come in to him and dine with him, and he with Me. (Rev. 3:20)

I realized I had never invited Christ into my life, and I did so a few days later by talking to God through prayer and asking Christ to come into my life to be my Savior and Lord.

Jesus began to live in my life and supply me with the understanding and power to live the kind of life I knew I should live.

My goals and motivation in life are different now that God is a part of my life. Golf used to be my god. I lived to shoot good rounds, to win tournaments, to make the pro tour. When I asked Christ to take over my life, I realized that had to include my golf too.

Now before every round of golf, I commit it to God, then go out and compete as hard as I can. I know God wants me to be a winner. He wants me to give 100 percent of everything I have—in my practice, in using my mind, and in playing the best I know how—and then thank Him for the results, whatever they are. That takes a lot of pressure off because if you do that, you are a winner in God's eyes, no matter what happens.

Memorable Moment

On the golf course, I guess my most memorable time came in my rookie season when I finished with the rookie record at the Masters. I birdied the fourteenth, fifteenth, sixteenth, and seventeenth holes that last day to finish at eight under par and with a 280 total for the tournament. That was an amazing stretch I'll never forget.

The other memorable moment, at least to a lot of people because it is in one of my videos, occurred at the 1978 Western Open. I hit a long shot and my ball rolled down a hill in the rough. I thought I was a goner, but when I got there, the ball was resting on an ice cube—which kept it from rolling down into some very thick bushes! Needless to say, I played that lie in a hurry!

Tip

In the nearly thirty years I've been teaching the game, I have found that the most common characteristic that destroys a golfer's play on the golf course is focusing on too many things—trying to make the swing happen by compartmentalizing it.

If I could get into the mind of the average golfer, I would find all kinds of body commands going on: left arm straight, right elbow bent, keep the elbow in the pocket, keep the knees bent, keep the weight on the inside of the hips, turn the hips forty-five degrees, the shoulders ninety degrees—information that the body can't relate to. Very few of the touring pros are even able to relate to these terms, and they've played golf for many, many years, competitively and professionally.

There's a Chinese proverb that states, "Ship with many captains sails up the mountain." In golf, I would translate this to: "Golfer with many swing keys spends much time in trees with squirrels."

Too much information can destroy a golfer and immobilize his swing. The swing takes about a second and a half to make, and during that period of time a proper swing is needed—a repetitive, consistent, smooth swing, with centeredness of contact, and centrifugal force to gain the maximum clubhead speed.

So what is the one single focus that a golfer should have when he or she is out playing the game? The thousands and thousands of swing thoughts that I've had and the teaching that I've done through the years have led me to believe that the most effective way to play the game is to think simply about making a circle with the golf swing through the ball.

Most golfers don't have a concept of swinging the golf club in a circle. They're deceived by

Photograph by Carroll Morgan

many things that pull them off that simple, functional, circular swing. They don't understand clearly that a golf club was designed so that the club could swing in a circle around the golfer's body or spine.

My tip to any golfer is to stand up with a golf club, with their arms outstretched and their back straight, very much like a baseball player, and swing the club around their body in a circular manner, letting the club shaft touch the tip of their left shoulder on the follow-through and the tip of their right shoulder on the backswing.

Then I have them bend from the hip sockets, stick their bottom out, bend their knees a little bit, and continue to swing the club like that, touching each shoulder tip—all the way down to where the club is brushing the ground.

If a ball were to get in the way of this motion, which is very much like a tilted merry-go-round or the propellers of a helicopter, the clubhead would square at the bottom of the arc. And if a ball were put there at that moment of centrifugal circular motion, the ball would come off the clubhead and be sent in the very direction that the clubface was pointed at the moment of impact.

This is the essence of the golf swing.

In other words, there's no backward and forward motion or upward and downward motion. This is an excellent way to test yourself and develop a feel for the circular power that you have when you swing the golf club correctly. If a golfer creates a circular motion like what I've described, and the circle comes around, and the face is square to the target, the clubhead will run into the ball and the ball will run into the target.

That is the essence of a great golf swing.

So the key elements that are involved in swinging the club are: creating the circle, empowering the circle with a good ninety-degree wrist set and reset, supporting the circle with a good lower-body coil and uncoil and stable legs, and setting the circle to the ground so that it can consistently strike the ball—all of which involve good posture with the back straight, the knees slightly flexed, the bottom out, a small arch in the back, and the chin up. This allows the shoulders to turn around the spine with the arms following, delivering the clubhead to the ball.

Being a circle maker is the name of the game.

It's as simple as that.

Paul Azinger

SURE, PAUL AZINGER HAS won eleven tournaments. And no doubt you know that he's won tournaments seven years in a row. You may even know that he's earned more than seven million dollars on the PGA Tour. And you probably watched the improbable bunker shot on the eighteenth green at Memorial. But none of Paul Azinger's accomplishments match his defeat of lymphatic cancer.

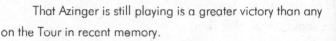

That Azinger is still playing is a greater victory than any on the Tour in recent memory.

Azinger isn't all the way back. He hasn't won a tournament since the 1993 PGA Championship. And it may be a

Photo courtesy of PGA TOUR

while before he's atop the earnings board once again. But Paul Azinger is a winner for now and for all time.

His heroic struggle with lymphoma, his gutty comeback, and his inspirational message have all touched more people—golfers and nongolfers alike—than he'll ever know.

And when you've come back from the brink of sudden death elimination on life's eighteenth hole, every day from there on is the best day of all.

Ask Paul Azinger.

I was probably the happiest guy on earth.

On the last hole of the 1993 Memorial Tournament, I holed a bunker shot to win. There's just no greater feeling than to win a tournament that way.

It was the bunker shot of my life. I was just hoping to get the ball out softly on the green. So when it coasted toward the hole and into the cup, I was in shock. The birdie put me one shot ahead of my good friend, Payne Stewart, giving me my first victory of the year and extending my winning streak to seven consecutive years.

It was the thrill of a lifetime.

Reading about myself the next day and enjoying the satisfaction that came with winning that tournament gave me the contentment that only winning can bring.

The next week at the Westchester Classic, I was looking forward to explaining to the press how I hit the winning bunker shot—about that little lump of sand behind my ball. And how it was all I could do to whack the sand so the ball would float over the lip and trickle gently into the hole.

But they didn't ask me about the bunker shot.

The first question was, "Paul, now that you've won the Memorial, you're probably the best player in the world who's never won a major. What do you need to do differently to win a major championship?"

Suddenly, all the contentment I felt from winning the Memorial was stolen from me—just like that. So much for being the happiest guy on earth.

Now the pressure was on me to win a major championship.

A few weeks later, I had a chance to do it at the U.S. Open at Baltusrol. I ended up finishing third—losing by only three shots. I was pretty satisfied with my performance, but I was also greatly disappointed that I had let the opportunity get away. But I figured with the PGA Championship coming up, I'd have another chance.

During the practice rounds at Inverness for the PGA, I was nervous. I knew how good I was hitting the ball and had every reason to believe that I could contend. After shooting 69-66 the first two rounds, I was four shots behind the leader, Vijay Singh.

Before coming to the PGA Championship, I was having a lot of pain in my right shoulder. My doctor was concerned and did an MRI to look at the bone a few weeks earlier. The results came in, and on Friday night, two rounds into the tournament, I received a phone call from Dr. Jobe.

"'Zinger, that shoulder looks abnormal to me," he said with a serious tone. "I'd like to do a biopsy."

"When do you want to do it?" I asked.

"Tuesday or Thursday of next week."

"Dr. Jobe," I pleaded, "I'm playing great. I've got a chance to win the PGA. The Ryder Cup's coming up. Can't we do it later?"

"Well, it could be some kind of infection," he said. "I'm going to give you some antibiotics. Keep taking an anti-inflammatory, and we'll put it off."

The next day I shot a 69, followed by a 68. I birdied four of the last seven holes and was fortunate enough to get into a play-off with Greg Norman. And I was even more fortunate that a couple of his putts didn't go in. After two play-off holes, I had won my first major championship.

Talk about contentment and happiness! I really was the happiest guy on earth. I'd gotten the press off my back for life. This was the ultimate. I had won my major championship, and I would probably never have to deal with pressure from the media again.

That is, until after the Ryder Cup.

A few weeks after the PGA, the press was at it again. Now the big question was, "Paul, now that you've won the PGA and two other tournaments this year, you have a chance to be the leading money winner and player of the year. What are you going to do differently? Are you going to continue your schedule?"

I thought, *Is this* ever *going to stop? It just never ends!*

The joy I felt from winning the PGA started to wane.

It's almost like buying a new car. At first, you don't want anybody touching it. You wash it every week. Then, a couple weeks later, you might wash it again. Then you wash it every three months. The next thing you know, someone dings it, and you don't even care.

The contentment from being a major champion was slowly dissolving.

Nick Price ended up being Player of the Year and leading money winner. I was about $20,000 short. But, obviously, the year was a tremendous success.

I was still putting off the biopsy because I had a few more events to play. But the week before the Skins Game, I hurt my back and had to withdraw from the Shark Shootout. I was close to Los Angeles and Centinela Hospital, so I went to see Dr. Wadkins for my back and Dr. Jobe for my shoulder.

They ordered a bone scan from head to toe and another MRI. The MRI was to isolate the shoulder, and the bone scan was to look at my back.

When I saw the X rays of the bone scan, the area of the shoulder was pitch black. It didn't look good.

"There are no ifs, ands, or buts about it," Dr. Jobe said. "We're doing a biopsy Tuesday after the Skins Game."

After not winning a single skin, I went back for the biopsy. They removed a little window out of the bone and said it looked good. It didn't look like any kind of malignancy. But it would be seven to ten days before I found out the results of the biopsy.

Two days later, I got a call from Dr. Jobe's secretary. She said Dr. Jobe wanted to see me in his office at 1:00 P.M. on Friday.

I knew something was wrong. I didn't eat dinner. I didn't eat breakfast. And I didn't each lunch. When I got to the hospital, I saw Dr. Jobe in the hallway and didn't even say hello.

"How am I?" I asked.

"It's not good," he answered. And we went into his office. My wife and kids were there when he told me I had cancer of the bone in my shoulder.

I was in shock. That was the last thing I expected to hear. I thought maybe it was some kind of weird stress fracture or an infection of some kind. But I didn't expect him to say _cancer_.

"How do you treat it?" I asked nervously.

"With chemotherapy and radiation," he said solemnly.

"Well, what do we do next?"

"We're going to go across the street and see if the cancer spread."

The shock was still ringing. Here I was, thirty-three years old. Fairly bulletproof. Suddenly, that wasn't the case.

The next thing I knew, I was in an X-ray room lying on an ice-cold table—shivering from nervousness.

It was an awful feeling.

As I lay there while the technicians adjusted the machines, a genuine feeling of fear came upon me: _I could die from cancer._ But then another reality hit me: _I'm going to die eventually anyway._ Whether from cancer or something else, I'm _definitely_ going to _die._ It's just a question of when.

In that same moment, something Larry Moody, the man who leads our Bible study on the PGA Tour, has said to me many times came to mind: "Zinger, we're not in the land of the living going to the land of the dying. We're in the land of the dying, trying to get into the land of the living."

My major championship, my ten victories before that, everything I had accomplished in golf, became meaningless to me.

All I wanted to do was live.

I don't know how successful you are. I don't know how big your house is, how much money you have, or how nice your car is. But I'm here to tell you, we came into this world with nothing, and we're leaving with nothing. And everything we get along the way is a blessing from God. If you're finding your contentment and happiness in your accomplishments or from the amount of money and possessions you own, I'm here to tell you *it doesn't last.*

I've made a lot of money since I've been on the Tour, and I've won a lot of tournaments. That happiness is always temporary.

The only way you will ever have true contentment is in a personal relationship with Jesus Christ. I'm not saying that nothing ever bothers me and I don't have problems, but I feel like I've found the answer to the six-foot hole. I know I'll spend eternity with God.

And I have a promise that, as a child of God, He'll help me deal with anything. He promises to give me contentment no matter what life brings—even cancer.

God did not intend for this world to be the best of all possible places. But it's a place where we can prepare for the best of all possible places.

We need to recognize that we are separated from a perfect God because of our sin, and by placing our faith in Jesus Christ, we are promised eternal life. It's the only way to experience the "peace that passes all understanding" that the Bible talks about.

Even though it's great to be called a PGA Tour player, and it's probably even greater to be called a PGA Champion, no greater gift is mine than to be called a child of God, because I place my trust in Jesus Christ.

Memorable Moment

Probably the shot I will most be remembered for in my career is the bunker shot I hit on the eighteenth hole at the Memorial Tournament in May 1993. I was tied with Corey Pavin on the last hole—one shot behind Payne Stewart. I hit my second shot into the greenside bunker with a five iron.

Payne followed me in the bunker. He hit a seven iron for his second shot and buried his ball, then knocked it out about ten feet behind the hole, which was a great shot.

All I was trying to do was get close, because I knew Payne had a hard putt.

Many times when you're trying to make a bunker shot or a chip shot, you gun it way past the hole. I didn't want to make a bogie and miss a play-off by a shot. I needed to hit it hard, but I needed the ball to come out of the bunker with a great deal of spin.

So I rehearsed everything about the shot in my mind before I even picked up the club. Then I took my stance in the bunker and swung the club as hard as I could.

The ball came out high and soft with some spin, just clearing the lip. It landed about ten feet from the hole and began to trickle back. It broke about two feet and actually went in the *back* of the hole.

I went to my knees. Since then it has been written that I "howled toward the heavens."

This clearly was one of my most memorable moments.

Tip

I used to be a horrible bunker player. Very rarely could I get up and down out of the trap. I would either leave the ball in the sand or scull the shot across the green. So I set out to improve my sand play with a lot of hard work and practice.

I used to stand very close to

Photograph by Sam Greenwood/PGA TOUR

the ball. I was always told, "Open the clubface, pick the club up, and cut across the ball, hitting two inches behind it." Unfortunately, it is not that simple. So, with significant help from some very good bunker players, I developed my own technique.

When I take my stance in the bunker, my weight is evenly distributed: 50 percent of my weight on the left foot and 50 percent on the right foot. I also get further away from the ball than normal, in a bit of a sitting position.

Next, I make sure that the ball is positioned evenly with my sternum. Then I make a fairly low stroke, with a very open clubface.

As you practice this technique, try to hit somewhere behind the ball. If you're hitting the ball fat (which, in golfing terms, means too much turf is taken with the clubhead upon impact), move your sternum slightly ahead of the ball. If you're hitting the ball thin, move your sternum slightly behind the ball.

Sometimes golfers will hit the ball fat, and the club will bounce into the ball, and they'll think they're hitting the ball thin when in reality, they're still hitting it fat. You have to be aware that if that's the case, you should move your sternum ahead of the ball.

The key to success in the bunker is to never let your clubface turn over after you've hit the shot. In order to practice this, put your left hand in your left pocket and hold the club with your right hand. Make a swing with your club and you'll notice that the clubface naturally does not turn over.

A right-handed swing will usually be the perfect swing. Make sure to get further away from the ball, in a sitting position, with a slightly open stance. The club can go back as low or as steep as you want to take it. I initially take it back fairly low and then let it come up.

From a fifty-fifty weight distribution, you have to determine what is a normal, comfortable swing for you. Take notice of how far the ball flies in the air. That distance is your normal result produced by your normal swing and your normal weight distribution.

Now you can fool around and figure out what happens if you put 70 percent of your weight on your left side and use the same normal swing. What happens if you put 70 percent of your weight on your right side and make that same normal swing? I found if your weight's right, the ball goes further. And if your weight's left, the ball goes shorter.

We get many different lies in bunkers, and I try to adjust my bunker game based on how my current situation differs from my normal situation. If my normal weight distribution is fifty-fifty, will my present stance change the weight distribution? If my normal ball position is even with my sternum, will that have to change based on my lie? Will I have to change the speed of my normal swing? Does the sand I am in differ from the texture of my normal sand at home?

When I dig into the sand in a bunker, I'm not digging in to get good footing. I'm digging in to see how deep it is. I know if there's less sand than normal, the ball will go further with the same swing. Or if there's more sand than normal, the ball will go shorter.

So when I'm digging in, I'm trying to figure out if there's more or less sand than my usual home course sand—the sand I practice in the most.

This brings me to my final observation. There is no improvement without practice. If you want to be a better bunker player, you must practice long enough to find a technique that works for you.

Pat Bates

PAT BATES IS YOUNG, handsome, and appears to have a brilliant future ahead of him in professional golf. His third-place finish in the 1994 NIKE Tour gave Bates a well-deserved exemption for the 1995 PGA Tour.

The three-time All-American had a memorable career at the University of Florida on a team that included Dudley Hart, Chris DeMarco, and Jeff Barlow. He won three collegiate tournaments, including the 1990 *Golf Digest* Invitational at the TPC at The Woodlands.

Photograph by P. J. Richardson

Bates was one of the longest hitters on the NIKE Tour, but he's had an equally strong impact as a faithful, supportive member of the Fellowship of Christian Athletes (FCA) and the PGA Tour Bible studies.

I was raised in a Catholic environment. We went to church every Sunday—my mom and dad made us go! We went to Confraternity of Catholic Doctrine (CCD) and stuff. I had great parents and a great upbringing. Even though they may not have known they were doing it, they taught me the ways of the Lord through CCD. I had a recognition of God and a foundation in the faith.

Throughout high school and college, especially college at the University of Florida, I got into all kinds of trouble. I strayed from the faith, like so many young adults do. These days, a normal college life is not serving the Lord! I was into all kinds of bad things, but I still thought I was a good person. I was as far from the Fellowship of Christian Athletes as you could go.

During my senior year of college, I began to feel guilty about some of the things I was doing. I think it goes back to my upbringing: knowing what was right and what was wrong.

I was heading to South Africa to play the South African tour after I'd just turned pro in 1992. Before I left, I stayed with my best friend's parents—the Alfieris—who were also from a Catholic background. They'd rededicated their lives to Jesus about five years before. They were on fire; they preached the Lord to me all week. I heard the things they were saying and I was getting scared because I knew I hadn't lived a solid life. I knew I was in the midst of sin. I thought I was in trouble.

"I'm getting scared," I told the Alfieris. And they said, "Hey, that's okay! 'The fear of the LORD is the beginning of knowledge'" (Prov. 1:7). That really hit home. I thought, *Wow—maybe I'm having the right kind of feelings.*

Later they showed me the movie *Jesus of Nazareth,* and they explained the Bible to me—and all of this made perfect sense. I felt like I couldn't dispute it. I became a Christian that week on January 8, 1992.

The Alfieris have been great—they've been right there for me over the past few years.

Have you had the opportunity to speak out on your faith since that time?

I do some things with FCA, especially the Bible studies, but I haven't done any speaking engagements for them. I've spoken at a few churches, but most people don't know who I am. That probably has something to do with it. Not a lot of public speaking yet, but I'd like to.

How has having a personal relationship with Jesus affected your life on a day-to-day basis?

Since becoming a Christian, I've tried to walk in the Spirit and let the Spirit lead me. It has been an incredible transformation because I used to look at everything through my eyes and how I thought things should be. Now I try to look at everything through godly eyes by asking, "How does all of this fit into God's plan?"

That's how I try to lead my life, day in and day out. I never had that before I had a relationship with Jesus Christ.

Toward the end of 1993, I was playing in a Canadian Tour event, and during the tournament I was in third place going into the tenth hole on the last round, so I had a chance to win. I hit my second shot on a par five into some high grass. I looked and looked around for it and couldn't find it. Just as I reached the five-minute limit, I found the ball. I closed out the hole with a five-foot putt for a six.

But when I pulled it out of the cup, I realized that the ball was an old Titleist 5, all nicked and cut up. I realized, "Oh my gosh—this is not my ball!" What were the chances of my finding another Titleist 5 in there?

I went to the scorer, thinking I was disqualified—DQ'd. But he said it was only a two-shot penalty for hitting the wrong ball, plus having to go back to the place where the ball was hit. So I ended up with a ten.

I'd done the same thing once before in college, and I thought, *This is crazy. I need to mark my ball—there's no doubt about that.* So I opened my Bible that night and realized I needed to start marking my balls with Bible verses. For a while I alternated Old and New Testaments—every ball would be a different Bible verse. That was okay for a while, but I finally had so many I couldn't remember them all. So now I just stick with one Bible verse for the week. I'll read something powerful and put it on the golf ball all that week.

At one point in 1994, I flew to three straight tournaments, including a Monday through Wednesday tournament. For those tournaments I wrote Hebrews 10:36: "For you have need of endurance, so that after you have done the will of God, you may receive the promise." That was to give me endurance for a couple of weeks—and it worked! I finished second, second, and eighth in those three tournaments!

Also in 1994, while playing in the NIKE Tour in Shreveport, going into the third round, I was around fourteen under for the tournament—just a couple shots behind the leader. But on the eighteenth hole, I hit it right into a creek, right into the heart of the swamp.

The marshal said, "Do you want your ball?" I said, "No, just leave it there. I'll drop another one." I smiled and finished the hole. And I ended up with a bogey. I was pretty disappointed; I went to four shots back and had been just a shot or two back on what should have been an easy birdie hole.

The next morning, the first person I saw on the course was that same marshal from the eighteenth hole. He said, "You know, I went down there and picked your ball out of the water. I saw the Bible verse on it, and I went home and read it. I have to tell you, I just became a Christian a couple of weeks ago, and those were real encouraging words for me!"

That really humbled me. Here I was all upset over a bogey, and God was using it for His church's glory. I figure if I need to take a bogey for God—that's fine. It puts it all in perspective.

It really helped me understand that I'm not in complete control. It is something that I accept. Hopefully, I do the best I can—and leave it up to the Lord as to what's going to happen.

Memorable Moment

On the NIKE Tour, winning the Dakota Dunes Open was my highlight. The thing that made it so neat was that I'd just recently lost the tournament in Shreveport earlier by finishing second. A couple of weeks later, I finished second again. A month after that, I was leading by three shots going into the last round and shot a 74 and lost by a shot again! Even though I was playing well and making some money, I was wondering if I'd ever close one out.

So when I finally had a chance to win in South Dakota in August, I shot a 65 in the last round and birdied the last three holes to win by two shots. So the way that I won and the way that it all happened—it was an exciting time for me.

As I came down through the stretch on the sixteenth hole, I was fortunate because I had a sixty-foot putt in the middle of a slope. I just smacked it, and it hit the hole for a birdie. I got up to the seventeenth and said, "You know, this just might be my week." I birdied it and the eighteenth as well.

All those second-place finishes kept me strong mentally to win, and that's what growing is all about—learning from experience. The win and the other good finishes put me third on the NIKE Tour money list and guaranteed me a slot on the PGA Tour in 1995. So it was a great time, a great win.

Tip

I think you should try to get into a good setup position where your head, your shoulders, your hands, your knees, and your feet are all going parallel in the same direction. I see so many amateurs line up to the right and come up over the top of their shoulders.

But my main tip would be to get lessons because golf is a skill. Nobody is born a great golfer. It's something that you develop over time. If you can get somebody to help you with your golf swing and your game, you're going to improve. There's almost nobody who plays golf without a teacher. Even the best players in the world all have somebody to look at their swing. So I would suggest that you go see your local PGA pro and say, "Do you see any stroke savers?"

I see so many amateurs who go to the range by themselves and swing. They don't have anything to work on; they're just hitting balls. Then they don't find themselves getting better. But if you'll go see somebody like the local pro or somebody that you've heard about—anyone who has some golf knowledge—he or she is going to be able to help you and improve your game.

Of course, the instructor shouldn't take you out of your natural swing. If you have a particular swing, and somebody has a theory about a different swing—that everybody should swing that way—that's not taking into account a person's natural tendencies.

But seek out a pro for regular lessons—that would be my tip.

Photograph by Pete Fontaine/PGA TOUR

Brad Bryant

THEY AFFECTIONATELY CALL him "Dr. Dirt," and the sad-eyed man with the big dimples is one of the most popular pros on the PGA Tour. Period. And it isn't because of his golfing prowess, either—although he's had a wildly successful career, with more than $2 million in winnings, despite some debilitating injuries.

But Bryant was probably the guy that inspired the phrase "Nice guys finish second." He's had an incredible seven second-place finishes since 1982, including the Kmart Greater Greensboro Open and the Doral-Ryder Open, both in 1994. He was the only non-winner invited to

Photo courtesy of PGA TOUR

the Tour Championship, finishing one stroke behind the Mark McCumber-Fuzzy Zoeller playoff. Bryant then turned around and won the unofficial JCPenney Classic (with Marta Figueras-Dotti). His sizzling 1994 ended by finishing first in the year-end PGA Tour Statistics in birdies with 397.

Maybe it would have been more appropriate if he'd finished second!

My father is a Baptist preacher and pastored his first church when he was seventeen. So, of course, I've been going to church since I was born. I grew up in the church. My dad (W. H. "Dub" Bryant) went to Southwestern Seminary, so we lived in Fort Worth for a time. He pastored two churches in central Texas before moving to New Mexico where he pastored a church for seventeen years.

We had a phenomenal time growing up, especially at the church in New

Mexico. We had so many wonderful things happen. The people were great, and my dad was one of the best pastors I've ever known. He really understood what being a pastor was all about—he equipped the people, then got out of the way and let them do the work.

He's now the director of evangelism for North and South Dakota and Montana and works with the pastors there.

I was seven and a half when I met the Lord. It was really something. My mom said she was afraid for me to go to school because I had to cross a couple streets, and she knew that I was really searching at the time! But even at seven and a half, I understood that we are all sinners, and because of that I was going to hell. I also understood that Christ died for my sins, so I gave my life to Christ because that was the only way to go to heaven instead of hell! My dad got to baptise me, my brother, and my sister—so that was pretty neat too!

It wasn't until I became older that I really began to understand that God also had a plan for my life, more than just saving me from hell.

Since then, my life has had a lot of peaks and valleys, including some very emotional times. I had a very bad injury to my left shoulder for a while. But I have been fortunate because of the way my parents taught me and the way my parents lived. I never distrusted that God would take care of me and my family.

Plus, no matter what the state of my spiritual life is, I realize it's not up to me to be a saint. I can't do that; I can't be perfect.

In 1987, after I was hurt, I lost my playing privileges and was off the Tour for a year—and that was probably the best year my wife and I have had. I slept in my own bed four straight months! That was the first time I'd done that since I was sixteen—and it's been that long since I've done it again! My wife and I really had a chance to start setting some groundwork in our marriage. We had some difficult problems to work through, but that enabled us to go back and work on the foundation of our marriage.

We've been married twenty years, and our marriage is better now than it was a year after we were married. We're finally beginning to understand each other better.

As for golf, I've had a bunch of seconds. I've played nearly twenty years without winning. Of course, every time someone writes an article about me, it begins, "Brad Bryant, who currently holds the record for the second-longest run on the Tour without a victory . . ."

But I know that when God is ready to let me win, or when I'm ready to win, it will happen. There have been times in my life when I was glad I didn't win because I would have done my testimony and my witness a great deal of harm. So when God is ready to use me in that way, He'll let me win. But I think I still need preparation to get me to the point that I can do that.

No matter where Sue and I have been, there's been one Scripture verse that we've always really believed is true. It says no matter what we have to face in this world—whatever pain or suffering or joy that we face in this world—it will not compare to the joy we will have once we get to heaven and are with Christ (Rom. 8:18). It gives me a huge amount of satisfaction in life to know that no matter where I'm at, ultimately I know how all of this is going to come out—that the battle has already been won.

Memorable Moment

I've been fortunate in that I've always known that God doesn't care if I'm the world's greatest golfer. I've never once worried that He was involved in my golf game. I don't think that's His responsibility. I go out and play to the best of my ability, and I try to live my life as best I can. Then it is up to God to take care of the rest. It's not whether I get good bounces or bad bounces—I figure that's just part of living.

I don't really have what I would call outstanding golf memories. I know when I got the ball on the green on the seventeenth hole in 1982 in the Players Championship, I was pretty happy. I had played very, very poorly that entire year, but I had led that tournament the whole way until Jerry Pate birdied the last two holes to beat me.

I still remember hitting that ball on the green, because if I could hit that ball and make a par, my career would be secure for another year. But if I missed the green and hit the ball into the water, there was a chance I wouldn't be secure for the next year.

But when I walked off the green, I had made $68,000 that week, and I thought, *Gosh, I've done the best I could and I've provided for my family.* And anyone who complains about making nearly seventy grand in a week ought to be shot! I don't think I'll ever forget that.

Conversely, I'll never forget losing a tournament in Canada in 1993, and how frustrated I was when I kept hitting good shots that kept turning out so badly. In the last seven holes, I hit three shots that I couldn't have hit any better. I hit great golf shots, but each time they turned up in the worst place possible on the hole.

Tip

I've always paid attention to my equipment, making sure that the shaft—the particular length and weight of the golf club—fits my body. One of the biggest problems in golf is that amateurs have no idea how to fit themselves for equipment. They don't even think about it.

Through the years, everything has been toward swing weight, length, and that sort of stuff—which really doesn't matter. Swing weight is the static weight of something that you're going to use while it is in motion. That's really not a good measure of what you're going to be doing. Instead, I think that you can take some measurements of yourself and find out pretty quickly what you need to do.

Most people, especially men, if they are barrel-chested, swing too far. If you're built like me—kind of thin in the chest and not real strong in the shoulders—you can take a pretty long backswing. But if you're big-chested and you have strong

Photograph by Pete Fontaine/PGA TOUR

shoulders, strong arms, and a strong back, you should take a very short backswing. Most people take the club back way too far. Most people use their legs way too much.

That is the number-one problem I see with amateur players. The thing I would tell them first is not to use their legs at all. Period. Their legs have to remain absolutely passive in the golf swing, and they have to learn to turn their chest and upper body. That is the number-one problem amateurs have.

Once you learn to do that, then you can easily fit clubs to your size. I think that most people play clubs a little bit too long and a little bit too heavy for them. When you swing a club, it becomes exponentially heavier because of the centrifugal force pulling on the head. All of a sudden you have something very heavy in motion that may have been very light when it was static. It is also something that is now uncontrollable.

Having too light a shaft makes the clubhead too heavy, which, when you swing it, increases that weight. People just can't control it.

That's the biggest problem they've had with graphite shafts. And that's why back in 1990, I tried to get the manufacturers to build heavier graphite shafts. It took about two years before the Loomis company started building heavier shafts like I wanted. Now, of course, nearly everybody on the Tour who plays with graphite shafts is playing with shafts that are nearly the same weight as steel. They're much heavier than what the engineers originally envisioned.

So . . . learn to hit a golf ball without moving your knees. In fact, don't move your knees at all. Hey, if you can only hit the ball fifty yards, without moving your knees, that's great. And as you can increase your distance, *then* begin to move your knees slightly.

Always remember that your knees only move as much as your shoulders move. They can never move farther. Most people move their knees considerably farther than they move their shoulders. They'll move their right knee to the right on their backswing, their left knee will come in, and both knees will get out from under the shoulders—and they lose the support in their golf swing.

The thing that has helped my game, and I'm probably one of the more improved swingers on the Tour right now, is that I learned to keep my knees underneath my shoulders throughout my swing. My shoulders and my upper body are always supported by my legs, and my balance remains good. As soon as you get off balance, you can't hit good golf shots.

Strangely enough, no one teaches much about balance.

The way to achieve balance is to stand with your spine fairly erect and straight—not curved—and then get your knees under your shoulders. Don't get too bent over. If you get so bent over that your shoulders are closer to the ball than your knees, you'll be out of balance. The way your body is made, to hit a golf ball you need to stand where your knees are almost directly under your shoulders in a vertical position, with your spine fully erect and straight. If you'll do that, you'll have good balance.

Note: As *The Way of an Eagle* went to press, in October 1995, Brad Bryant finally broke through, winning the Walt Disney Classic by a stroke. It was Dr. Dirt's 460th career start on the PGA Tour.

Barb Bunkowsky

BENEATH THE DAZZLING smile and great mane of beautiful hair is one tough little golfer. Barb Bunkowsky has steadily become a force to be reckoned with on the LPGA Tour in recent years after a long, difficult apprenticeship.

Despite winning the Chrysler-Plymouth Charity Classic in 1984, the Canadian-born Bunkowsky struggled through a number of tough seasons. Eventually, however, the poise and skills that made her a top amateur golfer (1981 AIAW National Champion) began to emerge.

In 1993-94 alone, Bunkowsky earned more than $300,000 and punctuated her all-around strong play with a

Photo courtesy of LPGA TOUR

third-place finish at the Sprint Championship, a third-place tie at the ShopRite LPGA Classic, and a fifth-place tie at the Youngstown-Warren LPGA Classic.

Both of my parents were Lutheran, and we went to church regularly every Sunday. I didn't go to a lot of Bible studies; it was mostly just church on Sundays. I went to church because I had to go to church.

I first accepted Christ as my Savior in about 1986 in Hawaii. I'd been going through a lot of stuff through the off-season. The Hawaii tournament was in March, so the January and February before that I'd been going through a lot of difficult times. I was struggling a bunch.

I was on a path to destruction, and I knew it. I'd been drinking a lot, and I'd been very promiscuous—I was in that whole scene. I was on a road where I knew I had to make a choice. The Lord eventually just humbled me to make that choice. Sometimes He has to break us first before we learn. Sometimes it takes pain. Everybody can relate to that; everybody's had a painful experience in their life. And while I'd made some friends along the way in the Fellowship of Christian Athletes, I had never really committed my life to Christ. Finally, I thought, *I need to give my life over to Christ to run—I can't do it any more.*

So I went to be with a group of Christians on the Tour. I went to the fellowship because I wanted to go there. I was hungering for the Lord. I was thirsting for knowledge, thirsting for the answers. And over a period of time, I came to know Jesus through the Bible study.

I don't seem to trust like a lot of people do, so it took me longer. It had nothing to do with my original religion; I just don't trust much of anything. Or didn't. Since then I've had to remove the walls, layer by layer.

I was struggling with so many different things in those days: self-esteem, confidence, so many, many things. Becoming a Christian was a gradual sorting out of all of those things—and still is.

It didn't really hurt when I parted from my old friends because I knew I had to. I didn't have that many friends, so it wasn't such a big deal. But the friends I did have weren't real friends anyhow—even though I thought they were. I knew they were on a path to destruction, and I didn't want to keep going down with them.

I didn't make friendships easily back then because I didn't know how to. I was hiding behind drinking. When I'd get bored with life, I'd be promiscuous. I like my current lifestyle much better. I'm much happier, and it is less frustrating.

And now I can go back to them and give them support, when at that time I couldn't.

But there are times when I'm more frustrated now than when I wasn't a Christian, because now I have to deal with my sin. Before I never had to deal with it; I just kept on going. I'm certainly more humble now! I'm convicted more—sometimes right away! So becoming a Christian has made a definite impact on my life.

One big thing I've noticed lately is that I have more hope and more purpose in coming out to play golf. Before it was just chasing the white ball.

Now there are more opportunities where I can spread the gospel—such as getting to know people in the Wednesday pro-am tournaments. I used to struggle on Wednesdays with pro-ams. Meeting four new people every week and having to go out and play a game of golf with them was really a struggle for me. But the more I prayed, and the more I asked for opportunities to arise during the day, the more I enjoyed it.

Now I talk about it all the time. It seems like any question I'm asked can always bring me back around to my faith. I don't do it on purpose to get somebody to "come to the Lord," but when someone asks me a question, if I want to answer it honestly, the Lord has to be involved.

Cris Stevens's Bible study has had a definite impact. It helps me during the times my faith is wavering a little bit to go there and have fellowship with the other girls on tour, to get out of my own little environment. To be with other Christians on tour, to have some support, to talk about your faith—all of that is important.

I learned a little bit from all of the Christian players on the Tour just by watching them. When they shot bad rounds, I watched how they handled the situation—that made me realize that they had a lot of hope, a lot of joy, and a lot of peace in their lives. I wanted a part of that. I could see those qualities in every Christian I came in contact with.

I use my faith all the time now when I'm playing and practicing. When I'm filled with anxiety because I haven't been practicing, I ask God to give me peace about that. When I'm playing with a partner who is going through a tough time, I ask the Lord to give me the opportunity to share with her and encourage her all week.

I speak a lot to youth and college groups on the LPGA Tour. It's really neat to see a kid come to know the Lord—I wish I had done it when I was younger. But then, the Lord always has you in a different place, and He wants you to meet Him on *His* timing—not on *your* timing. Now I'm just thankful that I did find the Lord at all. It is neat to see and hear the young people, to know there could be a couple of kids that very morning committing their lives to Christ. You never know who it will be.

So, in the end, it was the hope that attracted me. Definitely the hope. When I did it for myself, I got all frustrated. When I did it for the Lord, my life immediately began to have more meaning and more purpose.

Memorable Moment

I used to quit when I'd start playing badly; I would really quit. Now with the Lord, I'm more at peace. When things start going badly, I can make light of it. I don't take life so seriously; I'm not so hard on myself.

I was in a tournament in late 1994, and I was playing very well. But on the third day I started playing badly. I just asked the Lord to get me through, because it was a tough day, and I asked Him to put everything in perspective—even though I wasn't going to finish as well as I thought I was going to.

I finished up and realized what was more important. That was a special time.

Tip

I feel like I'm a pretty good driver. I finished seventh in accuracy in 1993. I just can drive the ball right up the middle.

So from an amateur's standpoint, I'd say: Try not to go at it too hard; try not to kill it every time. It didn't take me long to realize that being in the middle of the fairway is better than being in the trees or being in the rough with a bad lie.

As a result, I say to golfers all the time, "Don't try to go at it as hard. Try to put a controlled swing on it."

I try to set up the same way every time and look at the green. I set up according to where the trouble is. If the trouble is down on the left side, I'll stand on the left side and hit out to the right. If the trouble is on the right side, I'll stand on the right side and hit off to the left. This gives me more green to hit away from the trouble. And it gives me more fairway to look at as well.

Photograph by Jeff Hornback

Bobby Clampett

YOU'VE PROBABLY SEEN handsome, articulate Bobby Clampett announcing some of the televised golf tournaments. But first-time fans may not know that Clampett's a pretty fair golfer in his own right.

In fact, his amateur days were little short of spectacular. The pride of Cary, NC, was the winner of the 1978 and 1980 California State Amateur tournaments, the low amateur at the U.S. Open in 1978, the winner of the 1978 World Amateur medal, a three-time All-American at Brigham Young University, and a two-time winner of the Fred Haskins Award as top collegiate golfer.

As a pro, Clampett won the 1982 Southern Open and to date has earned more than $1.4 million in prize money on the Tour.

And while broadcasting has cut into his playing time in recent years, he still managed to play sixteen tournaments in 1994, finishing in the money eight times and in the top ten twice—including a seventh-place tie at the Freeport-McMoRan Classic.

I was born of an American father and a French mother. I never went to church on a regular basis. There were times in my growing-up years when I went to church on a trial basis, but Christianity was never professed by anyone in my family. I had several stepfathers as well, and none of them were professing Christians. My father died when I was eleven. His father was a minister, but I didn't really have a chance to develop my relationship with him.

The first things that started to happen were in high school, where I really felt that something was lacking in my life. I didn't know what, but I found a certain void beginning to develop. Some friends invited me to go to a Young Life meeting. It was the first I'd ever even heard of the group.

About that same time, my golf coach, who was a Christian Scientist, began encouraging me to attend his Christian Science church. I spent a lot of time in that church. On the positive side, in the Christian Science church, I saw how the Bible could be directly applied to our personal lives and how it contained a tremendous amount of wisdom.

Then, as I began to grow and get involved more in the church, I went off to college at Brigham Young University. At BYU, I was one of the 3 percent of the students who are not members of the Mormon church. I saw—again, from a positive standpoint—the good aspects of the Mormon faith: the tremendous emphasis on family, the strong moral values, the discipline, and that the way Mormons lived their lives was different from other people.

But as I began to study the Bible, certain things started to happen. I started seeing the differences between what the Bible and Christian Science and Mormonism taught. It put questions in my mind, basic theological questions. I saw differences between what Mary Baker Eddy wrote and what Jesus Christ said. I also saw differences between what Joseph Smith wrote and what Jesus said.

So I came out of college confused, never having joined a church, still searching, but not really knowing where to turn.

I found myself in a period of time where golf became my god. What became important to me was success, fame, and winning tournaments. My life really got wrapped up in that. My whole identity of who I was as a person reflected who I was as a golfer. And, once again, it left an emptiness within me. I really sensed that something was missing in my life.

Little did I know that people were already beginning to pray for me. There were some people who came into my life at that time, most notably my wife Ann. When I met her, my third year out on Tour, she was the first Christian I'd ever dated.

As our relationship began to unfold, with the topic of the Bible at the forefront of the relationship, we literally spent hours and hours debating religion. I was trying to win her over to the Christian Science side; she was taking a biblical Christian stand.

I finally came to the point, even with my very stubborn nature, where I began to see her side. Then, as I began to meet with pastors and other Christians, it became evident to me that, theologically speaking, there were flaws in both the Christian Science and Mormon doctrines.

It was actually a long process, but to make a long story short, right after we got married, I made a public profession of faith. A lot of that was due to a home church we'd found, but we also had a lot of people working with us: Bill Lewis with FCA Junior Golf; Rik Massengale spent a lot of time with me on a long bus ride on the Tour; and Morris Hatalsky also spent some time with me.

And then, shortly after Ann and I got married, Paul and Toni Azinger, good friends of ours, invited us to a Bible study meeting. I'd been to one years before and initially kind of turned away from it, for whatever reason, but mainly it was, "Aw, I don't want to be one of *those* guys."

Larry Moody was speaking that night during the Anheuser-Busch Classic in 1984. I really didn't want to go, but my wife said, "They asked us to. We really ought to go." I said, "Well, I've been to those things before." Finally I said, "Oh, all right. I'll give it a try this time."

I just loved it. And that began a relationship with Larry that's been very fruitful and has grown ever since.

Memorable Moment

When you're talking about the greatest impact on me, two things come into my mind. One was when, as an amateur in 1979, I lost a three-way play-off at the Spaulding Invitational, which was then held at Pebble Beach. I was eighteen years old, this was a professional tournament, and it was a big thing for me. I had a chance to win on the last hole with a twelve-foot birdie putt—which I missed.

The following year I really focused in on trying to win that tournament. I worked hard beforehand and ended up winning it. But what I can remember after the tournament—the same one I had worked so hard for, the one I'd played something like eleven practice rounds for prior to the tournament—is that after I'd won, I had this feeling of *Is this all there is? Wow! I thought it would be so much bigger and greater than this!*

It was a letdown. My focus at that time—and the only thing that mattered then—was the winning. It left an emptiness in me that carried on through college and early on in my professional career.

The other pivotal moment in my life came after I'd been saved. A very difficult time occurred in our third year of marriage, right after the birth of our first child. We'd been trying for a couple of years to have a baby, and the Lord hadn't opened the womb yet. So when it finally did happen, it was a very exciting moment. My wife had a wonderful pregnancy, and it was the first grandchild on both sides of our family.

On the day of Sara Elizabeth's birth, everything went pretty normally. But within a few minutes of her birth, they took her away for some tests. She was having trouble breathing. The doctor ordered some X rays and they found a diaphragmatic hernia. It's a timing disorder in the development of a child. In it, the diaphragm closes too late and it pushes the lungs into the upper chest cavity. This cramps the development of the lungs. They operated on her six hours after she was born. It is a very serious operation.

Just thirty-one hours into her life, the Lord took her home.

Right at that moment, a fully staffed jet landed in Raleigh to transport her to New Orleans for treatment. Today, that treatment is readily available, but back then there were only three places the operation was being done. Had she been born today, there would have been a much greater chance of her surviving.

It was a difficult time for both of us; it was a sad time. It was a time when close friends really comforted us with their prayers, prayers we felt very strongly.

It was also soul-searching time for both of us. It was a crossroads in both of our lives. We were confronted, for the first time, with a real tragic event. We had to decide: Is the Bible really the inspired Word of God? Are God's promises really true? Do all things *really* "work together for good to those who love God, to those who are the called according to His purpose" (Rom. 8:28)? Or are things just as they seem? Is it something we did that we deserved?

My wife and I began to search the Scriptures for the answers. Eventually, it became clear to us that, as we read in John 9:2-3:

"Rabbi, who sinned, this man or his parents, that he was born blind?"

Jesus answered, "Neither this man nor his parents sinned, but that the works of God should be revealed in him."

Those verses and others spoke very strongly to us and helped us get through it.

And through the Bible and prayer, we came to grips with the truth that God will use this for good and that there's a greater good. I really sensed His grieving in this loss, but I knew that He had an ultimate higher good, a purpose for it. And looking back on that time, I see many of the signs of the higher good—though we won't know all of them until we get to heaven.

He's since blessed us with three healthy children. He allowed my wife to get pregnant almost immediately afterward. She gave birth to another girl within thirteen months, our daughter Katelyn. So it was a time where our faith really grew through that. And through our trials, God revealed Himself. It's sad that with our human nature, with our stubbornness and humanness, it so often takes something as strong and as powerful and as emotional as that to draw us to Him.

Sara was born on September 25, 1986, and died the following day. That occurred toward the end of the 1986 Tour season. I was not having a good year on the Tour. In fact, it was a bad year. I needed to go out and play several tournaments toward the end of the year to stay in the top 125. When I went back out at the Disney, with only two tournaments left on the Tour, I was 138th on the money list.

I can remember what a difficult time emotionally it was at Disney. It was just a strong emotional time trying to play with this heavy burden laid on me, but I really felt God's power and presence.

The following tournament was the Texas Open, and it could help me because it was a one-million-dollar tournament—and I was still 138th on the money list.

They had a couple of rain delays for the first two rounds, so the tournament didn't get started until Friday. God gave me a real sense of peace and a sense of strength that I had never encountered before. In fact, I hit forty buckets of balls before the rounds, something I'd never had a desire to do before!

I was in good position after two rounds; I'd made the cut. And on the third day, Sunday, we were playing thirty-six holes. I started making some putts on the back nine of the first round, and after the third round was completed, I was tied for third. If I could stay there, it would be more than enough for me to keep my card. But my game was very shaky. I didn't have much confidence at all.

On the first hole of the fourth round, I made a bogey. On the second hole, I managed to get it up and down for a par. On the third hole, I made another bogey. But as I was missing a four-foot putt for par on that hole, the rain-delay siren went off! It had been a beautiful day in San Antonio, and suddenly this big, dark cloud loomed over the course. It dumped two inches of rain on the golf course. The whole final round got washed out. So the bogeys didn't count, and I finished third in the tournament!

As I recall, I made $48,000 from the Texas Open. The money bumped me from 138th on the money list to 87th. It was more than double what I needed to keep my card.

I couldn't help but think and relate back to the story of Job. After Job went through his trials, God gave him back at least twice as much as he had had before the trials began.

It was the start, for me, of a real sign that God had a purpose for all of this.

Tip

The thing I see all pro players do when they get to the top of their backswing is that they store all of the energy in their down-swing as long as possible until the centrifugal force releases it. And what I see amateur golfers do is that when they get to the top of their backswing, they start to un-cock their left wrist right away. It just breaks down at that point. Then the reverse pivot happens as

Photograph by Julie Pettibone

they cut across the ball. All of those things are related: it is a releasing of the power (or stored energy) too early in the start of the downswing.

There are two things you can do about this. One is the sense that the ball is simply in the way of the swing. Golf is a game where the focus is on the golf swing. The ball is just in the way, and where the ball goes is simply the result of what you put into it through the swing.

Second, as you start the downswing, you should start the downswing by trying to set it with your feet, your knees, and your hips. The last thing to move—again, at the start of the downswing—are your hands. If the hands are the last thing to move at the start of the downswing, the energy gets stored longer. Therefore it sets up that chain reaction so the energy can be released through centrifugal force at impact.

In other words, resistance is established in the backswing. As the start of the backswing occurs, the hands just stay back and the feet plant, the knees and hips start to turn, shoulders start to move—and *then* the hands follow. That way the power is stored and released when you want it, *where* you want it.

One of the things that God's blessed me with in my game is the ability to do that. I'm not big. I currently weigh the most I've ever weighed, 165 pounds, and through most of my career I was playing at 135 pounds. But I was still in the top 20 percent of the Tour in driving distance. The reason was that I had the ability to be able to store that power on my downswing.

Jay Delsing

WHEN BIG, RAWBONED Jay Delsing drives, you can see that he comes from an athletic family—his father Jim played for several American League teams, including the New York Yankees and St. Louis Browns. And while attending UCLA, Jay was teammates with well-known golfers Corey Pavin, Steve Pate, and Duffy Waldorf.

Photo courtesy of PGA TOUR

But Delsing's earnings slipped in 1994 after back-to-back great years in 1992 and 1993. In 1992 he won nearly $300,000 on the PGA Tour. In 1993 he barely lost by a couple of strokes to Paul Azinger at the New England Classic. And he started strong in 1994, winning nearly $125,000 in the first eleven events, but faded at the end.

Still, Delsing has maintained his genial good humor throughout and in 1995 looked to have his stroke back, finishing with a second-place tie at the FedEx-St. Jude Classic and taking home a whopping $110,000.

I was born and raised a Catholic. I went through twelve years of Catholic education by the Jesuits. We came from a religious—I would say, very believing—background. Unfortunately, when I was a kid, the Catholic faith used guilt a lot more than I would have liked. But as far as believing in the Lord—and obviously I've gone up and down since I was younger—I've always felt like I've had that faith with me pretty much my whole life. I feel pretty lucky in that regard.

I think I kind of grew into my faith. A lot of people are able to pinpoint it and say, "at eight o'clock on the third of January 1965." It wasn't like that for me. I do remember the lowest point in my life, right when I was getting out of college and coming on the tour. That was the part of my life when I strayed the farthest from Jesus.

Then I remember reading some things about Medjugorje in Yugoslavia, where the sightings of the Virgin Mary were taking place and lives were changed. It really sparked my interest in my faith again. It was interesting just to read some of the things people had written about what they had seen. So my wife Kathy and I researched it a little bit, and we saw some videos on it as well.

And in the days that followed, we talked about Medjugorje a lot, what it meant to those people and what it could mean to us. Kathy remembers those days vividly. We'd go and pray, and it was incredibly powerful and emotional for us.

We never talked specifically about how that affected us both, but I'll always remember the feelings we had at the time and just the casual conversations we had after a lot of the prayer meetings we went to—it was very inspirational for both of us.

It really got us back on track and back to what we believe in and think. It was really nice. I realize it's a strange sort of thing, but your relationship with God is so personal that there's no telling what it can be for you.

In retrospect, as I look back, it may have been a reflection more of the low point I was in—straying from my original faith—and maybe that's why this particular time and that particular incident stick out in my mind.

Another point came at the birth of our first daughter, Mackenzie. We had some serious medical difficulties with the baby—and Kathy as well. She had some major complications with the birth, so both went into intensive care.

But somehow, I just had some sort of resolve, whether it was the Holy Spirit or whatever, but I knew things were going to be okay.

Now I look back on it as an incredible time in my life when He was there, and I *knew* that everybody was well taken care of, even though I'd look at them in the hospital and have no idea what all the tubes were for! That was an incredibly strong part of my life as well.

On the Tour we really enjoy Larry Moody; he's a wonderful man and a great example. I had always shied away from the Bible study when I first joined the Tour, but once we got to meet and know Larry and listen to him speak his wonderful daily applications that really help you get along, we were fine. He's just a nice man and a big help, and now we go to the study as much as we can.

We still belong to the Catholic church in St. Louis, and our daughter has just entered the Catholic kindergarten there. I pretty much feel like Catholics and Protestants are all on the same team. We're all just human. The problem is when you act like you're perfect and know all the answers.

In this life, you just have to do the best you can do.

Memorable Moment

As far as highlights, in 1993, I shot a 61 at Memphis on Sunday and had an opportunity that particular day to shoot an incredibly low score. It was one of those days when just about everything I did went about the right distance and went right at the hole.

Did you know early in the round something special was happening?

Not really, because you try not to think about it; you try to enjoy it. This is what we practice for; this is what we work hard for. It was one of those things where I just didn't want to run out of holes. I wanted to keep enjoying the day, to keep having fun with it, and it was just a great, really fun, fun day.

Another time, I was playing Hilton Head with Paul Azinger on Sunday's round in 1991. I hit a shot from the right-hand side of the fairway on the fifteenth hole, which is a dogleg par five. I pulled it slightly and it hit a tree.

There's a lake down to the left, and I thought, *Nuts, that ball's gone into the lake.* Instead, I heard a sound like someone had hit a coconut with a hammer. A real hollow sound. Then I heard all of these people groaning. We were probably 130-140 yards away—it was a nine-iron shot—so I couldn't see anything.

But when I got there, I saw what had happened. There was a turtle in the water, and my ball hit the turtle on the shell and came back on to the land! I came back and chipped the ball almost into the hole, tapped it in, and finished tenth in the tournament! That made my week!

That's just one of those things that make you smile and think, *Okay—remember those couple of bad bounces I got the day before? We're evened up.*

Tip

Here are a couple of the standard things I see that get people fouled up with their putting. First of all, they let their mind get preoccupied with too many thoughts: left arm straight, right arm up, right elbow at a forty-five degree angle, and on and on. Those sorts of things, those abstract things, don't really have anything to do with making a putt.

There're really only a few things you do need to know. You really need to keep your head still while you're watching the ball, and your hands need to be even with the ball. Those are basically the only two things you need to know.

Other than that, if you can knock a ball into a hole, you're a good putter. That's all there is to it.

Putting is the most individual way of expressing yourself in golf. I guarantee you that if you keep making putts, someone is going to come up to you and say, "How do you do that?" That's how you're recognized as a good putter.

Still, there are a couple of things that really might help—and golfers can use these in their entire game: chip, swing, everything.

The first is to really loosen up the feel. Loosen your forearms and shoulders. If you tense up the muscles in your hands and arms for five minutes and try to hold it, you'll see how stiff your

Photograph by Sam Greenwood/PGA TOUR

shoulders feel. That feeling can work its way all the way through your back. It is a very unnatural way to play, and the bottom line is that it is no darn fun!

So, I'd like to see people really loosen up their hands. It gives you a much better feel for the putter, much better feel for what you're doing, and it'll also loosen up your mind. That's the second thing: Free your mind of all of those abstract thoughts and just think of making the putt. I would love for a golfer's last thought to be: *Just make the putt.*

So many times you get up over the ball, and you're thinking, *I just want to make a good stroke.* Well, heck! I'd much rather make a bad stroke and make the putt than make a good-looking stroke and miss! If you can get it in the hole, it doesn't matter how it looks.

Pros are definitely more confident in their putting, but if you're going to go ahead and let your mind get freed up and untangled from all this junk it carries around in it, so far as techniques are concerned, you're going to be able to have that confidence too.

There are bad putters on the PGA Tour. You can watch them putt. They're tentative. There's no athlete in any sport who is any good when he or she is tentative. A lot of athletes get hurt then; their bodies are on the defensive side, and that's not good. That's not the way you want to try and perform.

So that's one of the things that's important in golf. Untangle those goofy thoughts you picked up from the twenty-five minutes you spent reading that magazine before you went out on the course—and try and remember it's still a sport.

Michael Jordan, when he drives down a lane, isn't thinking about how he is going to shoot. He is thinking about whether he is going to jump to the right or left, or go over or under the defender in front of him, to get the big ball in the hole. And that's really what you do now, except in golf, your "defenders" are mostly mental.

Everybody who reads this book has had a day when they stood over their putt and *knew,* absolutely *knew,* they were going to make that putt. And that's what I'm trying to get you to do. If you think, *I'm going to make this putt,* if you *feel* like you're going to make this putt, chances are you will.

This is going to do a couple of things: First, chances are you're going to come much closer to making it, and even if you don't, you're going to have much more success in the long run. And second, you're going to have more fun. That's what I stress when I do my clinics and corporate outings; I really try to increase the amount of enjoyment people get from golf.

After all, this is not supposed to be some sort of white-knuckle fight for these guys. This is supposed to be: *I'm out of the office. Let me enjoy a beautiful course on a beautiful day outing and relax a little bit.* Right?

Bob Estes

BOB ESTES LOOKS LIKE he still ought to be enrolled in the University of Texas (where he was named the Fred Haskins and Jack Nicklaus Awards winner as 1988 College Player of the Year), but he sure doesn't play like it. The modest Texan was Tour Rookie of the Year in 1989 and has just gotten better with each year.

In 1994 Estes scored his first PGA Tour victory, easily winning the Texas Open at Oak Hills in San Antonio. That little feat followed a second at the Phoenix Open, a third at the Greater Milwaukee, and a fourth at BellSouth. He finished with a whopping $765,360—good for fourteenth overall on the Tour.

Photo courtesy of PGA TOUR

He also won the all-around category in the 1994 PGA Tour statistics. The baby-faced Estes was tenth in scoring average, sixth in greens in regulation, sixth in sand saves, and sixth in birdies.

I grew up in the church. Both of my parents are Christians; my brother is as well. I've gone to Sunday school and church ever since I can remember. A lot of my friends who went to my church then are still my friends now, so it was a great atmosphere.

I think I was eleven when I made my commitment to Christ. I'd been around the church all that time, and so I felt that that was the right time.

To be honest, it has been up and down since then. In high school, my family always attended church and Sunday school. But when I went away to college, my days were so filled that I got away from going to church and Sunday school. When I was in college I felt like I crammed fifteen years into four. You hate to use that as an excuse, but that's the way it happened. Add to that trying to make the PGA Tour, combine a little bit of a social life and, well, something had to give. I was so busy with school and golf that most of the people I really got to know were athletes I lived with or close by.

During my first week at school in Austin, my roommate and I attended a Methodist church, even though I grew up Baptist. We went that one time, and I'm not sure he ever went again—and I know I only went that one time!

I did feel bad that I was not attending church and Sunday school regularly, but it happens. It's not like I didn't want to go, it's just that I felt so much time pressure. Once you get in the habit of going, it's easy to go. And once you get in the habit of not going, it's easy not to go.

There were many times when Sunday morning was the only chance I had to sleep in after a tough six days. Or sometimes we had a tournament to go to. Or we had one coming up soon, so I would get up early and go to the golf course on Sunday morning.

I would go to church when I went back home to Abilene to visit my family, but when I was in Austin, I only went that one time the first week of school. That was it.

Once I got on the Tour, I started going to the Bible study right away, probably my first week or two on the Tour. I'd heard about it when I qualified. Not only was that going to be a great way to learn about the Bible, it was going to be a great way to meet other Christian players and wives on the Tour. And that's exactly what happened. I've been going ever since. I will admit that I haven't made every single Bible study. Sometimes when you have a 7:00 A.M. tee-time, you tend to go to bed a little bit earlier than normal!

Larry Moody's Bible study was pretty much my church during my first five years on the Tour. Then in 1993, during the off-season, I knew I needed to find a church home in Austin. I went to four or five Baptist churches in town and ended up at Hyde Park Baptist Church—a block from where I lived during college! I started out going there and finally made it to Sunday school about a year later for the first time, and I quickly made some good friends there—some of whom came to see me when I won the Texas Open in San Antonio shortly thereafter in October 1994.

Meeting guys like Larry Nelson, Morris Hatalsky, Scott Simpson, Tom Lehman, Loren Roberts, Bobby Clampett—so many guys who are just super people—has meant so much to me on the Tour. They've got super wives, great families, and to see them be successful out here and still be such strong Christians really means a lot. And the younger pros, like myself, really look up to those guys for inspiration.

Memorable Moment

As far as a golf-related memory, I guess there were two. During my rookie year in 1989, I went into the fall not having made nearly enough money to qualify for the Tour the following year. I missed the cut in Milwaukee. Still, I had two really good days of practice, Saturday and Sunday, before heading into the B. C. Open. Then I really worked hard on my putting Monday, Tuesday, and Wednesday in particular, because I knew if I was going to score and finish higher up, I was going to have to putt well.

When the B. C. Open came, I got myself into contention. I had a one-shot lead going into the final round. Mike Hulbert caught me from behind, and we tied for first. That put us into a play-off—which guaranteed me at least second-place money. I didn't win the tournament, but the second-place money got me over the top and exempted me for the following year. And, as everybody knows, once you are bumped from the Tour and have to go back through the Qualifying School, there's no guarantee you'll be back right away—or ever. So that was a really big week in my golfing career.

Then I'd say my other favorite memory was my first career Tour victory in San Antonio in October 1994. Not only was it close to home, it was in front of many family and friends. My parents were there, as were my uncle and aunt (my original sponsor) with a friend and his wife, some other friends, a couple other family members, and a lot of people I didn't know but who had gone to the University of Texas—UT fans one and all. There was a lot of cheering just because I'm an old Longhorn! That all made it special.

Actually, before the Texas Open, I hadn't given myself as much time to practice or to prepare the way I had wanted. But I shot a 62 the first round and just kept going. I didn't make quite as many putts as I did on Thursday, but I made enough to win.

Tip

I want to talk about how you practice. It depends on how much time you have. You do need to balance that, of course. But a pretty good little rule of thumb is that you need to spend at least half of your time putting and chipping and hitting other shots around the green.

Amateurs love to get out there and whack at it—especially with the driver. That's part of the game, too, and that's fine. But one of the things I've learned that's really, really important is how to balance your practice, to cover almost every phase of your game every day, even if, for instance, you may only hit five bunker shots. Go in the bunker and hit those shots. There are plenty of days when that's all I hit. I may only hit three or four or five. You don't have to stand in the bunker and hit bunker shots for thirty minutes or an hour.

When you're playing a round of golf, you're doing a little bit of everything—you're hitting a tee shot, and you're hitting an iron shot, and then you're either putting or trying to recover. So I feel it's best to practice like that too.

There are different ways to do that. I spend a balanced amount of time on all phases of my game. The only thing I might spend more time on in one practice session is hitting full shots or your basic putting stroke. Anything else I do in moderation.

The most important thing in playing great golf and scoring well is to remember that you're going to spend half of your round on the green, so putting is now

Photograph by Sam Greenwood/PGA TOUR

my primary focus. Whereas when I was younger, I spent most of my time chipping, pitching, hitting bunker shots, and putting. Developing your short game may not be such a bad way to go when you're younger. Hopefully, you'll be able to carry that with you for a long, long time.

Typically, what I'll try to do in a practice session is start out putting. I'll putt for only ten to fifteen minutes, and I'll putt with only one or two balls and from all different lengths. I try to make it as much like it is on the golf course—unless I'm just working on repetition or something mechanical.

When I'm done putting, I'll hit chips for maybe five to ten minutes with various clubs. I may chip with the six iron first, then the wedge, then the eight iron, while moving around the chipping green, playing from different places uphill, down-hill, and sidehill. And then I might go to the area where I can hit a few bunker shots or pitch shots. I may only hit five bunker shots and maybe five to ten pitches with my different wedges.

And only then will I go to the driving range. Again, depending on how much time I have and how much I want to accomplish, I may only hit balls for thirty minutes.

So the main thing I'm trying to say is that I don't typically spend an hour or two on any one phase of my game. I keep moving around. Not only is that good for you because that mirrors what you do on the golf course, but your practice doesn't become boring and stale.

It's not like I have a strict time limit on myself either. But I feel like I balance my practice well enough now that I know when it is time to move on to the next phase of the game. You can definitely practice too much.

I finally discovered a couple of years ago that, especially in college and high school, I would spend an hour or two just hitting bunker shots—straight—until I had that down. Well, if I went from there to the driving range and hit full shots, all of a sudden my blade is open, my stance is open, I'm taking the club to the outside, and all I can do is cut the ball. I can't finish my backswing because I'm still setting up and working at the target as if I'm hitting bunker shots!

I didn't really learn how to practice and prepare myself for each following day until I got out on the Tour.

Rick Fehr

RED-HEADED RICK FEHR has increased his earnings for the past six seasons, culminating with a whopping $573,963 in 1994 and his first PGA Tour victory since the 1986 B. C. Open. But the big win at the 1994 Walt Disney World/Oldsmobile Classic almost didn't happen. At the last minute, Fehr put off hernia surgery, felt bad all week, and, because of a transportation mix-up, arrived just fifteen minutes before his tee-time on Sunday!

Photo courtesy of PGA TOUR

Fehr's career in golf has been one of unbroken success: winner of the 1979 Washington State Junior and PGA National Junior Championships, winner of the 1982 Western Amateur, two-time All-American at Brigham Young, low amateur at the 1984 Masters and 1984 U.S. Open. He's also on the PGA Tour Policy Board and is a sweet-spirited, self-effacing family man.

And, oh yeah—a month after the Disney/Oldsmobile Classic he did have the successful hernia surgery.

I was recruited heavily out of junior golf, and I had my choice of any place to go. And, being from the West Coast back in the late 1970s and early 1980s, the premiere program was Brigham Young University. I made some visits around the country, but I got to BYU and said, "Boy, this place has a great atmosphere. I love it here." It had a great golf tradition and great players. I wanted to be someplace competitive, play in the best college tournaments, and have a chance to win the NCAA. So I ended up at BYU.

For all students at BYU, it is required that they take a course each semester in religion. During my first year I studied the *Book of Mormon.* I made it through that class—which wasn't easy for someone who is not a Mormon. During my sophomore year I took two semesters of New Testament. For me, that was something totally new. I thought, *Hey, this is pretty neat—we're reading the Bible.* So I started reading it and studying it. By following the course outline, I read through the entire New Testament.

All of a sudden, I felt like, *Whoa! This is speaking to me! This just isn't some old book!*

I had had a very successful junior golf career and had achieved one goal after another. And yet, deep down, I wasn't satisfied. I'd reach a goal, but when I got there, it wasn't what I thought it would be. So the answer was either: "Figure out if it is something different" or "Keep pushing on to the next level—and keep hoping that answer is behind the next door or the next goal."

During my freshman year I finished in the top ten individually in twelve of the fourteen tournaments we played. Our team won the NCAAs, but I only got honorable mention all-America—which I thought was a little bit of an injustice—but I really was doing well. During my sophomore year I won a couple of tournaments, so I did even better.

It was a natural progression, but still, at the end of the day I felt like, *This can't be all there is.*

At the same time, I was still reading through the Bible and discovering, for the first time, about this stuff called "sin." The gospel was just jumping off the pages at me. I soon saw that I didn't have a relationship with God. Worse, I saw that I couldn't have that relationship—the Bible is pretty clear on this—because I was separated from God by sin. Not only that, I couldn't do anything on my own to solve that problem.

But the good news is: Jesus Christ did that for me. It was all very simple. All of a sudden, it leaped off the pages. This wasn't with anybody else's input or direction, just the Bible speaking directly to me. For the most part, it was the book of Romans; going through Romans just led me right along.

The only problem was that I was getting conflicting messages in the classroom at BYU! Naturally, that confused me a little bit. I saw everything as so simple and clear—and now I know that that was the Holy Spirit's touch revealing God's plan for me. But at the same time, I was sitting there in class going, "Wait a minute! That's not what I'm reading in the Bible!"

That began a year-long investigation into the Mormon Church and its claims—and where they line up and don't line up with the Bible. I was hearing from some teammates who were Mormons, and I was hearing from a couple of friends at home who had become Christians. It was kind of a final analysis before I made the decision which way to go.

The summer after my junior year, I made an intellectual and mental decision about what God had done for me, but I really hadn't acted on it yet. But one Sunday that summer at home, at Overlake Christian Church in Kirkland, Washington, I knew exactly what I needed to do, and God just called me forward. I went forward at the altar call. That was the seal of that transaction, that God took first place in my life. I turned my life over to Him, and He became my Lord as well as my Savior.

Because of my experience at BYU, I really encourage people to read the Bible. I believe if you get somebody sitting down with the Word of God, He's going to be there with them revealing Truth.

After my junior year, things got more difficult at school. I didn't have the fellowship I'd enjoyed at home.

I still had a great experience at BYU. It was great for my career and the people are wonderful. They really intend to seek God. But their teachings, the foundations of their church, just aren't right. They just don't line up with Scripture.

It's interesting that another couple of golfers from BYU—Bobby Clampett and Pat McGowan—are now solid Christians. I think it is a great testimony of God's power. You can't put the credit in anybody else's hands. It's always His doing; the transaction takes place by His power.

From that point forward, I was on the Tour. My wife and I still fellowship and are involved in the Christian church where I had my beginnings, and I love being home, but one of the things that I regret about my career is that we're not as involved locally as we could be.

But that's the story; that's how God brought me into His family. To sum it up, I had all the success I ever wanted—but it didn't meet my needs.

God blesses people in professional sports with a lot of things, but I view these blessings as an opportunity to be a responsible steward. That's one of the things my wife, Terri, and I enjoy the most—being able to take the resources that God provides out here and use them to help ministries. It's a wonderful life, but we have great responsibilities too.

We've been through tough times, although not in the last few years because God has really blessed what we've been doing on the Tour in that time. But I've been back to Tour School three or four times, and nobody wants to go back there. For a professional golfer, going back to Tour School is kind of traumatic. Still, any life is a struggle.

Also, Terri and I lost a baby back in 1992, and that was the hardest thing we've been through. We thought even then, *How can somebody go through some of these struggles in life without a relationship with the Lord?* With some of the answers that we have and through what He reveals in Scripture—as well as the things we don't understand—we know that we're in the hands of a God who loves us and has our best interests at heart.

I also know that my significance, my security, aren't tied up in how well I play golf, whether I'm number one on the money list or 65th or 180th. This life is a short period of time, and we're just passing through. So you sure don't want your treasure to be down here.

Memorable Moment

My victory at the Disney/Oldsmobile Classic in October 1994 was my first victory in nearly eight years, so everybody was saying it was my time, that I'd worked hard, that I'd been playing well lately, whatever. So it may not have been such a big surprise. But there was more.

Our church, Overlake, was going through some changes—a big fund-raising program for building a new facility. It's a real alive and growing church. We were relocating into Redmond, Washington, which is an adjacent town. With any building program, some people say, "Uh, that's a lot of money," and some people are skeptical.

But this is one of those things where we finally decided, "You know? We're in the world, we're not of it, but we're in it. And in order to have a place where we can meet needs and minister, we need a facility." We just outgrew the old one. So my wife and I decided we were going to be involved.

October 16, 1994, was commitment Sunday at Overlake. We had an all-church banquet where everybody came and made their commitment as to what they were going to give.

A month earlier, Terri and I sat down, prayed about it, and discussed what it was that God would have us commit to for the next three years. It was a little bit by faith, since golfers aren't salaried—we're essentially freelancers. There has been a plentiful amount in recent years, but you never know down the road. So we made a commitment at that time concerning how much we were going to give. It was a sizeable amount and would involve some sacrifice.

And then I was in Columbus, Georgia, and Terri was home with the kids, and they were going to come down to meet me at the Disney tournament in Orlando. That Sunday, Terri sang at the service—she's a gifted singer. The message that morning was about passing your faith on from generation to generation. It was tied into the building program, because the kids would need a place to bring their friends and neighbors, and we'd simply outgrown that place. So the message was on the importance of passing on your faith to the next generation. Terri was touched as she heard it, thinking about our two boys. She really felt moved that we needed to do more than what we had decided on a few weeks earlier.

So, while she was driving home, she got to thinking, *Wouldn't it be neat if Rick won—if he wins anytime soon—and we could give it all to the building program.* So when she arrived with the boys the Tuesday before the Walt Disney World/Oldsmobile Golf Classic began, she shared that thought with me.

"I don't know what you'll think about it, honey," she said, "but I was really thinking next time you win, let's give it all to the building program!"

I said, "Great! We've got everything we need. Let's take that next step and lay it out before God."

That very week, I broke an eight-and-a-half year winning drought!

Everything fell into place. We are convinced that it was no coincidence.

We honored that pledge—although I had to pay my caddie first since he wasn't in on the plan!—and gave the balance to the building fund. With a lot of joy.

It was really a miraculous thing. It is probably one of the most clear-cut evidences of God in my life. A lot of people would say, "Oh, it's just a coincidence."

Giving has always been a very private thing for us. And it's not like, "Look what we did." It's, "Look what God did!" I don't take any credit for any of that. We shared what had happened at the banquet as something to encourage others, to say, "Look what God's done. If you've wondered if God's behind this building program before—here's confirmation received on our part!"

It's just another way I've always been taught and challenged: You can't outgive God. Even with the right motives and the right heart, can you really ever outgive God?

Tip

I see it every Wednesday in the pro-am tournaments. It's a common mistake, even by people who've played a long time, not just those who occasionally play. It's the inability to hit a shot from near the green that gets up in the air and lands softly.

There's a shot that's termed the "lob." Most people are afraid to hit it because it uses a club they shy away from—their sand wedge. They think it's just for the sand, but actually most golf professionals in most situations around the green are using that club. It's a club they probably hit more than any other, save for their putter and driver. They chip with it and use it for those challenging shots where they are hitting it over a sand trap or over

Photograph by Sam Greenwood/PGA TOUR

water and they want the ball to stop quickly. It's really just a matter of understanding the physics of how the club and the ball meet and what the result is.

If you take any golf club and open up the clubface, you add loft to it—effective loft—which makes the ball get up quicker and higher and not go as far.

So what I do for the lob shot, and what I think most people should be able to do, is aim left with an open stance and open shoulders. I open the clubface, as most people have been taught to do when playing out of a sand trap—and do it off of grass. I suggest you lay the clubface more open than a sand shot, and then have very relaxed hands, and make sure your body and your hands don't slide ahead. Just stay really still with soft, relaxed hands, and let the club do the work.

Of course, that comes from practice and working with it and trusting that you can take a big swing from that distance, because you're adding so much loft that the ball isn't going to travel as far, but instead is going to get up high and land soft. It's something that we practice all the time. As with any tip that you might get, you need to practice. You need to find a situation where you can practice and spend a lot of time with it.

If you really wanted to elevate and get fancy, you'd use more wrist, but I think for this shot to be effective for most people, you don't have to. The key is *not* to have your hands way ahead of the club when it meets the ball because then you end up delofting, taking the loft back off of the club. What you want to do is return your hands to the same setup position and have the open face, because if you move ahead of it with your hands and with your body, you're going to end up hitting it too far and across the green. So you need to stay back and let your hands and the club meet the ball pretty much at the same time.

You do follow through, but you don't create an angle with your shaft forward. You want to keep everything still—just kind of dumping your club underneath it with an open face.

And this is a difficult shot to hit if you don't have a good lie. If the ball's not sitting on a good piece of grass, or if the ball's sitting on some hard pan or whatever, you probably shouldn't use this shot unless you're very well-versed and practiced. But if you've got a decent lie in the fairway or the rough, it works quite well.

Jackie Gallagher-Smith

THE PRETTIEST MEMBER of the golfing Gallagher family (brother Jim is a member of the PGA Tour and brother Jeff is currently on the NIKE Tour) has been playing golf since she was five. She was the 1983 and 1985 Indiana State Junior champion and an All-American at LSU in 1989.

As a pro, Gallagher-Smith competed on the Futures Golf Tour, where she won three tournaments, the Asian Tour, and the Central Florida Challenge mini-tour. She joined the LPGA Tour in 1994, and her best finish was a fifteenth-place tie at the HEALTHSOUTH Palm Beach Classic.

Photo courtesy of LPGA TOUR

My parents were very devout Catholics, and my brothers and I went to Catholic grade school, went to mass every week, and said our prayers. When we were younger, especially around Eastertime, the boys would get all bummed out because my parents would say, "Okay, now we've got our little prayer time," and the boys would have to recite the stages of the Cross.

We learned a lot from my parents and developed good morals and values from them. They always loved and supported us. And now that I look back on them and how their relationship was, I can see that they have a true love for the Lord.

I remember my mom having surgery one time, and my dad was constantly praying. I didn't grasp what it was all about until much later—which is the case in many things in life. You don't learn much from your parents until you've experienced certain things on your own.

We were always a close-knit family, and my parents always kept on us about going to church and thanking God for all that He'd given us. It was a good background; it just has taken me a little more time to really develop a true relationship of my own with the Lord.

There was a girl on our golf team in college who was a Christian. She was always so bubbly, and we could never figure it out. We'd think, *Golly, what is up with her?* But she always read her Bible and talked about how she was born again and saved. My thought was: *I go to church and pray. This is my way, and that's her way.*

Unfortunately, when I was in college, I didn't hear a lot about the Fellowship of Christian Athletes. I wish I could have had the chance to be a part of it then.

But the terms "born again" or "saved" always scared me. I didn't understand— and I didn't want to be a part of it because I'd heard the downside of it. Some people always degraded it.

Once I was out of college, I played the mini-tours because I missed the LPGA Qualifying School twice. It took me two more times to get my card. After the second try, I thought the world was coming to an end.

But God blessed me with my husband, Eddie Smith, whom I met at another friend's wedding. We went through the Pre-Cana—the counseling process you go through before you get married in the Catholic church, where you meet with a married couple and talk with them. We also had a class we had to go to.

And at that time I started to think a lot about God. I knew for our marriage to work, we needed God to be a part of it. I guess this is when my curiosity really went wild.

Once Eddie and I were married, we lived in Ponte Vedra Beach, Florida, and it seemed like we were surrounded by Christians! Friends of Eddie's visited us after Christmas of 1992. We started discussing God, the Bible, and being born again with them because they were Christians. I started asking a lot of questions, and so did Eddie. They'd spoken to him about ten years ago about his relationship with Jesus Christ, and that's when he took Christ into his heart. Being around this couple, I could see they had a really neat relationship and there was something unique about it.

Eddie had kind of gotten away from his faith, but when we were brought together, it renewed his relationship with the Lord, because that's when we started talking about things and began trying to build our relationship. He really led me in the right direction. I was asking a lot of questions. I was very inquisitive.

Eddie then started going to a Bible study for men in our neighborhood. He would come home each week, and I'd ask, "What did you learn this week?" Finally one week I asked him if I could come along, even though it was for men only. He called O. W. McCurdy, the man who held the Bible study in his house, and O. W. said, "Yeah, sure—tell her to come along." So I went to that study.

They had been discussing the book of John. That week, though, O. W. went off on a different path. The topic was relationships. I remember Ephesians 5:22-23: "Wives, submit to your own husbands, as to the Lord. For the husband is head of the wife, as also Christ is head of the church; and He is the Savior of the body." That kind of hit me hard.

That night while we were there, I accepted Jesus into my heart. I felt like there was a big load lifted off me. And then I knew that God would take care of me and that He would always love me, no matter what.

It's a nice thing to know after not playing well on the golf course that, no matter what, He'll always love me.

Then I realized that I could glorify Him through the talent He gave me by ministering to other people. The fact that He surrounded us with all of those Christians in Ponte Vedra—that was all part of His plan. It was interesting for Eddie and me to see all these little things working together.

A couple weeks after that night, I was baptised in our hot tub. That was all in early January 1993.

Memorable Moment

I could tell you about the golf cart wreck I once had—but I'm not sure how fond a memory that is!

A better memory would be when I won LSU's tournament when I was a sophomore—and clueless! I was in the last group. I don't remember what I shot the first couple days; all I knew was that I had to keep all the other girls' scorecards. And I remember not wanting to write down any of their scores because I didn't want to think about what they were shooting; I wanted to stay in focus in my own game. I wrote down the numbers at the turn, but I never added them up! I just wanted to keep playing my game.

And when I finished, I didn't even know that I'd won because I was so wrapped up in what I was doing. In fact, I even bogeyed the last hole and thought for sure I didn't win. But I ended up winning, and it was pretty cool, especially because I beat a couple of good players.

And once in 1993, I got to play in a foursome with Jo Ann Carner and Sandra Palmer in the U.S. Open. It was great—Jo Ann was really funny and Sandra was really nice, though I think my dad got more of a kick out of it than I did. I was the first alternate when someone pulled out, and so I snuck in there!

Strangely enough, I hadn't been feeling very good that week, so it wasn't as fun as it could have been. I wasn't on the LPGA that year and was just playing the mini-tours. Still, both Jo Ann and Sandra were comforting, encouraging, and caring.

Tip

One thing I think is important is knowing how far you hit every club. It's important to know if it is, say, 155 yards to the hole. I think a lot of times the normal amateur doesn't necessarily know how far they hit each club—they're just guessing.

So something I've done, and it is something we did in college that I still do today, is to either go to a field or driving range and measure off the distance in increments of ten yards. Then I hit each club and see

Photo courtesy of LPGA TOUR

where it ends up. Or, to be more accurate, I have someone watch to see where the ball lands. Then I go through every club doing that.

I hit each club as hard as I can, then I hit it easy. This way I have both of those measurements. I've found if I hit a six iron easy, I'll hit it about 145 feet. But if I really hit at it, I'll hit it 155.

Of course, the short irons are more important because that's where scoring is done, along with your putter. That's what I worked on a lot in the past year, especially with my wedges. I spent time marking off forty-five, fifty, fifty-five, sixty yards, and measuring exactly how far it takes with each swing.

When you're practicing, watch the yard markers. If you're just out there hitting balls, and you don't know how far you're hitting them, it doesn't help much.

Also, realize that all of this is give or take ten yards. A lot of times people under-club more than they over-club.

The other thing I'd suggest is working on your preshot routine. When you get behind the ball, try to achieve some consistency in your thought processes and habits. Do you take one or two practice swings? And once you're set up, do you waggle with your hands or do you stand still?

It's just repeating whatever method you go through before hitting each shot. If you go through that routine before you hit every shot, it'll help.

Another part of your preshot routine could be picking out a spot a couple of feet in front of you to align your club.

But there are all different kinds of good routines; everyone makes up their own. Whatever you do, it gives you consistency—and usually it will pay off in your club hitting and ball striking because you get comfortable with that routine.

Larry Gilbert

WHEN THEY TALK about golf in Kentucky, sooner or later Larry Gilbert's name is going to come up. In 1992 the modest, friendly Gilbert was inducted into the Kentucky Golf Hall of Fame. And with good reason! His accomplishments include: winning the PGA Club Professional Championship in 1981, 1982, and 1991, capturing ten Kentucky PGA Championships, three Kentucky Open Championships, and nabbing both a Tennessee Open and a Tennessee PGA title.

Photo courtesy of PGA TOUR

So it isn't all that surprising that Gilbert should do equally well as a member of the Senior Tour. His rookie season (1993) was marked by thirteen top-ten finishes, including a pair of second-place finishes. When the dust settled, he ended up seventeenth overall on the money list by earning a nifty $515,790.

Nineteen ninety-four was just more of the same—only better. Gilbert won both the Dallas Reunion Pro-Am and the Vantage (where he fired three consecutive rounds of 66), finished in the top ten twelve times, and earned a cool $848,544—good for ninth on the final money list.

How good was Gilbert in 1994? In the Senior PGA Tour statistics, he was first in the total driving category, second in greens in regulation, fifth in all-around, and tied for sixth in eagles. If he keeps going at this rate, Gilbert's next stop will be the Senior Hall of Fame!

I had eleven brothers and sisters—we were a very large family. Unfortunately, some of them passed away very young. I wasn't very close to Christianity back then. That happened to me quite a bit later in life. I was struggling as a club professional, running into various problems, including the man I was working for—but really, most of my problems were with myself. Along the way I kept meeting and associating with very devout Christians. It finally kind of dawned on me one day that maybe the Lord was trying to tell me something. I became very interested.

There was a man named Will Criswell in Kentucky who had a church there and who was also a very good golfer. He'd done some prison time over some things he'd done. But while he was in prison, he found the Lord. He's now an ordained minister. It's an amazing story of how his wife and children stuck with him through the whole ordeal. He told me that if the Lord could use him this way, He could do the same thing with me. And that's what happened.

Well, actually, it was a series of things that happened. About the same time, I wasn't happy in my job as a club professional. I felt an awful lot of pressure from the membership. It was time for me to leave and give my career a shot. I did a lot of soul-searching and, later, a lot of praying, because it was definitely a big gamble for me. I invested my life savings to come out here and play this Tour.

Do your Christian beliefs have an impact on you as a professional golfer?

Well, I really don't know if those beliefs help certain putts go in the hole or help certain shots bounce out of a bunker or whatever, but in my mind it's the peace and serenity that my faith gives me that's so important. You feel like things are going to go your way.

The Christians on the Tour all know each other. The thing of it is, most of the people out here are Christians, although maybe some are a little closer than others.

But that means we've got to be aware of what we're doing at all times. For instance, I see a lot of people on the golf course who take things out on their caddie. That's not me. When it comes to hitting a golf ball, I'm the last person to hit it. I'm also the last one who decides which club it is going to be. And if I make a wrong decision, or my caddie and I together make a wrong decision, then it is my fault—not his.

So there is an extreme battle among egos out here—and I think that's probably natural for that to happen. I have had people kid me now that I've won a couple of tournaments and been somewhat "successful." They come up to me and say, "I guess you'll change now, just like all of the rest of the jerks, and be a big star." I hope Larry Gilbert never changes. I tell them, "If you ever see me change and become one of those jerks, I'd like for you to tell me about it." I'm very sincere when I say that. I just want to be good ol' Larry Gilbert.

And one thing that helps is the Tour Bible study. We kind of look at it as our Sabbath, so to speak. We very much enjoy it, and there are some great speakers that have come to it. We even met at Glen Campbell's house one night.

Memorable Moment

It's hard to pick out one point that is the highlight. I do remember that in 1993, my rookie year, I was tied for the lead at Sleepy Hollow, New York, in the NYNEX Commemorative Championship. I had a good chance to win going into the last round. I was tied for the lead with Bob Charles and Chi Chi Rodriguez.

It was looking like I was going to lose the tournament when, all of a sudden, on the back nine, I got hot. I birdied the thirteenth, fifteenth, and sixteenth and got myself back into a tie for the lead before I bogeyed the seventeenth. But the guy I was tied with also bogeyed seventeenth. Then he made about a thirty-footer on the eighteenth.

And on that day, my son Chris was caddying for me. And to come walking up the eighteenth, with your son carrying your bag, knowing that you've got a shot at winning the golf tournament—now that's quite a thrill. I finished second, by the way.

I've got so much that I have to be thankful for. After my wife and I had been married for several years, they told us we couldn't have children. And to see our boy, Chris, who was born in 1973, grow to be a healthy, happy young man, that's got to be another highlight of my life.

You can win a lot of golf tournaments and win a lot of trophies and money, but that's not as good as seeing your children grow up.

I just wake up every morning and pinch myself to make sure that this whole thing's not a dream.

Tip

One thing that I believe is the key to the whole golf swing is good rhythm. I see people all the time with a fundamentally good golf swing, but who don't have good rhythm and are therefore not very good ball strikers. But yet you'll find some people who don't have good, sound swings, but they've got good rhythm and they are good ball strikers. I think rhythm is the key to the whole game of golf.

I'll tell you what I do—and I've done this for thirty-something years, I'd guess, almost ever since I started playing the game. I listen to one of those classic singers: Barbra Streisand, Barry Manilow, Sammy Davis Jr., even John Denver, singing soft and soothing music. I'll listen to that on the way to the golf course. And I'll find a song that just kind of sticks with me. I'll keep that song in my mind all day long; I'll just hum it to myself. And that helps me maintain rhythm.

So that's my suggestion: find a tune and hold on to it over the whole course as a way of improving your rhythm.

Photograph by Steve Greenwood/PGA TOUR

Gary Hallberg

SOMEHOW, GARY HALLBERG always manages to do what it takes to win. His first tournament at age nine was a father/son affair at Callaway Gardens. At Wake Forest, where he won the 1979 NCAA Championship, he was the first four-time first-team All-American in history. He was the first player to earn his PGA Tour card by winning the $8,000 needed at that time (1980) to obtain his playing privileges without going through Qualifying School.

Photo courtesy of PGA TOUR

As a pro, he won the Chunichi Crowns in Japan in 1982, the Isuzu/Andy Williams Open in 1983, the Chrysler Team Championship (with Scott Hoch) in 1986, the Greater Milwaukee Open in 1987, the Jerry Ford Invitational in 1988, and the Buick Southern Open in 1992 at—you guessed it—Callaway Gardens.

In 1994 Hallberg won more than $200,000 for the fourth time in his career, with his best finishes a fifth-place tie at the Southern Bell Colonial and a ninth-place tie at the Players Championship. He remains one of the friendliest, most approachable players on the Tour.

My mother and father came from Sweden when they were in their late teens. Actually, my dad was born here but went back to Sweden to get married, and that's when they came to the United States. Most Scandinavians are Lutherans. I used to ask my mother, "What religion are we, Mom?" She'd always say, "Lutheran." I'd say, "Okay." I just needed to know.

I used to go to my grandma's house for a month every summer. She was a Seventh-Day Adventist, and she read the Bible every day. In fact, every minute she wasn't cooking or ironing or knitting, she was reading the Bible. She was an incredible lady. And she was so wise; she had incredible wisdom. She always answered my questions just perfectly. I'd say she was very instrumental in my life, especially with my kid curiosity. So the Lord was working that way.

I don't think my folks ever went to church. I remember my mother saying, "We're not good enough to go to heaven. Very few people are going to go." I'd think, *You're not good enough? And you do everything just right! So what chance do I have?!*

Then in high school, my best friend's brother was having a Bible study, so I went to that one time. It was very interesting; I really enjoyed it. I was never one for history; it was my least favorite subject in school. I didn't care about those kings and guys who were all gone. I was more interested in what was going on right now. But this was very interesting to me, especially about Christ and the eternity aspect of it. At that age you're starting to think, *Gee whiz, where am I going? What am I going to do? What's this all about? You mean, someday I won't be here anymore?* That's a pretty scary thought—you get almost worried about it because you have no real assurance of eternal life.

My best buddy and I shared that common denominator of concern about the eternal. We went to Bible studies together, but he eventually moved away. And when he did, I got into drinking beer, hanging out with other kids—those teenage kinds of things.

From there I went to college at Wake Forest. There came a time there again, my sophomore year, when something happened. My best friend lived with a guy who was from somewhere in the Bahamas. This guy was incredible. He was a happy, friendly guy who loved the Lord. There was something special about him. He had an affect on my best friend while he was living with him. Everywhere we went, we were doing things together, having Bible studies, and we were really getting into it, reading more and more.

But it was more of a head thing. I was reading, learning, and getting educated, trying to find out about it: "What is this? What's this mean? What is that?" I was still not attending much church. Instead, I was doing my thing, playing a lot of golf, not doing real well in school, just getting by, looking forward to meeting a nice girl.

I turned pro right out of college. Things almost immediately went very well for me. That was a problem. I was swept up in my success, thinking that this was the way it was supposed to be. For most of us, it is a gradual improvement. But I turned pro, did well, slumped, did well, slumped, and continued to go up and down, up and down, up and down. I was very inconsistent.

Part of the problem was that I put so much emphasis on golf. I went out one time and played twenty-six weeks in a row; that's half a year. I didn't go home; I just stayed in hotel rooms. I was single, by myself, and lost. I was floating around out here and staying busy: you go here, you go there, your tee-time is so and so, you go to the hotel, you go to dinner, and you go out after that. I didn't have to think. Time was just flying by. But my golf game was not going very well.

I felt like I was letting a lot of people down, because I was out there trying to play golf, and I was *supposed* to be this great player, and I wasn't living up to the billing. So I worried about it. All these guys I used to be quite competitive with—and beat most of the time—were passing me. Take Fred Couples, for instance. I'd hardly heard of him when we were younger, and suddenly he was winning tournaments. It wasn't like I was better than the others, but they went right on by me. It had an impact on me.

I had built my self-esteem on golf—and it was pretty low. I wasn't really searching for anything, although I'd met my future wife by the middle of 1987 and we had started dating long-distance. It wasn't long before we got pretty serious. It was about then that I started to reflect on my life a bit, and I started to think, *Maybe this Christianity business . . . maybe I ought to focus in on that.*

So I started to pray and read the Bible—and suddenly it started to make sense! Instead of being a bunch of head knowledge, it was becoming clear.

My wife-to-be, Shirley, was living in Las Vegas at the time, and I think she was about like me, as far as where she was in her faith.

I'd prayed for a wife; I'd said prayers a lot: "God, if You're up there, I wouldn't mind a nice wife. I'm not going to look." I didn't have a date for a year after that! By then, I just wanted to talk to somebody—anybody! Finally, I met Shirley. She was working in a health club in Las Vegas.

It was hard to date while I was traveling, but we stayed in touch. During this time she started going to a church.

Also, during this period of my life, Jim Hiskey was very instrumental. Throughout the 1980s, from high school until I turned pro, Jim was there. He was always approachable and always pleasant. He is such a gentle spirit.

I'd always been the kind of person who didn't want to approach people who looked busy. Jim never looked busy. He was just kind of sitting there, looking around. I'd see him and say, "Hey Jim! How are you doing?" I'd sit down and talk to him lots and lots and lots. And through that, Jim introduced me to Christ.

It was about then that I experienced a turning point in my golfing career. I was playing worse. I had a lucky win at the Greater Milwaukee Open in 1987—I got into a swing thing and happened to pull it off—and I played better for a time.

In 1988 I took most of the year off to get to know my wife better. I stayed home most of the time because I was exempt for two years.

One Sunday we ended up in Calvary Chapel in Costa Mesa, California. We went to church because I was home and wasn't playing. We went in there, and the pastor said, "Anybody who wants to make it public, we're called to tell others, not to just keep it to ourselves." I think Shirley and I were thinking the same thing at the same time. But I hadn't been talking to anybody about what I was thinking. So I stood up, and Shirley stood up at the same time. There were hundreds of people in the church, and every eye was closed, and we both stood up with our eyes closed. When we opened our eyes, we were the only two standing. Then everybody else opened *their* eyes, and we were exposed to everybody!

If I'd been in school or anywhere, and I stood up with two hundred pairs of eyes on me, I would have been embarrassed. But I wasn't embarrassed then. It was a different feeling. We both went down to the front and talked about why we wanted to make it public.

That was a turning point.

Memorable Moment

The year I made my decision for Christ, I went to the Texas Open. At the time I was losing my Tour card; I'd only made $40,000. Until then my responsibilities had been first to my golf, and then to being a good guy. *I'm okay,* I thought. *People seem to like me. But now that I'm playing badly, suddenly I'm a loser, and nobody wants to talk to me. If I'm not a golfer with a capital "G," then what am I? What am I exactly?*

But for the first time, I went to Texas thinking, *Hey, God loves me. I'm okay.* I went to the Bible study that night. I had always been one to sit in the back of the class in school. That was partly because I didn't speak English when I went to kindergarten because we'd just come back from Sweden, and partly because I later sat with the jocks in the back. So I had an inferiority complex about academics.

But when I went to that Bible study, I wanted to talk all the time! I'd raise my hand, I'd talk about the issues, I was right in the middle of it with everybody, and I wasn't being judged. When you're a kid in school and you answer the wrong way, you feel really humiliated. But with believers, you don't judge each other. Not feeling judged is a wonderful feeling. It's such a judgmental world.

So the next day at the tournament, I let go. I needed to make $80,000 to keep my card, with only a couple of tournaments left. So I needed a second-place finish or two third-place finishes. And I'd never made the cut at the Las Vegas Invitational, so this was it. I was already thinking ahead!

From the first tee, I let go. I wasn't controlling it. It's hard to explain, but I went out there and played seventy-one holes, just floating along, having a real good tournament, and ending up tied for the lead with the last hole to go!

I got real scared on the last hole and made a bogey and lost by one. I finished second.

I'd prayed all week: "Lord, if you want me to continue in this fashion, if this is a loss, I'll consider this Your message." It was kind of like putting Him on the spot—this is it. But if I don't play golf, I'll do something else.

Well, I did it. *He* did it. And I've played better ever since.

Tip

One of the most important—and I don't know how to rate these because they're all important—aspects of your game is the swing. Because if you are not comfortable with your swing, you're going to have problems fighting with your swing, and you're not going to hit the ball where you want it. And if that's the case, then you're going to end up shooting high scores!

When you are standing at address, the face of the club should be facing directly at the target. At the top of your backswing, the toe of the club should then be pointed directly at the target. Amateurs, on the back swing, tend to pull the club too far inside or pick it up too far outside. And if you can't start your swing correctly, it is very difficult to finish your swing correctly. So you want to start your backswing correctly.

I feel that if I turn and get that toe up, I've made a nice, level shoulder turn and I've got good extension. If the toe is short, then I'm losing some of my extension. Having the toe up gives me my extension. I want the toe of the club pointing into the air. If you're doing it right, you could draw a line through the club and it would be pointed at your target.

That gets the club in the position that you want it in on the backswing. If you'll watch professional golfers hitting balls on the practice range, you see'll that the guys who are playing well are in some of the best positions on the backswing. It starts the swing and it sets up the swing. As a result, this is something I try to be conscious of and always work with. It helps my game.

Our hinges—our elbows, our hips, our knees—have to be hinging the right way throughout the swing.

The average amateur takes the club too far inside on his backswing, and it points to the right, so the ball is going to the right unless he makes a number of compensations for his swing. And when you have to compensate so much, you're eventually going to have injuries. It is a frustrating thing because it weakens an otherwise good swing. When your lines are off, the ball goes crooked.

Photograph by Pete Fontaine/PGA TOUR

Morris Hatalsky

IT WOULD BE DIFFICULT to find a more respected, more loved member of the PGA Tour than Morris Hatalsky. Half the Christians on the Tour point to Hatalsky as one of their spiritual mentors. The other half know him as an excellent player with four tournament victories to his credit (1981 Hall of Fame Classic, 1983 Greater Milwaukee Open, 1988 Kemper Open, and the 1990 Bank of Boston Classic).

Photo courtesy of Mary Darden

But then, Hatalsky has always been a winner. He won the 1968 Mexico National Junior Championship and was the captain of the 1972 U.S. International University team that won the NAIA championship.

But if he never leads in another Tournament, there are a couple hundred guys on the PGA Tour who will always consider him a winner—on and off the greens.

I am of Jewish heritage. It was mostly a culturally Jewish family, but we did acknowledge the high holidays such as Rosh Hashanah and Yom Kippur. I was raised by a mother and a grandmother—my father died when I was two years old. In other words, I was raised by two Jewish mothers! I was still brought up being very proud of my Jewish faith. And that's kind of the way my life was led.

I grew up understanding that there were Jewish people and there were those we called *Gentiles*—whom I equated with *Christians*. And I grew up having some strong prejudices because I was singled out as being a Jew. I received some very strong comments through my junior high school and high school days and definitely received some prejudice because of my faith. But God works things out for the good, though little did I know it at the time, because I developed some very strong feelings about what I deemed to be the hypocrisy in the Christian faith. Still, I always had a feeling that there was a God.

I came to know the Lord through a golfing friend, Don Pooley. Don and I first met when we were in Southern California. We had known each other through the years of competition in junior golf and later in college golf.

Meanwhile, golf was a vital part of my life. My identity was so tied into it that it was the god of my life. It really dictated my feelings toward myself, and it dictated my feelings toward other people. If I played well, I felt good about myself; if I played badly, I had a very low self-esteem. I was totally wrapped up in golf.

I finally got married. My wife, Tracy, had grown up Episcopalian, but she grew up with only an intellectual belief in Christ—she didn't have a relationship with Christ. Our understanding of our relationship was built on the premise, "If you're okay, I'm okay. There are different ways to come to know God." That way it was comfortable for our relationship.

There came a point when I went through a very difficult time in competing out on the Tour, and I started looking for answers to questions. I started asking myself deeper questions than just how to fix my golf game, questions like "Is this my purpose in life? Is chasing a little white golf ball what life's all about?"

There was an evolution of asking profound questions such as: Who am I? What am I? Where am I going? And why would I have my security and significance wrapped up in golf?

Through all this I was still friends with Don Pooley. Now Don was and is a very competitive person. He loves golf as much as I do. But he had a different perspective on God. He knew that I was Jewish; he respected that very much.

We would share our feelings and thoughts while on the courses and in the clubhouses. Basically, I shared about my Judaism and he shared about his Christianity. But when he did, he shared about the person of Jesus Christ, about a relationship with God.

One day he asked whether I was perfect, or whether I knew anybody that was perfect. I said, "No, not really." I had some tough times with that one, because I had a hard time with the word *sin*.

In time, though, I came to grips with that. Then I asked him a big question: "You know, I grew up believing that Jesus was a good man, a good prophet, and a good teacher, like Isaiah, Moses, and all of the great people—and I've just kind of put him in that line. So why did He die on a cross?"

Don shared with me from Isaiah 53. I was very much into, at that particular time, my Jewish heritage, the Scriptures, and what they said, and it really started coming alive to me in a way.

I suddenly realized that this prophecy in Isaiah 53 was written about seven hundred years before the actual event of the Cross. There was substantial historical evidence to prove that this Jesus was who it was referring to. It wasn't something that just slipped into the Scriptures. The Jewish people had a history of being very meticulous in the way that they wrote their history.

Don said, "Well, he died on a cross to bridge the gap between a holy God and sinful man—'not [your] works, lest anyone should boast'—as Paul says in Ephesians 2:9."

And at that moment, it made sense to me, because if God is a holy God, He is sovereign, omnipresent, omnipotent. His character in essence is holy, perfect, flawless, a perfect will. And if anything falls short of that, it is foreign to God.

I came to grips with that.

But I must say I was really just like Saul: I was the persecutor—the verbal persecutor—of what I thought Christianity was. Back then I saw a lot of hypocrisy because I wasn't focusing so much on the person of Jesus Christ as I was focusing on those people that said they knew the person of Jesus Christ.

So for some years after that, Don and I continued our heated discussions. But the thing that probably spoke strongest to me and helped me more than anything else to accept Jesus Christ as my Lord and Savior was the fact that Don Pooley stuck to what he believed the truth was. And that was Jesus saying, "I am the way, the truth, and the life. No one comes to the Father except through Me" (John 14:6). Don didn't waver from that, and yet he showed enough tolerance to be my friend even though I treated him poorly because of what I thought his faith was all about.

I was very, very strong-headed and indignant when it came to Christianity. I would dwell on what was happening with the Christian world at the time, such as the televangelism scandals.

But because Don continued to be my friend, and because he accepted who I was, I was motivated to continue to read the Scriptures, to continue to investigate what the truth really is. It was probably because of his friendship that I came to know the Lord. And the night I came to know the Lord was at a PGA Tour Bible study, where Billy Graham was the speaker and there were about thirty to forty people in attendance—a pretty intimate group. It was, incidentally, the last time Reverend Graham was out on the Tour.

But that night I accepted God's free gift.

Since that time I've tried to share a discerning spirit about what the good news of Jesus Christ is. I've tried to be vocal. I've been involved with many people's lives out here on the Tour. With some it has been a sowing process, and with others it has been a cultivating process, and with others it has been a reaping process.

It has taken me a long time, but I know it is God's business. I'm always available to talk. Or listen!

Memorable Moment

My first tournament win (the 1981 Hall of Fame Classic) was very special, and my second tournament win (1983 Greater Milwaukee Open) was also special, but probably the most memorable was my third win. And the reason is that I had gone five years without winning a golf tournament.

Along the way, there was an interesting journey I went through with my golf, and with my relationship with my wife, and with how this all evolved into what I can best describe as the "sanctifying process of a Christian."

That's why I think 1988, when I won the Kemper Open, was probably my most memorable moment, because it absolutely clarified God's faithfulness to me. The God I know through Jesus Christ is a sovereign God. That fact was shown to me so much throughout those five years, and it was consummated when I ended up winning that golf tournament.

Tip

I would venture to say there are as many different types of putting styles as there are different individuals on the Tour. So because of that, I would say it's important to allow every individual to have his or her own particular putting characteristics.

But there are some fundamental things you have to adhere to to be a consistently good putter.

One of the most important things that a person has in putting is the way they grip the club—the grip pressure. Grip pressure might even be more important than the grip itself because what you're trying to do is maintain the angle of the putter to make a good solid hit without having to manipulate the putter head.

Therefore, constant pressure, whether it is firm or whether it is light, is the most important factor. It's important that both hands feel like one when on the putting grip. You shouldn't have the right hand holding tighter than the left hand.

It's important that you "milk" the putter. Milking that putter is the regripping of the putter until you've got constant grip pressure in both hands. If you monitor that, you will not manipulate that putter head.

And while I believe that is probably the most important thing, I do like to see complementary angles in terms of the way a person grips the putter. In other words, the angles of the way your wrist and arms hang when you're setting up for your stance and when you're going to stroke the putt should be complementary.

I will also say this: To go along with the grip pressure and the proper grip, it's important to have complementary angles in terms of your shoulders, your hips, and probably your knees. Maybe not so much with your

Photograph by Pete Fontaine/PGA TOUR

stance. If you like to open up your stance a little—that's okay. If you like to close your stance—that's okay too.

But the fact is that closed shoulders and open hips are not complementary. It causes you to have different planes, and therefore you will have to manipulate the putter. Everything is on the premise of having complementary angles and not having to manipulate the putter.

Joe Jimenez

YOU'D BE HARD-PRESSED to name a more humble, more self-effacing Senior than Joe Jimenez. The soft-spoken Texan played the PGA Tour with middlin' success in the 1950s (he won the 1960 Puerto Rico Open), before working as a club pro for more than thirty years in the Midwest. After winning the old PGA Seniors' Championship in 1978, he joined the Senior Tour in 1982 and became fully exempt in 1986.

Photo courtesy of PGA TOUR

While Jimenez's most successful year came in 1990 (with $246,067 won), he's made a greater name for himself as a Super Senior. In 1994 he defended his Super Senior title at the First of America Classic and finished sixth overall in the money rankings. He currently stands second behind only Don January with twenty-nine Super Senior victories.

But what raised many eyebrows in 1994 was that the sixty-nine-year-old Jimenez shot his age or better six times at five different events. At age sixty-five, during the second round of the 1991 GTE Northwest Classic, he became the youngest Senior ever to shoot lower than his age with an eye-popping 63 at the Inglewood Country Club.

I was pretty much raised in a Christian environment from an early age. My folks were Catholic originally. When I was about six years old, they decided to join the Baptist church. My older brother, I think, was the first one to turn to the Baptist church, then my mother and father. I accepted the Lord when I was about ten and was baptized then. I was raised with a lot of Christian boys and girls, including the Baptist minister's children, and we all became very good friends. And we still are.

So that's pretty much how I came to believing.

Did you really have a good understanding of your salvation at age ten?

Well, the full understanding came a little later on. My mother was the strong one in the family, and she was always talking with us, telling us about our faith and our beliefs. I'd say I was in high school before I really learned more.

In my mind, everything happened for a reason. I knew early that the Lord provides everything. One of the things that I couldn't see right away, but I found out later, was that with the Lord everything is possible.

By the way, I married the minister's daughter too! She is a very strong believer; she reads her Scriptures every morning. Sometimes I forget the readings, but I always thank the Lord for her and for everything He has provided me.

Do the other Seniors know who the Christians are out on the course?

They probably do. You hear little things back and forth. They may kid around with you some, but they know. There are probably some fellows that should go to the Bible studies and pay closer attention to things of faith, but that's between them and the Lord. I don't know their hearts.

We won't know about some people until we get to heaven—if your name's on that list and you get there! There are a lot of temptations out here. You have to be yourself and try to live your Christian life.

Don Massengale is a good example of someone who is an inspiration out here. And I've had the opportunity to give my testimony as well.

Memorable Moment

I was a club professional for a long time, and before that I played a little bit on the old winter tours.

But I would say winning the PGA Seniors in 1978 was a big highlight of my life. That's why I'm out here today—because of winning that particular event.

But you know, just being out here is wonderful. You meet a lot of nice people. Actually, I haven't met any bad people on the Senior Tour, even the people I play with in the pro-ams or meet in the galleries; they're all good folks.

It's also great just being out here and playing with fellows that years ago you dreamed of playing with. Now I'm in foursomes with some of them. They are all pretty much down-to-earth guys. Probably because most of these fellows' families have gone and married—it's a lot more relaxing type of Tour. I think everybody gets along together.

Tip

Most of the time pros talk about proper grip or balance or keeping your head steady and other things, but along with all of that comes the mental game. If you can find that within yourself, if you can find what you can do, how much you can do, you can only get better.

The other thing is, if you can perform probably at the 80-percent level of your swing, you will do better. Don't let anybody you play with intimidate you. Instead, you've got to think, *I can hit it as far as he can.* But then, don't try to kill the ball; just try to finish your swing every time—and it *will* go farther. If you'll do that, just performing at 80 to 85 percent of your power in your swing, you'll get more distance because your swing is better and your timing is better. If you'll just do that, the distance will come with practice.

Too many golfers want to hit

Photograph by Pete Fontaine/PGA TOUR

it too hard; they're thinking, *Kill! Kill! Kill!* They've got to get over that. They've got to get that mental part of their game in order.

So don't worry about the weight transfer and all of that stuff. I think once you get the proper grip, stance, and the fundamentals, the amount of power you put behind the swing can make all the difference in the world in your driving success.

Steve Jones

A BAD MOTOCYCLE wreck nearly ended the career of one of the PGA's brightest young stars. Steve Jones won one victory in 1988 (the AT&T Pebble Beach National Pro-Am) and three more the following year (MONY Tournament of Champions, Bob Hope Chrysler Classic, and the Canadian Open), before the accident put him out for three full seasons.

Photo courtesy of PGA TOUR

Jones, who was a highly recruited multi-sport letterman in high school (including all-state in basketball), began concentrating on golf full-time at the University of Colorado, where he earned second-team All-American honors.

Still, his golf career suffered from a series of stops and starts before putting it all together in 1987 when he won the JCPenney Classic with Jane Crafter and began showing up regularly on the leaderboards.

Today he's back on the Tour, having completed a rigorous rehab program and competed successfully on both the NIKE and PGA Tours at the end of 1994. By early 1995, the affable, gentle-natured Jones was once again a force to be reckoned with on the links—and one of the best comeback stories in years.

As a kid, I went to a church that wasn't very evangelistic. It seemed like their message was that you just need to be a good person. At least, as a young person, that's what it seemed like to me. When I got older, church faded a little bit, and I finally quit going completely when I went to college.

In June 1984 I was about twenty-five years old, and someone asked me to go with them to a Bible church. I said, "Sure, that's no problem." After all, I grew up going to the church. I had a "religious TV movie" belief in the Bible—that if I were to die I'd go to heaven, and all that kind of stuff. But I never really was convicted about God in my life.

But in June of 1984, when I went to that church and heard what Dr. L. Strauss was talking about, I suddenly realized I was being spiritually convicted by the Holy Spirit! It opened my eyes. What he was talking about made me realize, for the first time, that I was not a Christian. I realized *Hey! I'm not doing what God wants me to do.* Through all those years, I thought I was okay doing my own thing.

So for six months I went to this Bible church between tournaments and listened to the gospel. Finally, on November 11, 1984, there was a guest speaker, and he gave a great message. He said: "Quite simply, you're either a son of God or a son of Satan. You're going to heaven, or you're going to hell. There's no riding the fence."

It was just what I needed at that time to make a decision. For six months I'd said, "If I'm going to make a decision for God and accept Christ, then it is going to be 100 percent—it's not going to be half-hearted. I just want to make sure I know what I'm doing."

And so that's exactly what happened. After six months, I finally said, "It's time." And that's when I accepted Christ and started growing from then on at Scottsdale Bible Church.

I'd been out on Tour one year, 1982, and then I busted my thumb and got that operated on in September of 1982. I dropped out of the Tour for almost a year and had to requalify. In 1984 I got my card back for the 1985 season. That was about two or three weeks after I became a Christian. But I lost it again and went back to Tour School, got it back, and lost it again. Finally, in 1986, I won the Tour School—and that was my last time back. But through the years I've gone back to Qualifying School five different times.

At the time, I wasn't married and I didn't have anybody in my life. In 1986 my life was God, and golf was my work. I finally met Bonnie, my wife-to-be, at the very end of 1985. When I first met her, I figured she was going to be the one I married. And sure enough, she ended up being the one I married! In February of 1991 we had our first child. Two years later, we had another.

Bonnie was a Christian when we met, and she understood my background, and that I had a different perspective on life, and we've really fit together well. It has meant a lot to our marriage and our family—and it has been a very good thing.

We've grown in our faith together too. There's nothing like being married to a woman who believes what you believe and really desires to please God in her life. There are so many people who are married to somebody that maybe isn't 100 percent in their commitment—and that's hard. I can't imagine it.

When I got married, I wanted to make sure I was marrying the right person. So before I married, I talked to a lot of people first. My desire was to marry a girl who was right with God and really wanted to please God and was a true believer. And Bonnie is all of that and more.

My goals for my family are simple: First, I want my kids to become more godly Christians than I am. And second, my family is to be a light to people in this age of divorce and noncommittment. I want to be able to say, "Listen, my wife and I are committed to each other and our kids. I love my job. *And there's nothing wrong with that!*"

Today, I look at golf as a job. Sometimes it is fun; sometimes it is not as much fun. It's more fun when you play well. Regardless, you have to just grind it out a lot of the time.

I've had a few injuries, but I've never really had a golf injury. We all put our faith in something, I've put my faith in God. If I'm supposed to be playing golf, I will be. I'm at peace with that. While I'm playing golf, I'll give 100 percent to that, and that's what I'll stick to.

You see, I had a bad motorcycle wreck, and that's what cost me virtually all of the 1992, 1993, and 1994 Tour seasons. I still just trusted God and said, "Hey, if He wants me back on Tour, fine."

But because of those years off the Tour, I now feel more comfortable than ever before being out here and witnessing and doing that type of thing.

Still, it was a different time for me. I'd been playing golf since I was eleven years old and, all of a sudden, to have two and a half years off—I just took it.

So you never know how long you've got out here. You've got to make the best of it, whether you're out on the PGA Tour or you're a janitor or whatever. Whatever you do, you've just got to be faithful. God hasn't called everybody to be working on the PGA Tour. Or to be CEO of a company. He wants faithful people. You don't have to be rich, just faithful. Wherever he puts you, just be faithful.

I've never prayed to win, I've just prayed, "Help me to be a good witness and to give it my best shot, Lord. You've given me the skills, and I want to use them for Your glory, whatever the outcome." There are a lot of Christians out here, and I don't know that any of them pray to win.

Memorable Moment

One of my strongest memories comes from a time when I had an interpreter in Japan back in 1990, and I was able to share the gospel with her. She didn't know at the time that I was a Christian. She knew after I started talking to her. I'd given her a New Testament written in Japanese and had talked to her about the Lord. Her job was to interpret for me. That's what she got paid for—as an interpreter for the golfers. And that's what she's still doing today.

But it wasn't until late 1994, four years later, that I found out she'd accepted the Lord. Now she's helping support one of the guys who has a golf ministry in Japan, helping him go to seminary. He was the one who told me the story, and it was really neat. It was nice to know I had a part in someone's salvation.

Who knows what effect you've had on other people. You'll never know until you get to heaven.

Of course, there have been a lot of times when I haven't been faithful, when I've messed up and missed sharing with someone I should have shared with.

When you're out in the public eye, you've got to walk in your faith, not just talk it.

People think, "How come this guy's different? Why is he different from that guy?" For me, here's the reason: Before, my desire was for the flesh. Now my desire is for the Spirit.

Before my conversion, I was the absolute worst. I used to drink ten to twelve beers a night just to get drunk, and I thought it was okay. I believed in a lot of weird stuff. But after I became a Christian, I quit drinking, I quit cussing—it was an incredible turnaround for me.

All of a sudden, people were saying, "What happened to you?" Some people felt weird about that, some people were real happy for me, and some people weren't happy for me. Well, maybe not unhappy—but they were really stunned at the commitment I had made. Hopefully, it had an effect on them as well.

I'm friends with almost everybody out here on the Tour, players and caddies alike. I can say hi to everybody with a straight face and know I have nothing against them. And if they ever want to talk, I'll share my faith. If there's ever a moment or an occasion that arises, one of the Christians out here—and there are a lot of them—will be ready. If one guy can't talk to someone, then someone else can.

So, I wait for the right moment and understand that that's why I'm out here. To make a change. Not only to glorify God, but to help change other people's lives by sharing the gospel with them.

So for all of us, the Tour Bible study means a great deal. It sure is nice to have a study where you can come and worship and learn and grow in the Word. Larry Moody does a great job. You can't do it alone. That's why the Bible talks about the body of Christ. You can't swing without your hands, and you can't swing without your feet— you need all of the body parts working together. Which is the way the church should function.

Tip

I use a putting board that's about eighteen inches long, and I line it up just left of the hole. It's called a putting track, and I put the heel of my putter on it, which keeps my stroke straight back and straight through and basically keeps me lined up. Mentally, that's what I'm trying to accomplish in the putting stroke so I can repeat it over and over and over. Hopefully, that will help

Photo courtesy of PGA TOUR

me repeat it out on the golf course.

I think the putting track is one of the best putting tools that anybody could use. Anybody can use it. I've seen a lot of different golfing aids, but I've never really used any of them until this one. It came along in 1991, and it has really helped me.

The great thing is that you can buy it commercially, or you can make your own with a 2 x 4 or 2 x 2 or anything.

But really, there are a lot of things you can do to help your game. I've run my putter up along a wall in a hotel room before. That really helps me.

Some people's strokes are maybe a little more inside or outside, but I pretty much keep mine straight back and straight through and just make a pendulum out of my shoulders, keeping my hands still. When it does right, after I read it correctly, that's the way I like to putt.

Of course, first of all, you always have to read the putt correctly, because if you don't read 'em right, you'll never make 'em.

Do whatever it takes; use whatever helps you like. Your goal is to make it automatic. The more you putt, the easier it becomes. And that's the way you want it to be.

Patty Jordan

YOU WOULDN'T KNOW the pretty lady with the sparkling green eyes is such a fighter. Her entire career has been a struggle, physically and emotionally, as she has overcome a series of career-threatening setbacks (including chemical imbalances that affected her adrenal and thyroid systems) to carve a niche for herself on the LPGA Tour.

Patty Jordan capped a fine amateur career by joining the LPGA in 1986. Two years later she captured the Mitsubishi Motors Ocean State Open and enjoyed her best year financially. And while 1994 was only the latest step on her road to full recovery, Jordan still managed to shoot a career-

Photo courtesy of LPGA TOUR

low 67 during the Jamie Farr Toledo Classic and finish tied for eleventh at the State Farm Rail Classic.

But those who know her—and her friends are legion on and off the links—know that the best is still yet to be for Patty Jordan.

I was raised in a churchgoing home where both of my parents believed. My father is Catholic and my mother is Presbyterian, and they continued to go to their respective churches during my entire growing-up period. It was "Dad's church" or "Mom's church"—never "my" church. Or my faith, really. They both had very strong personal beliefs, and neither one wanted to attack the other. It was wasn't exactly a hands-off subject at the house, but it was definitely Dad had his and Mom had hers. So my brother and I were kind of a little bit of both and not much of either.

So I wasn't totally Catholic and I wasn't totally Presbyterian; I just kind of floated along. Both of my parents felt very strong about their own faiths, and yet I didn't have a lot of training in either. So it was up to us kids as we got older to try and find our own way.

I started playing golf when I was young, and what attracted me to it was that on the course I had total control over what was going on. If I lost control, it was me that lost it. That is both the most appealing aspect and by far the most difficult part of this sport. It's a love/hate thing. It's the thing that makes you totally frustrated and the thing that makes you totally elated. It's all you—how *you* respond to every situation, the decisions *you* make, the preparation that *you* do.

Growing up, I really tried to pattern my life after my father; I loved him dearly. Unfortunately, he had a number of physical problems and died of cancer at the age of fifty-three. I was twenty years old and in college at the time. He'd battled for about five or six years with it.

And that became my testing ground; that created the need for me to find my faith. That's what set it in motion—for me to explore a little bit more of what they knew.

The other catalyst was going to college at Wake Forest. That was the first time that anybody I hung around with actually studied the Bible. That was a foreign concept to me—it was quite a new thing.

During my freshman year there was a girl on my hall who hosted a Bible study in her room, and any girls that wanted to could come. At that point I was sort of sitting on the fence. I would hang out with all of the other scholarship athletes, and a lot of them were good at playing hard and working hard. I had the playing hard part down pretty well. But then there was a part of me that was drawn to attend some of these Bible studies. For a while I was swinging in both directions.

As things got much more difficult with my dad, and we knew he wasn't going to be able to overcome this illness, I was really challenged. He was everything to me; who I strove to be. I wanted to do all the things he used to do. If he was the captain of his high school basketball team, I wanted to be captain of my high school basketball team. It was that kind of relationship.

Then, all of a sudden, that person I'd tried to chase after wasn't going to be there any more. It was really tough. I had to really think about who I was and what motivated me, because he meant all the world to me.

It was at that point that I really became humbled. Through the Bible studies, I realized that there was such a thing as a personal relationship with Christ and that Jesus died for each one of us. I had never felt that before.

There were a couple other tragic things that happened in our family within about a three-month period of my father's death, including a very young person whose life was taken and the death of my grandfather, who took his own life.

As all of that was coming down, I was finally at a point where I no longer thought I was going to live forever. Or even be healthy forever. We really don't know how long we have. So all of that raised some real questions in my life.

Finally, I accepted the Lord as my personal Savior prior to my dad's death. As I look back on all of the difficulties from that time, I can really see the Lord's hand pulling me through when I was very discouraged.

Some people say, "All things work for the good." Well, I don't know that God necessarily creates every circumstance. But I do know that in every circumstance, He can create something that *does* work for the good.

Sure, I've been disappointed in some aspects of my career. A few years ago, I had some necessary surgery, and it took quite some time to come back from that. I really felt like I was back 100 percent from that, but in 1990 I got very sick. It took almost a year before we found out what it was, what was going on, and what it was causing.

Turns out I had a chemical imbalance, but even now I can't get a consensus as to what's wrong. So it took several years to rectify; it was a slow process. It really hurt me physically, mentally, and emotionally because the imbalances caused extreme fatigue. I would bend down to make a putt, and when I'd stand up, I would get so dizzy I'd almost black out.

It also gave me huge emotional mood swings—which isn't my personality, and that's not how I know myself. As I was going through it, I just couldn't understand it: *What the heck's going on?! This isn't me!* I really struggled.

I stayed on the Tour anyway, which was probably a mistake. Playing through it during the most difficult times really hurt my confidence. I didn't perform very well.

As a result, it has been a struggle to pull it all back together since then. Sure, I have some regrets about that. I would have made a few different decisions if I could do it all over again. The frustration is to know that you have it within you, and you feel like you haven't pulled it all out yet. That was a tough thing to get tested on.

As Christians, God calls us to be the very best we can be. Being Christians, it's almost like there's a mattress underneath us. When we fall down, we're not going to break apart. We keep striving and we keep climbing, and when we fall—we're not going to break into pieces. We gather back up and go at it again.

As for the folks who don't have that faith, I'm not sure what happens to them when they fall. They don't have that cushion that says, "You're a whole person no matter what you shoot. You're a very, very special person. You're a created being with an eternal value that is much more important than whatever your scoring average is."

Do you have many witnessing opportunities on the LPGA Tour?

You respect the other people out here. With young players, there are definitely opportunities for them to see your faith—without your even having to verbalize it—in the everyday situations and stresses you go through. There are so many opportunities as a player to interact. It's unbelievable how many people you come in contact with. We're not on a playing field, separated from everybody else. We're not covered with helmets and pads—the people are up close and get to see our faces and hear what we say.

Being so public, we're constantly reminded that we're not there yet. There's a part of you that's constantly thinking, *I wish everybody didn't have to see me in my less-than-best state.* When you do or say something you shouldn't have, you can never get it back. If you are curt or snappy, how many times do you have to be gracious and loving to overcome that?

So there is a certain pressure out here to feel like you've got to rise to the occasion every moment.

How do you keep in close contact with your faith out on the Tour all of the time?

For the players, the Bible studies and chapel are where we get fed. That's where we encourage one another as players and continue the learning and growth process. And, in some cases, we've been able to hold one another accountable. Cris Stevens is good about that—she's been there before. She can say, "Maybe you're losing your perspective a little." We can help each other to be accountable—and, gosh, that's a rare thing in this world. It's a delicate balance out here because these are strong egos; these are all people who feel like they're capable of winning at any given moment.

To get real close to each other, with all of those dynamics, it's really a tough thing. You know that there are certain boundaries that you've got to keep because you're still competitors. A lot of players are real protective of that. So that's a constant battle. I have some friends from some other walks of life, and it seems easier to get into a closer relationship with them, but I realize now that some of the boundaries on the Tour are healthy. We spend a lot of time traveling together, playing practice rounds together, but we're still competing and we have to have certain boundaries.

If you know someone is going through a tough time, and you're playing with them in the last group, you have to keep this competitiveness healthy. You want to be their friend, but you want to be a competitor, too, and focus on your own thing.

The greatest gift I ever had was when I accepted the Lord, and now each day since that is a great gift as I'm growing more in Him. For me, I want to share that great gift.

With each new tournament, I stand on the edge of the tee box and pray, "Lord, help me to be a good servant to You. Help me to be a good witness. And whatever happens on the golf course today, help me reflect Your grace in my life." Then I tee it off.

Memorable Moment

My first year out, I qualified as a conditional player on the Tour. I didn't make enough money to keep my card that year, so I went back the next year to Q School. It was such an emotional week. The first couple of days, I shot pretty mediocre scores. I wasn't out of it, but I wasn't ahead either. The course was rough, it was wet, and it was extremely windy.

After the second night of play, I was really frustrated. I felt like I was trying to do it all by myself. People kept telling me I had some talent, but it wasn't happening.

So that night I got on my knees and prayed. I turned it all over to God again. I felt like I had been trying to do it all on my own. As I looked back on that first year, I realized that I hadn't really given Him my golf.

And so I did.

The next morning I went out and it was like the guy in the movie *Caddyshack*. I was making everything. I played great. The first nine, I think I shot a 32, and I still missed two or three putts inside of five feet! I was really going pretty well and on the last few holes I started thinking about what was happening, and I think at that point I took it back again and ended up with a 68.

But I've never forgotten that night before the third round, to be so confused and frustrated and to have this happen.

I did qualify and I got my card. God gave it to me. Spiritually it was a victory just to go out with the attitude that "It's golf. It'll still be here next year if I don't make it. It's in His hands. Whatever happens to me, it is still in His hands."

How many times have I had to relearn that lesson? But it is still a good one.

Tip

I don't want to spiritualize it too much, but if you start with a good thing and maintain a good thing—you're going to get good things. The setup is the key in golf: the fundamental things like posture and grip. People just

Photograph by Sandi Higgs/LPGA TOUR

don't want to hear it. You think it is too basic and you just want to get by it and get into the real meat. Well, that *is* the meat. Start with the good fundamentals.

Assuming you have a good grip and balanced posture, you need to maintain your triangles. You form the triangle by using your arms and your shoulders and your hands. The base of the triangle is where your hands combine—that's the nearest point of the triangle. The center of your sternum is the center of your triangle. So when you start taking it back, it stays at the center of your triangle. If you look at a player at the top of the backswing, it's still at the center of the triangle.

When one leg of the triangle outpaces another—or when you're swinging your arms faster than your body is turning—the triangle is destroyed. Likewise, if you turn your body faster than you swing your arms, the triangle is destroyed.

So if you start with something good and maintain it, you're going to be able to get consistent results.

I tell people to stick to the fundamentals, just as you need to stick to the fundamentals of your faith. Know that God is God, and He's the thing.

That's the same thing with golf. Stick to the fundamental things: get the best setup you can, and what you start with, try to maintain. When you change the angles in the triangle and add a lot of new things, you create a whole series of compensations, and then you're in for an awfully tough time.

Brian Kamm

BRIAN KAMM HAS been a model of consistency the last couple of years. In 1993 he won $183,185 to finish ninety-fourth overall, while in 1994 he won $181,884 to finish ninety-eighth overall. Likewise, his short, compact swing and excellent sand play (Kamm finished fifth in the PGA's Sand Saves category in 1994) make him a fine role model for young golfers.

Photo courtesy of PGA TOUR

The Florida State grad finished with a flourish in 1994, with strong finishes at the Walt Disney World/Oldsmobile Classic (tied for seventh), the Texas Open, and the Las Vegas Invitational. Then he began 1995 with a bang, briefly challenging at the tough Buick Invitational before finishing with an eleven-under-par 277 and a share of fifth-place prize money.

I come from a Lutheran church. When I was a kid, we went to church with Mom and Dad, but we never really desired to go to church. I went through confirmation classes and was confirmed. I was even an usher for a while. But after high school I started going just during the holidays. My mom and dad believed, but we never talked about it. To tell the truth, I never really knew what it meant to be a Christian until 1991. I always believed in God, but I didn't know much else.

I grew up playing golf. By the time I was fourteen, I'd decided I wanted to become a touring professional—that was the life I'd set up. Golf dominated my life from that point on. I told myself, *I'm going to turn pro, and I'm going to give myself three years to see if I'm good enough.*

After two years of college golf, I realized I was good enough, and two years later I got my Tour card and went out on the PGA Tour. Golf dominated my life. There was absolutely nothing important to me except getting my Tour card and playing on the PGA Tour.

From when I started playing at age eleven, right on through to the present day, I've improved every single year that I've played golf. I've spent twenty-four years improving in golf. It was a total obsession: "I *will* get that card, and I will do whatever it takes."

I went to college. I wasn't that great when I entered college, but I worked my way up, and by the end of the year, I was an All-American. But when I turned pro I didn't do very well at first. After a couple of years, I was doing well on the mini-tours. Then I won on the mini-tours. It was the same when I got my Tour card. I had a terrible 1990—I made $10,000 and made only five cuts that first year on the Tour.

Midway through my second year on Tour, the same thing was going on. I had basically only made about $7,000 *that* year to that point. So we're looking at a grand total of about $17,000 I had made on the PGA Tour in about a year and a half.

But beginning in 1990, I started playing on both the regular and Hogan tours with a friend of mine, Fred Wadsworth. Fred's a Christian who was on the Tour at the time.

He and his wife had talked to me about my faith from time to time, and they asked me to go to a Bible study one night. That evening Fred planted a seed: "Just because you're a good guy doesn't mean you're a Christian." That started working on me. This was about April 1990.

Later that year, I went for the first time to a Tour Bible study with Kenny Knox. David Krueger was speaking—and he's a fantastic speaker. I still love to hear him talk. From that point on, the beginnings of a religious faith just sort of got into my consciousness a little bit at a time.

I never really did anything about it until 1991. I was in Hattiesburg, Mississippi, playing in the Deposit Guarantee, and I was rooming with Fred Wadsworth again. That week he really sat down and *talked* to me. We spent some time in the room that night talking about God and talking about what a Christian is and how it is a personal relationship with Jesus.

This was something I never really understood before. That was the first time I'd ever heard it and understood it. As soon as I understood it, I made a commitment right then and there. I started reading the Bible that week; I read it pretty much every day until I'd read through the complete Bible. It took me probably two to two and a half years to finish it.

I made that commitment to Christ about April. In June I found myself in the U.S. Open. I had a chance to win the 1991 U.S. Open in Haseltine with nine holes to go. I was in the third-to-last group, playing with Fred Couples. My golf game took off after that point. That one tournament, that confidence builder, and I took off.

I almost got my card that year—I probably should have. I was leading the Canadian Open through six holes into the fourth round before Nick Price birdied five holes in a row to beat me. I ended up finishing eighth.

My career started taking off. Why? Mainly, I think, because golf was *not* the most important thing in my life anymore. It was still *very* important, but it was not the most important thing in my life. I had God, and I had my wife, Yvette, and two children now—and they were more important than golf.

I still worked at golf just as hard. I just didn't let it consume me as much. I felt like, *I'm playing golf to try to please God.*

Sure, I still find myself, as all Christians do, getting mad sometimes. Sometimes on a golf course, I think: *Why am I getting mad at a white ball?* I find myself not acting the way I should. I think we all do that. That's where I stumble a lot in my Christian life. But I'm working on it.

To be at this level, a PGA Tour player, you almost need to dominate yourself, to make golf the main focus in your life. But to become the best that you can be—there's no way that you can do it alone. The better you get, the more you play at that top level, the more self-doubt you begin to have.

I'm in it right now in October 1994, trying to finish in the top 125. Even four weeks ago I was sitting 160th on the money list, before finishing sixth at the Canadian Open, vaulting myself right into contention.

But maybe I won't finish in the top 125 this year. Maybe God doesn't want me to. But I can tell you this: When I didn't make it back in 1991, I went back to school and spent that whole year of 1992 on the NIKE Tour, and it taught me how to handle the pressure. I won out there, and I won out there in the heat. Certainly I want to play on the PGA, so I'm not working on being number 125 out here. I'm working on trying to improve myself as a person.

I'm also trying to win instead of just trying to keep my card. I've got three tournaments left this year, and I did not meet my expectations at all. In 1993 I finished ninety-fourth on the money list. I was shooting in 1994 for the top-30 list, not trying to struggle to keep my card. I struggled in 1994; I really played poorly. But you know what? I've got three tournaments left. What if I would go out and win one of those? All of a sudden, it would be my most successful year ever. And here I am in the first week of October saying it's not a very good year—even if I were to finish third somewhere. You just don't know how it is going to be. That's why you've got to remain patient—and faithful.

Memorable Moment

I think during the 1991 U.S. Open was when I realized I belonged. Playing there and playing close—that was one of my highlights.

But what I remember best about that day was one certain shot. The sixteenth hole is extremely difficult at Hazeltine. I was playing into the wind on Saturday with Sandy Lyle. I had been hitting drivers and four woods off the tee, but I hit a driver off the sixteenth tee that day because the flag was way in the back, right next to the water. For my second shot, I wasn't able to use a long club—it wouldn't have been smart. So I took my six iron out instead. My caddie was very experienced. He gave me the club and said, "Yes, the wind will get it. You can hit it!"

And I hit that shot within five feet of the pin. Those two shots could have been the best two shots of that tournament. They were definitely among the best on that hole, where golfers were getting doubles and triples left and right. I hit it within five feet for a possible birdie. In the grandstands around us, twenty thousand people were going crazy. I was so nervous over that putt, I missed it. They still went crazy when I walked off that green because I was the only one who had hit the ball back by that pin. I went on and birdied the seventeenth hole after that.

I also remember my first NIKE Tour victory in Panama City. I made about a twenty-footer down the hill, from the fringes, on the last hole to win by a shot.

Tip

When I drive, I like to eliminate one side of the golf course—usually the left side. So when I'm swinging, I pick a target on the range, start the ball at it, and try to have it fall a little bit right. I try to do the same thing on the golf course with probably 80 percent of my shots.

I pick a spot out in front of my ball, an immediate point, one that's maybe three or four yards between that spot and the point that I'm hitting. If I can line up over that spot, usually I can tell that I've aimed pretty well. If you try to aim by looking out over the practice range or the course, you're going to line up wrong. Picking a spot out in front of you is the best way to line up. It's something Jack Nicklaus has done forever, and I've been doing it for a long time now, probably twelve years.

It also helps if you have a proper stance and proper weight distribution, so your weight is between the balls of your feet and your heels. This is really important so that you don't get too far forward or too far back.

Also important is hitting the ball lower, which keeps the ball from going off-line. Because the lower it is, the less chance it has of going off-line. This way the ball will hit the ground first before it flies into the trees. You tee a ball lower and try to hit it lower when you really need to hit it straight. It makes that hole play a lot easier.

Photograph by Pete Fontaine/PGA TOUR

Let's say you have a hole with trouble on both sides. You've got trees and water, so you have to hit it straight. Take your fundamental shot that you like to hit. Then eliminate the left side.

I'll then set it up at the left edge of the rough, tee low, and try to hit at the left rough and let it go to the right—still very low. How far right can it go? As long as I know it's not going left, and it's going low—how far off-line can it really get?

Al Kelley

AL KELLEY ISN'T going to let a bad year or two get him down. The quietly determined veteran has persevered through lean times and remained humble through the good times as well.

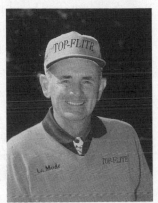

A well-respected amateur, Kelley won the 1960 and 1962 Florida Amateur Championships and the 1962 Air Force Worldwide Championship before joining the PGA Tour late in 1962. Alas, his stint on the pro circuit wasn't much to write home about.

Kelley joined the Senior Tour in 1986 and struggled until 1990, winning his first tournament and taking home $253,011 in year-end prize money.

Photo courtesy of PGA TOUR

Recent years have been a little tougher, but he did manage to card his first hole in one on the Senior Tour in the second round of the Franklin Quest Championship.

I was fortunate to have parents who went to church. My mother was an organist for several years in the church. My father was a school teacher, a Sunday school teacher, and was also Sunday school superintendent at our church. So we were involved in church from the beginning.

As for my personal faith, I think I'm developing it all of the time. Whether I'm signing an autograph or playing an actual game, I try to keep God in my life. I keep involved where I can in the church.

Nowadays I can't go to church every Sunday, of course, being on the Senior Tour. But this is where our chapel is so helpful because we otherwise don't get a chance to go to church. If I am playing great, I can make the early service a lot of Sundays! But sometimes I'm not playing so well and don't make it.

Still, you can build and grow so many ways: the Tour Bible study, your own study of the Scripture, or just hearing a good message. There should be some variety in what we're getting. And we can certainly learn a lot.

I don't think it is easier being a Christian on the Tour, but I do think it might be *harder* because of the fact that you want to do the right thing. Sometimes there are situations in your golf game or wherever that create negative feelings or aggravations. When you're out in the public like this, you have to be on your best behavior to keep trying to go the straight and narrow!

I try to witness by my actions. I haven't done as good a job as I'd like, but I try to get people interested in the chapel service.

And, in part because of my faith, I believe that if I didn't have the opportunity to keep playing, I could keep going on with my life and get into something else— and still be in golf to some extent.

For instance, my wife Norma and I are interested in Habitat for Humanity, so we'll probably be getting more into that in the days ahead. It's hard now because we're home for such short periods of time, so the situation really hasn't been right.

Plus, my shoulder was bothering me over the winter of 1994-95, so I wasn't sure I was up to pounding nails then! But I think in the future we might be able to do that. We like to be able to help the less fortunate when we can.

How did you come by the nickname "Mr. Monday"?

That came about back when I knew how to qualify on Monday! I hope I won't have to do that anymore. I finally started 1995 on the all-time money list, so I can hope I play well enough to keep on it in the future.

One thing I always remember is that if you're a Christian *and* you play golf, you have two of the most humbling things that there are in life. Both can really humble you in a hurry!

It's like Sam Snead once said to Ted Williams when they were out playing golf. Ted had said, "Sam, you've really got it made. You just tee the ball up and hit it.

It's standing still. I stand in the batter's box, and I'm dodging fast balls, and I'm trying to hit curves and sliders and everything they're throwing up there."

Sam hesitated a moment and said, "Yeah, but you don't have to play your foul balls!"

Memorable Moment

My first win in 1990 was a tremendous feeling. I was runner-up the week before and was never in the picture to win, because Chi Chi Rodriguez eagled two holes on the first nine and he was gone! I was probably ten shots behind him on the front side. But because I kept steady and ended up shooting a 69, I gained ground. We also had a rainstorm, and it was the kind of day where it was easy for the field to back up. I was six under, and all of a sudden a couple of guys who were eight under backed up to me. Then they bogeyed, and I ended up tied for second.

So I was going pretty good, and I just tried to play the same way the next week. I ended up going head-to-head with Lee Trevino, and I eventually won the tournament. It was just a case where I knew the golf course better than he did. It was the first year Lee had played the Newport Cup. We were rained out on the first day. During the first full round, everything went right for him, and he shot a 65. I hung in there, and the second day I made two or three birdies and he couldn't catch me.

I think that the Lord had a big part in it, because the week before, we'd stayed with some friends of ours, and they were praying each day that I'd have success. We went to their church on Sunday, and their minister told us that *he* was praying for me to play well! I felt very humbled that not only were my friends praying for me but the minister as well.

So I said to him, "With so many people in the world who need prayer much more than I do, I feel honored. At the same time, I hope that I'm not taking up their prayer time!"

He said, "Oh, not at all. I feel like everybody deserves to have prayer time!"

I felt like their prayers put me in the right mood at the Newport.

Since then, I've been trying to get my minister friend back on tour. We can't go back to his place because that was the only time we've ever played there!

T i p

Two of the most important things in the swing are movement and extension. This is where amateurs tend to lose it. It is so easy to hit with their hands that they lose their balance or fall away from the ball instead of trying to hit with their body and control their hands.

So if you're hitting with movement and extension—or stretching through the ball—then you've got a better chance of being consistent.

These are two of the easiest things to deteriorate in a golf swing, because it takes a little more effort to move and a little more effort to extend. It's more comfortable to pull with our hands and quit with our movement, but we don't get the results that we otherwise would.

Consequently, it is so important to keep that extension through the hitting area and try to finish things off.

If a person can't finish, then either they don't have the right balance or their hands are over-powering their swing. Backing down with the pressure in your hands and softening your grip or not swinging so hard will sometimes help.

There's also an exercise where you start with your hands to make the first move on your downswing. The second move is to get into the hitting area, and let go with your right hand, and pull the club through with your left hand, and finish and balance on your left foot. This is the best exercise I know for actually feeling like you're pulling the club through. It's the same whether you're hitting with irons or woods.

Photograph by Sam Greenwood/PGA TOUR

Betsy King

HOW DO YOU sum up the career of a superstar in just a couple of paragraphs? Betsy King is one of the most dominant players to ever play the LPGA Tour. There is, quite literally, nothing she hasn't accomplished on the Tour. And she's done it with grace, style, élan, and a strong, vibrant Christian faith.

Photo courtesy of LPGA TOUR

In college she was Furman's Athlete of the Year in 1977. She joined the LPGA that same year and won a tournament every year from 1984 to 1993. She has won a host of tournaments (not counting four unofficial tournament victories), including the 1987 and 1990 Nabisco Dinah Shore, the 1990 U.S. Women's Open, and the 1992 Mazda LPGA Championship. In 1994 she passed Pat Bradley as the Tour's all-time money-winner with more than $5 million in earnings.

And in the summer of 1995, she won the ShopRite Classic. The victory was number thirty in her illustrious career and automatically earned her a spot in the LPGA Hall of Fame.

But there's so much more to Betsy King than just victories and money. She is vitally active in a number of humanitarian and religious efforts both in the U.S. and abroad. She's been a pivotal member of the U.S. Solheim Cup teams in 1990, '92, and '94. And she's touched untold numbers of lives both on and off the greens.

How do you sum up the career of a superstar in just a couple of paragraphs?
You don't.

I grew up attending church. Mine wasn't an evangelical background, but I went to church fairly regularly, and I did become confirmed in the Episcopalian church.

I went to college at Furman, a Southern Baptist school, and at the time, a lot of kids were active in Christian activities. I can remember walking down the halls and seeing signs for Bible studies or for the Campus Crusade chapter on campus or FCA meetings. I never got involved with any of them for some reason—I guess I was too into school and golf.

But once I went out on the LPGA Tour, I got involved with the fellowship through a couple of people, especially Donna White, when she was playing on the Tour. And the very first activity I attended, back in 1979, was when I inadvertently went to a Fellowship of Christian Athletes golf day.

Bill Lewis was the first one who approached me, because he was originally from Reading, Pennsylvania, where I'm from, and that's where I got involved. Following that golf day, I rode to the mixed-team tournament at the Broadmore with a lady named Margie Davis. She was going to be coming out on Tour the next year, the way Cris Stevens is out now, and she invited me to come to the first Tee-off Conference, a weekend retreat for Christian golfers that was held the week before the first tournament on tour. And that's where I committed my life to Christ.

Before then, I'd never really heard that I should have a personal relationship with Jesus Christ, or that I needed to personalize that Christ died on the cross for *my* sin—not just the general sins of the world. And I didn't know that it was more than just going to church on Sunday.

I always was a "good person." I didn't get into trouble much, I didn't drink much, and I wasn't wild. So sometimes it's hard for people who are close to you to see a real big change. But I knew inside, in my heart, that I was not a Christian.

Golf takes a lot of practice, and sometimes you don't have a lot of time to do other things. But I've found—as I've gotten older, particularly—that there have been more opportunities to spend time with other people or to share my faith, and that's been good to see and be a part of.

A few years ago I went on a mission trip to Korea. We played golf with some different groups and shared our faith there. And I've done a couple of different things in Japan too—all because golf gave me a platform to speak. Sometimes you'd like to get away from that, but golf gives you a platform among golfers, and maybe some credibility among people in the business world if you've had success.

And sometimes it is just nice to do things where being a golfer doesn't make a bit of difference. Our trip to Romania was definitely that way. There they don't know anything—or very little—about golf. There aren't any golf courses in Romania. Being golfers didn't make much difference.

But a group of us went over and volunteered to do whatever we could to help. It originated with Cris; she wanted us to do something internationally, to help us get a feeling for the body of Christ around the world. It just so happened that Denny Ryberg had contacts in Romania. And that's how we ended up going there.

It was interesting going back a second time in 1994, because we spent some time with a couple of full-time missionaries, with some people who have committed a year, and with another guy who has committed four years. I found it very interesting to talk to them, to find out why they're there and what's the mind-set of someone that goes into full-time mission work. Just making the commitment to learn the language is a big effort—and something that needs to be done if you're going to have an impact.

But it's just nice to help people as one person helping another.

The level of comfort that Romanians live in is vastly different from here, so their concerns are not: "Well, are we going to get that second car?" or "When are we going to get a bigger house?" Instead, it's more "Are we going to have enough food to eat today?" and "Are we going to have enough fuel for heat this winter?" Their energies are tied up with just the basic necessities of life.

That's the hardest to understand. You don't realize how optimistic we are in this country until you go to Romania. We still have the feeling in this country that, if you work hard enough, you can make it. Most Romanians don't feel that, because they don't have a government that supports them. Instead, it represses them or makes it impossible to get ahead. It's not like here, where we say, "Well, if I just work a little harder, it'll eventually pay off." Because in Romania, it probably won't.

One of the things you do learn in missions is that everybody needs the Lord. Whether or not you're starving, you still need the Lord.

And the Romanian church really has grown. In some ways, because they are in more of a crisis situation, it causes people to question why and makes them think

There has to be something better than this life. So in that respect, maybe their situation makes more people turn to the faith.

I found that in Korea too. While we were in South Korea in 1985, they were still living under the threat of being invaded by North Korea—the guy that was leading North Korea then was kind of crazy—so they still had air-raid drills once a month. They had cables strung down the middle of golf courses so that planes couldn't land in the middle of fairways if there were another invasion.

It would be like living in Pennsylvania and being worried all the time that New Jersey was going to invade you! It would make you think, *You know, I could die tomorrow,* and sometimes when that happens, people are more apt to say, "What *if* I die tomorrow?" Whereas living here, people put that question off. And they sure don't say, "What if I die tomorrow—am I going to go to heaven?"

Sometimes when you're looking in from the outside, you think that if a player doesn't win on the Tour, then they have no reason to stay out here. When everybody first comes out, they think, *Oh, I'm going to win. If I don't win in the first year, I'm not successful.* By the time I finally won, I was thinking, *Well, I might never win out here. But I'm still going to make a nice living and I'm still going to stay out here and work to be the best player I can be, whatever that is.*

And as soon as I decided that, I started winning. It was strange. I have to give a lot of credit to Ed Oldfield too. He helped me make some swing changes that allowed me to hit the ball better and perform better.

I can't say that I won tournaments when I came to a personal relationship with Jesus. Sometimes people make it too dramatic. I mean, if that were true, then everybody on the LPGA would be at the Bible study each week! I have a hard time with that.

But certainly I feel that, as a Christian, you do almost have an advantage because you do have it in perspective a little bit, and you're not basing your self-worth on what you shoot on the course. I see players out here and their moods definitely go up and down according to how they're playing.

I admit that I get into that mode a little bit when I'm struggling. It makes it a little bit tougher to be out here, but when I know that God loves me the same whether I shoot 58 or 80, it makes it easier to put it on the line week after week.

There are a lot of people who are scared to say, "Hey, I gave it my best and it wasn't good enough." As a Christian you can say, "Hey, I gave it my best and if it's not good enough, that's fine. And if it is, that's good too—because my relationship with the Lord isn't going to change whether I win a tournament or don't win a tournament." For a player, that's reassuring.

Memorable Moment

The first wins are always special because until then, you're not sure you're able to win. I think the biggest thing I've learned is how many shots you can miss and still win a golf tournament. Up until that point, I felt like I had to play the game of my life in order to win. It really is amazing—you can shoot a round of 76 and still win a golf tournament! It's how you recover from those mistakes. It's just a little something here and there that determines who wins.

Probably my best performance, in my mind, was the LPGA Championship in 1992, where I shot seventeen under par for four days, and I didn't think anybody could shoot that. The course played long; it's a very tight driving golf course. I just played very well and kept the ball in play. I didn't really have a bad day in my four days out there. So that's probably been my best performance.

Tip

In playing with amateurs, I don't feel like I'm that great a teacher as far as the swing goes. But just by watching how they play, I think I can help their games

Photograph by Jeff Hornback

after playing eighteen holes with them. Usually amateurs make a lot of mistakes in strategy. Most pros play the percentage shots.

For instance, on a par five where I have a chance of reaching the green in two—if I don't feel like I can get on the green, then I don't take the risk. If it just means that I'm only going to get twenty or thirty yards from the green, I'm not going to take the risk. I'd rather lay up to a shot and avoid having to carry water with a wood or something.

So I would say as a pro to an amateur, the biggest thing is learning to play within yourself, to play the percentages. If you're a fifteen-handicapper, be realistic about how you're going to hit the ball. If you hit it in the woods, just trickle it out rather than trying to hit a shot where you have only a one-in-thirty chance of pulling it off!

If you have to take one more shot to get on the green, take it. You see that all of the time, players aiming at a pin. I say, just try to hit it toward the center of the green.

Bernhard Langer

IT'S NOT ENOUGH to say that Bernhard Langer is the greatest German golfer who ever lived. You have to add that he is one of the greatest golfers of our generation from any country.

Photo courtesy of PGA TOUR

In addition to being just one of three men to win the Masters twice, Langer has won more than thirty international tournaments since 1980, including virtually every major European Open. He has had at least one European Tour victory every year for the past sixteen years.

He is also a selfless team player, representing Europe and Germany dozens of times with the European Ryder Cup, the World Cup, the Dunhill Cup, the Nissan Cup, the Kirin Cup, and the Four Tours World Championship.

Alas, Langer's playing time in the U.S. has decreased in recent years, but when he does play a full schedule (as he did in 1993), he always acquits himself quite well indeed!

I grew up in the little town of Anhausen, about thirty miles from Munich. My father was a bricklayer and my mother was a housewife. I am the youngest of three children. In those days we were very poor.

At the age of eight, I started caddying to earn some money. There were eight boys from our town who caddied on a regular basis. We were paid five marks—which is about three dollars—for eighteen holes. The golf course was five miles away, so we rode our bicycles to get there and back. Out of those eight guys, three became golf professionals. We got four old clubs from a member and all of the caddies shared them. Those four clubs were a two wood, a three iron, a seven iron, and a putter with a bent shaft. Maybe that's where all of my putting problems have come from!

In the early years of my life, I grew up in a religious home. I went to a Roman Catholic church on a regular basis and served as an altar boy for seven years. I always believed in God and was very religious. By being religious, I mean I tried to keep all of the rules, like not eating meat on Fridays, going to church as often as possible, and going to confession.

In August 1972 I started my first job as an assistant professional in Munich. I had a wonderful time working on the golf course all day and playing a lot of golf.

When I finished my apprenticeship and got my diploma as a golf professional, I was eighteen and decided to try my luck on the tour for a couple of years. I bought a little Ford and drove two thousand miles to Spain and Portugal, where the first stop of the 1976 tour would be.

I immediately developed the "yips." Yips is an uncontrollable and involuntary movement of the muscles. It has destroyed many professional careers, such as golfers and surgeons. I think part of the problem was that I put too much pressure on myself. I did not have much money, and I wanted to succeed quickly. I was lodging in some terrible places, the cheapest places I could find. I didn't want to spend much money on food, and I couldn't afford a caddie. And I certainly could not afford to fly from country to country, so I drove many long hours on the road. The first two to three years were pretty rough, and the problem with my putting did not help.

In 1978 I still had putting problems. On one occasion during a match play tournament, I four-putted from within three feet. I was double hitting it. Those were extremely difficult and trying times. There were many times when I asked the Lord, "Why me? What have I done to deserve this?" There were also many days when I thought about quitting and going back to teaching golf.

The breakthrough came in 1979 when I won the World Championship at twenty-five years of age by a record seventeen strokes, which is still a record. I made every putt I looked at, and it was as if a heavy load fell off my shoulders.

Two years later, in 1981, I won the money list in Europe, and no one would ever have thought a German could do that. Oh yes, we have good soccer players, great tennis stars, and good skiers, but golfers? No way!

Nineteen eighty-four was a great year for me. The most important event of the year occurred in January. In 1983, I had met and begun dating a girl from Louisiana named Vikki. On January 20 she became my wife. That was the beginning of many great things. By the end of that year, I had won the money list again in Europe and finished second at the British Open in St. Andrews. I also played eight events on the U.S. tour and won enough money to receive my PGA Tour card for 1985.

In 1985, my first year as a member on the U.S. tour, I won the biggest event of my career thus far, the Masters in Augusta, Georgia—one of the four Grand Slam events. I also won the Sea Pines Heritage Classic in Hilton Head, South Carolina, the Australian Masters, the Casio World Open in Japan, the Sun City Million Dollar in South Africa, and two events in Europe. That year I won seven tournaments in five different continents. I was ranked number one in the world. I had a beautiful young wife and had achieved everything I could ever have dreamed of.

The problem was, there was still something missing. As I analyzed it, with a lifestyle like mine, it is easy to get wrapped up in things like money, cars, houses, and positions in the world rankings, the U.S. tour, the European tour, and so on. It seemed easy to be greedy, jealous, full of myself, and thinking I could do it all myself—and get a false sense of security.

My priorities were: golf, golf, golf, and more golf, then myself, a little time with my wife, and every now and then—the Lord. If my golf was not good, my whole life was miserable. I always hoped that being a good person and keeping some of the Commandments would get me into heaven. I was trying not to steal or hurt anyone on purpose.

As I got more and more successful, I thought I could do it all myself. I didn't need God so much when everything was going great. I still prayed every now and then, and I still went to church on Sundays.

Then in 1985, the week after I won the U.S. Masters, I was invited by a friend of mine, Bobby Clampett, to come to the Tour Bible study on a Wednesday evening. I told my wife that I would like to go, and she also came. There we met Larry Moody and a whole bunch of other professional golfers and their wives. That evening was the first time in my life that I heard that I needed to be reborn to be able to have eternal life.

That did not make any sense to me. So at the end of the study I asked Larry what he meant when he said that I had to be reborn. Surely, at the age of twenty-eight, I could not be born again.

He opened the Bible and showed me John 3:3, which reads, "Most assuredly, I say to you, unless one is born again, he cannot see the kingdom of God." And John 3:5 reads, "Most assuredly, I say to you, unless one is born of water and the Spirit, he cannot enter the kingdom of God."

I thought I was a pretty good Christian, but I had never heard this before. Larry went on to explain what it meant in practical terms. He told me that every one of us is separated from a perfect and holy God because of our imperfection and sinfulness.

He went on to say that many religious people think they can overcome this problem by doing lots of good deeds for God. But no one is so good that they can save themselves, and no one is so bad that God can't save them.

The reason Jesus Christ came to earth was to pay the penalty for our sins so we would not have to be forever separated from God. Through His death and resurrection, Jesus made it possible for us to have an eternal relationship with God. Romans 6:23 says, "For the wages of sin is death [which means eternal separation], but the gift of God is eternal life in Christ Jesus our Lord."

Instead of trusting in what I could do to get me to heaven, I needed to trust solely in Christ's death and resurrection as sufficient payment for my sins. The moment I trust Christ as my Savior, I'm born spiritually into the family of God.

To be born again means that I have experienced true birth. Everyone who has ever lived has experienced the first birth, but not everyone experiences the second birth. Only those individuals who transfer their trust from themselves to Christ experience the second birth. We cannot earn our way to heaven. Those who are born again do not trust in what they do, but in what Christ did to save them.

And Larry went on to say that once we accept Christ's free gift of salvation, the Holy Spirit comes to live permanently within us and guides our thoughts and actions.

Furthermore, Jesus promised not only to give us eternal life, but also an abundant life. The promise of an abundant life does not mean that we will not face pain and problems. But it does mean that God will give us the strength to face any circumstance.

After understanding that God loved me so much that He sent His only Son to die for my sin, and that I could never be good enough to get to heaven through my works, but only according to His mercy and free gift, it was natural for me to ask the Lord into my life and let the Holy Spirit reign within me.

My wife, Vikki, felt the same way, and she also accepted Jesus Christ as her personal Savior. Since then, I have seen tremendous changes in her life, my life, our relationship as husband and wife, and the way we treat our friends and anyone else in this world. Many of our prayers have been answered.

My priorities have changed a lot since that day in 1985. Now my number-one priority is God, number two is my family, and number three is my job. At times it is hard to keep this order, and I fall back into my old habits. But I believe when you have your priorities right, everything is much easier in life. Every morning when I get up, I give my whole day over to the Lord, I give over all of my thoughts and actions, and I ask Him to lead me through the day. I ask Him to help me treat other people in a loving and honorable way and to help me deal with the daily frustrations of life.

I'm never alone. He's always by my side, and things happen much smoother and easier.

God has truly blessed me, and I thank Him daily for my talents and gifts to play this game so well.

I'm still in the early stages of my spiritual life with the Lord. But I already know what a difference it has made. The Lord has given me peace, patience, confidence, and a sense of security that I did not have without Him.

I could only wish the same for you. I hope and pray that all of you will experience the same joy and peace that I now know through Christ. Accept His priceless gift of salvation. You will never regret it. On this earth, or in heaven.

By the way, I will give free golf lessons in heaven. I pray that I will see you there.

Memorable Moment

In 1991, I was one of the twelve Europeans chosen to play against the twelve best Americans for the Ryder Cup. It is the most important team competition of professional golf; it is the Super Bowl of professional golf.

My team captain put me in the so-called "anchor position," which is the last player out on the course. My opponent was Hale Irwin, and when we played the fifteenth hole, the U.S. team had a one-point lead, and I was two holes down with four holes to play. I won the fifteenth and seventeenth holes to draw even. If I could win the last hole and gain a point, I could win the match and keep the Ryder Cup in Europe.

So it all came down to the last putt of the last hole in the last match on the last day. Hale Irwin made a five and I faced a six-foot putt to win my match and retain the Ryder Cup for Europe. It was by far the most important stroke in my career, and millions of people in thirty-two countries were watching on TV.

I prayed for courage, strength, and a quiet hand. I didn't want to let my teammates down; I wanted to make that putt and become the hero of the Ryder Cup.

I missed. And as the ball slid over the right edge of the hole, the American crowd cheered and celebrated their team. All I could feel was pain, agony, and disappointment.

It would have been easy to blame God and say, "Why did you let this happen to me? Why me?" A nightmare like that can easily destroy one's confidence—even one's career.

But I came to see that it was an opportunity for me to test my faith and see if I really did love and trust Him, no matter what might happen. By having an eternal perspective and a personal relationship with Christ, I was able to cope with it.

I looked at it this way: There was only one perfect man in this world—and they crucified Him.

All I did was miss a putt.

Two days later I played the German Masters in Stuttgart, and I faced many reporters who asked the same question. I realized pretty quickly that people would remind me for the rest of my life about what happened on that Sunday afternoon at Kiowa Island. I received hundreds of letters from all over the world from people who felt for me and wanted to encourage me.

The very next Sunday, I faced a fifteen-foot putt on the last hole of the German Masters to get into a play-off. It was very hard to block out the negative thoughts about what had happened just seven days earlier. But I made the putt and went on to win the play-off and the trophy.

With God's grace and the encouragement of my family and friends, I went on to win more prize money that year than any golfer had ever won in a year.

Vintage Club
Palm Desert, California

PDI: Chris John

PDI: Chris John

Inverness Golf Club
Palatine, Illinois

PDI: Pga Tour

The NEC World Series
of Golf

TPC at Avenel

PDI: Chris John

Teton Pines Golf Course
Jackson, Wyoming

PDI: Chris John

Congressional Country Club
Bethesda, Maryland

PDI: Chris John

PDI: Chris John

Grandfather Golf and Country Club
Linville, North Carolina

PDI: PGA Tour

The Byron Nelson Classic

PDI: Chris John

Westwood Country Club
Vienna, Virginia

PDI: Chris John

Queenstown Harbor Golf Links
Queenstown, Maryland

Jackson Hole Golf and Tennis Club
Jackson, Wyoming

PDI: Chris John

My most meaningful victory, since I became a born-again Christian, came when I won the U.S. Masters for a second time in 1993. This time it was even more special, since I won it on Easter Sunday, which is the day we celebrate the resurrection of Jesus.

Tip

For me, there are three very important things in the golf swing. One is the grip, the next is the address position—the way we stand over the ball and how we aim—and the third one would be the swing path, that is the path and the way we swing the club.

I would like to talk a little bit about the address position because that's where I see the most players make a lot of mistakes. You can generally tell a good player from a bad player just in how he stands over the ball—without even seeing him swing.

Your alignment is very important. It should look like a railroad track. The outer line is the clubface, aiming at the target. The inner line is your feet, hips, and shoulders aiming parallel to the target.

That's very important—but it is not easy, because we're not looking at the target from behind the ball, we're standing to the side of the ball. That's one of the reasons why it is so difficult to aim correctly. If people aim wrong, they have to concentrate to bring the ball back on target. If I aim thirty yards right, I have to come over the top to bring the ball back to the left—and vice versa. And that causes a lot of swing problems.

The other thing is you want

Photo courtesy of PGA TOUR

to keep your back pretty straight and let your arms hang very relaxed so that there is no tension in your hands, arms, or shoulders. They all should be very relaxed. You should be in a very athletic position with a slight knee flex.

And from that position, you are just going to try to make a full shoulder turn—and some hip turn, obviously—to create a move you can always repeat. You don't want to try a half backswing or a three-quarter backswing.

Then, to come back to the address position, the ball position, is obviously very important as well. A lot of people have the ball too far forward, which means that their shoulders will have to be open to reach for the ball. They have to slide into the shot (or all sorts of things) just to get to the golf ball.

In my eyes, the ball position should be in the middle of the feet for the shorter shots, and between center and the left heel for the medium range shots. For the woods and long irons, I would have the ball opposite of my left heel because it is not a descending blow. It is more of a sweeping blow, especially with a driver.

Those things are extremely important. A lot of people look for some magic tips when their real problem is in their address position or line up or in the way they aim.

I would like to see almost every amateur set a club down when he or she hits balls on the driving range. Set one or two clubs on the ground, facing at the target. That helps you align your feet, your clubface, and your shoulders.

You could even set another club at a right angle to it where the ball position is so that you have one or two clubs pointing at the target and one or two between your legs where the ball position is—at a right angle—so that you can see where the ball is aligned.

Tom Lehman

WHEN YOU TALK about perseverance, you've got to cite Tom Lehman. His first foray into the PGA Tour from 1983-85 was—to put it kindly—a bust. But he honed his skills on the Dakotas, Golden State, South Florida, and Carolinas mini-tours and used the Ben Hogan/NIKE Tour as his springboard back to the Big Time in 1992.

Photo courtesy of PGA TOUR

That year Lehman won $579,093. In 1993 he won $422,761, and in '94 he took home a whopping $1,031,144 to finish fourth overall in earnings.

Nineteen ninety-four also included Lehman's first victory (at the Memorial Tournament), a second (the Masters), and a third (Bell Canadian Open). He continued his winning ways in 1995, capturing the Colonial and finishing second at the United Air Lines Hawaiian Open and third at the U.S. Open.

When you talk about success, you've got to cite Tom Lehman.

I was raised in what I would consider a Christian environment. For me, that meant going to mass on Sunday. My parents read the Bible, believed what it said, and had a definite faith in Jesus Christ. But for me, it didn't really hit home until I was fifteen.

I was an athlete and a student, and it seemed that my whole life was wrapped up in having to be good at what I was doing. But the ups and the downs, the successes and the failures, really gave me a sense of the emptiness on which I was putting the emphasis of my life.

It got to a point where I was feeling very hopeless and very despairing about what the meaning of life was.

Finally, I went to a Fellowship of Christian Athletes meeting where they talked about a personal relationship with Jesus Christ—how we're separated from Him by sin and how He forgives our sins. They talked about how He can give us peace and hope and joy and unconditional love and acceptance. And that's exactly what I was looking for.

There have been so many people who have been instrumental in my faith walk, but I think the most instrumental were the people I went to high school with. There were a bunch of guys on the football and basketball teams who were strong Christians: Jeff Leslie, John Donatelle, Rod Ripberger, and a few other guys whom I really looked up to. They were strong believers. Also, our football coach, Ed Christopherson, had a big impact. Growing up, I'd think, *I'd like to be like these guys.* So, more than anyone else, they had a big influence on me.

I think that everything you go through helps you develop character. And the Bible talks about how God allows you to go through good times and bad times so you'll be trained by what you go through. Then you'll learn how to persevere, how to develop character, how to be more open and, hopefully, how to be more like God. I really feel like every good thing and every bad thing you actually go through is experienced in order to make you more like Christ—if you'll allow it to train you in that way.

I've never been much of a worrier. I think I have a very simple faith in God. I felt strongly very early in my life that He cared for me, loved me, would provide for me, and would do the best for me. And that meant in golf, out of golf, whatever.

Is it tough living in a fishbowl like professional golf?

Not really. Yes, people are watching us, but I believe the most important thing is to be real. Being real means you are going to stumble and you are going to fail. I think it is important not to pretend you are somebody you really aren't. I'm not ever going to pretend that I'm perfect—because I'm far from it.

I think it is important that, when people realize a guy is a Christian, he doesn't pretend like he's holier-than-thou; he doesn't act like he's Jesus Christ and proud of himself. I think people can understand if you get upset on the golf course or get in a bad mood once in a while. I think it is important that people see the *real* side of you.

In our Bible studies, we talk about doing things for the glory of God and not for the pleasures of men. That's one of the ways you can keep yourself focused on being everything God wants you to be on the golf course. You need to play for God and God alone. Whatever else comes along is nice, but it doesn't really mean as much as having God saying, "Well done."

Do you see your golf as a ministry—as a way to spread the Word of the Lord?

God has definitely used the golf in a great way over the last several years. I think of myself as a Christian who plays golf, not as a golfer who is a Christian. So whatever kind of job I do, there is a way for God to use that as a tool. In society at large, especially the way golf is growing, there is a huge platform for golfers.

Do you do much public speaking about your faith? You spoke at the '95 Masters on Sunday morning.

Actually, I do quite a bit of speaking. I do quite a bit with FCA. I've also gotten heavily involved in Athletes in Action in Canada. Also Executive Ministries, Campus Crusade, Youth for Christ—all kinds of different things. I enjoy speaking.

I always try to convey to those groups—especially to professions that are very competitive—that there are ups and downs in life. For so many of us, happiness is derived by how well we perform. So the message I try to convey is that we are unconditionally loved, and we are eternally accepted by God, regardless of our successes or failures in business. Or in life.

I usually give my testimony: about how I felt so hopeless and despairing as a kid and how I really feel that meaning in life shouldn't be derived from performance and whether you won the golf tournament or not or whether you closed the deal or not. Meaning in life is derived from your walk with Jesus Christ. There are so many people who are empty, who are looking for something beyond just the daily routine of work and whatever else.

In my own life, I think maturity really helps. When I was a young Christian, I was surrounded by so many Christian people that it made being a Christian very easy. The downfall was, I counted so much on that fellowship that I never got too much into the Word like I should have.

When I got away from involvement at school and was a twenty-three-year-old kid out on my own, I learned that if you don't have that circle of supporters around you, it's a struggle. It's a maturity thing. I had to learn how to get disciplined, how to pray, and how to walk with God on my own.

Your story is interesting because you made the PGA Tour,
then were forced to return to the NIKE Tour,
then fought your way back to the PGA
more successful than ever.

At the beginning of my pro career, I put so much emphasis on money and in being successful that all of the things I felt from age fifteen to age twenty-two were shot down by the things I saw all around me. I went from doing things for God's glory and trying to be His kind of guy to trying to make money and be successful, just for myself. It took my being knocked way down to realize that God wanted me to be *His* man. He wanted me to be His man with my family, with golf, with everything I did. And to start putting the focus on God and say, "God, I'm going to be whatever You want, go wherever You want me to go. If You want me to quit golf, I will. If You want me to be a golfer, I will. Take me where You want and I'll follow."

That's the kind of perspective I think I regained during those struggling years of 1985 to 1990.

At the same time, you've got to be careful with your prayers, because God answers prayers. If you pray and ask that He help you develop character or integrity, He'll do it!

I wouldn't trade those bad years, golf-wise, for anything, because those were some of the best years of my life, especially in terms of meeting friends, growing spiritually, and growing as a person. The Lord helped me see what's important in life.

And, to be quite honest, all of the success of the last three years has been great and everything, but when I won the Memorial in 1994, I thought to myself, *If you have to spend your whole life looking for this thrill of victory, how disappointed you will be.* Because it just wasn't that thrilling. The round was great, and the money was great, but this is not what life's all about. Relationships are what matters.

I'm thirty-six years old, and as I get older, I see that relationships are what's important in life. I was talking with a friend earlier this year and talked about how the Tour at times can be on the unfulfilling side because it is such an individual thing, and it is difficult to develop close relationships—for a number of reasons. You're not on the same schedule as everybody else.

But relationships are what give meaning to life. A relationship with God is wonderful. He loves us unconditionally. And we need to love the people around us—hopefully the same way. And that's much more meaningful and lasts a lot longer than any success on the golf course.

Memorable Moment

I do have a memorable moment from the Tour School in December of 1990. I had struggled to that point with a lack of confidence and way too many feelings of anxiety. I just didn't trust in who I was as a golfer.

At Tour School that year, I went to the seventy-second hole needing a birdie to make the four-round cut and have a chance to get my card. The hole was a par four—about four hundred yards. I hit a good drive. It was the kind of shot where you need the ball to fade to hit it close to the hole. That was a shot I really didn't have confidence in. But I still had to do it, because that's what it called for.

To make a long story short, I hit a nearly perfect fade and had a two-foot putt for a birdie.

That was the turning point in my golf career. At that point, I felt like all the anxiety and fear that had been on my shoulders for so many years just lifted away. It was as if God had given me another chance to learn my lesson. It was as if God were saying, "I gave you the ability. I trust in you. Now you trust in yourself when you play golf."

From that point forward, I was a different golfer.

I'm a firm believer that God gives you all kinds of opportunities to learn these things. If God wants you to accomplish something in your life, He's going to put things in your life for you to learn from. It's often cumulative. You learn a little bit here and a little bit there. And then there's the final straw that puts you over the hump. Once you get it, you know you've got it.

Tip

I don't really think much about technique at all; I'm a "feel" player. Most of the time, I talk about taking a bag of balls out and trying to hit different kinds of shots to get a feel for the club—a feel for what it takes to make the ball hook or fade or go higher or lower. I learn by feel.

So on the range, I create different situations: If the pin's right, I try to hit a fade. If the pin's left, I try to hit a hook. If the pin's at the back, I try to hit a roll and watch it bounce up. If the pin's at the front, I try to hit it high and bring it in soft.

Just hitting different shots gives you a feel for the shots you'll have to hit when you get out on the golf course. Then it'll be like you've done it before. It's better than pounding away on the driving range. Golf is a lot different than just mechanically beating balls.

Golfers are people, and they're all different. Some have very analytical, scientific minds. And for them to know exactly why mechanically you have do

Photograph by Pete Fontaine/PGA TOUR

this to make a ball do *that* is important. And that's okay too. Nick Faldo is that way. Nick is a scientist. He needs to know exactly what *it* is. He needs to answer all the questions in his mind.

But I don't have these questions. I just watch how the ball flies when I do something. Then I try to figure out what made it do that. And if it is a bad result, then I do something different.

Steve Lowery

GETTING THIS SELF-EFFACING, soft-spoken Alabama boy to talk about himself is like pulling teeth—unless you ask about Crimson Tide football!

After a couple of years of knocking around the periphery of the Tour, Lowery exploded in 1994, winning his first tournament and finishing with nearly $800,000 in prize money. In fact, few players played better in 1994's closing tournaments, including an eighth-place tie at the season-ending Tour Championship. His opening-round 66 included only the second hole-in-one in Tour Championship history, on Olympic Club's challenging No. 8, no less.

Photo courtesy of PGA TOUR

I did not grow up in the church; we occasionally went, but I really didn't come from a Christian background.

I was led to Christ by some Christian golfers. I wanted to have what they had, the peace that I could tell was in their lives. I'd experienced a lot of success all through my life, but as I turned pro when I was twenty-four, things changed. I started going to a lot of the Bible studies, and people like Dick Mast made an impact on me.

One night during that time, I went home and started listening to Charles Stanley on the television. I made a decision to accept Christ in my life that evening. I acknowledged that I needed Him, that I was a sinner.

God had allowed a lot of great things to happen in my life, but through them all, I was searching for what I was supposed to be doing. Looking back on it, it was the only way that He could have done it, because I'd played golf my whole life, and I was basically led by the euphoria of playing well. The highs and lows of this life are very dramatic. But Jesus was the constant that I needed. In the low point in my life, He used that to bring me to Him.

If you'd continued to play successfully, do you think you would have ever come to a personal relationship with Jesus?

I'd like to say so, but probably not. I grew up playing golf; that's all I really knew. I thought I had the world by the tail; the reality was that I didn't know as much as I thought I did. I'm sure this is a similar story to many out here on the Tour, but it is still miraculous when it happens to you.

Because golf is an individual sport, when you do well, you tend to feel as though you are the one who's doing it, that you are the one in control of it, that you are the one who's deserving of it. But when God opens your eyes and makes you realize that everything you have is a result of Him and that you're totally dependent on Him, it makes a huge difference.

It's important for me to know that I can rest in the fact that God—not Steve Lowery—is in control of my life. I don't have the worries and anxieties of trying to be something I'm not. He sent His Son to die for me, so I'm already—in His eyes—all I need to be. I just need to be myself as He created me. I don't have to worry whether I'm witnessing for Him through a low point in my life or a high point—He thinks enough of me to send His Son for me.

Is it easier or harder being a Christian as a pro golfer?

If being a Christian is serving other people, it is hard to serve people on the Tour because they do everything for you. If you're trying to humble yourself and exalt other people around you and all they want to do is put you up on a pedestal, it's a challenge to try to make other people feel more important. People are always trying to do things for you, so you're constantly trying to serve from that position.

At this point, through October 1994, I've already had the best year I've ever had on the Tour, and I'm trying to constantly remind myself that God has allowed this to happen and that He's the one that's orchestrated my whole career. Not that I feel like I've done it, but I'm constantly reminding myself that He's given me the talent, He's given me the health, He's given me every opportunity—everything is from Him. I'm constantly coming back to that.

As a Christian, you always want to have the right attitudes, but the world is constantly pushing you up here, and you're trying to have this personal relationship separate from that, knowing, in your heart, that He's given you everything that you have. Even though people are telling you something totally different, that somehow you're some kind of hero, you have to constantly humble yourself before the Lord.

Is it possible to remain "fed" as a Christian on the Tour?

It's much harder, even though there's a Bible study and a group of Christians; we're just not constantly together. There are some weeks when half of the guys aren't playing. There are other weeks when you have a 7:10 A.M. tee-time, and you have to be out there at 6:30 A.M. warming up, and it is hard to be at a Bible study across town until 9:30 or 10:00 the night before. It's a challenge.

You have to push yourself to the fellowship and to the other things, because it's not like it's all there before you. It's not like you show up at church and there are three hundred people there with whom you can spend time. Basically, we have a couple hours on a Wednesday evening. If you're home, you try to go to church. But it's not like the normal eight to five, off on the weekends, go to church on Wednesday night and all day Sunday lifestyle.

I have my own Bible reading times. And one thing about this life, you have a lot of spare time on the road. If I'm on the road by myself, and my wife Kathryn and the kids aren't with me, I have a lot of time to spend praying and reading the Bible. There's lots of time on the airplanes. So actually you have a lot of quiet, quality time.

I guess missing the fellowship with other Christians is the one aspect that's harder than any other.

Memorable Moment

In 1994 I won the Sprint International. I eagled the seventeenth hole, the second eagle of the back nine. That was *the* shot that was really something else, something special.

You know that God is always working in your life, whether you shoot an 85 or a 65, but it sure is apparent at times when something is really amazing in your life.

My parents don't come to a lot of tournaments; they live in Birmingham. But my mom and my dad, my mother-in-law, my wife and my daughter, three or four other couples who are friends of my parents, and some other family friends all flew in to Denver that week. We were all there. My caddie had his girlfriend, his dad, and his stepsister there—and *they* were all at that tournament. It's a fairly off-the-beaten path tournament; it's not like Orlando, where I live. Still, they were all there, and I won it! It was so amazing, not only to me, but to everybody. Everybody said, "This has been decided on from up above. This is not something that is mere coincidence."

That was a point in my life where you can point there and say, "That was definitely God intervening." You see, my parents had not only never seen me win as a professional, they had always felt like they didn't want to come watch me, because it made me nervous and messed me up. They were not the type to even come out and watch.

But this one time, they all came, and they all watched, and I won my first tournament! A lot of people have their parents there every week, and their parents have watched them forever, but my parents always felt like maybe this was a distraction. They didn't really want to come out much—"it isn't the time" sort of thing.

That was a really amazing tournament for me, especially the way it happened.

T i p

Whenever I give a lesson, it's really tough, because I'm not a mechanical person, and I do not teach someone, "You need to do this" or "You need to do that." I'm more of a "feel" kind of player or a "react to the shot" type of player.

Putting is the strength of my game, and most "feel" type players are good putters: Ben Crenshaw, for example.

Consequently, I don't work on mechanics: perfectly straight back, keep it low, all that stuff.

Instead, with me, it's like you're a basketball player dribbling down the court. The defender moves left, and you just shoot. You don't really think about it—you just do it. I'm that kind of golfer.

My thought process goes like this: This putt's going to break a little bit to the left, so I'm going to play the ball off a little to the right. I'm looking at the point where I want the ball to go in.

Now, I will say, if it's real windy, widen your stance a little, but not a whole lot. That's kind of a feel thing too. If I'm uncomfortable, if I feel like I'm going to get blown over, I just do it. I don't worry about the structure thing; it's just another feel thing.

Then I line it up where I'm going to hit it and trust that it is going to go there. And, just often enough, it does!

Photograph by Sam Greenwood/PGA TOUR

Don Massengale

IT SEEMS LIKE there's always been a Massengale playing professional golf. First there was Don, then there was brother Rik, and now Don's son Donnie is on the NIKE Tour.

Photo courtesy of PGA TOUR

Don Massengale joined the PGA Tour in 1960 and eventually earned more than $200,000 along the way, in addition to winning the 1966 Bing Crosby Celebrity Pro-Am and the 1966 Canadian Open. After retiring from the PGA, he became a well-respected club pro and in 1972 even won the National Club Pro Championship.

Massengale joined the Senior Tour in 1987 and has enjoyed a number of solid seasons. He won the 1990 Greater Grand Rapids Open and the 1992 Royal Caribbean Classic. In fact, in 1992 he won more money than he won in his entire PGA Tour career—a dazzling $271,184!

Various aches and pains have cut Massengale's touring schedule in recent years, but he remains an affable, congenial player, and a wizard playing out of the sand.

I was raised in a Christian environment. My mother and father were Christians, and they went to church regularly and let me go regularly, although sometimes as a kid I guess you don't want to go. I always went. We went Sunday morning and Sunday night and did all of the stuff. It was a very good family environment.

Even so, I didn't really come to be a Christian until a long time after that. I thought that I was; I had gone down front and joined the church when I was twelve.

But it wasn't until quite a bit later in life—in 1967, and I was born in 1937—that I became a Christian!

I did that by going to a Tour Bible study with my wife, Judy, and my brother, Rik, and his wife, Cindy. Dave Reagan was speaking that night. He explained what you had to do to become a Christian, and that we were all sinners and that Jesus died on the cross for our sins.

At that point, I realized that I had not accepted Christ. And that very night I admitted that I was a sinner, and I invited Him into my life.

It was an instant change. One of the things I had had trouble with was bad language. I cussed—*a lot*. After the Bible study, I was playing in the Houston Open. I'd barely qualified to get in. This Bible study was on Wednesday night. And so I went out and played on Thursday. I was playing along, and I had some good holes and some bad holes. After about ten or twelve holes, I realized that something was missing. I hadn't said a cuss word all day!

Since that time—and we all slip from time to time—the Lord has taken that bad language away from me. That was quite an experience in my life.

Did the other golfers notice a difference in your life?

Yes, I think they did. I know a lot of the people who played golf with me knew that there was a difference. And I think it had an effect on a couple of people. One became a Christian some time after that. He was playing golf with me and wanted to talk with me about what changes had been made in my life and so on and so forth. So we talked.

Out here, a lot of our witnessing is just trying to conduct ourselves correctly more than trying to go around witnessing at every stop. I think a lot of people resent that, and you don't want to be getting into a big brouhaha about that. I think the way we conduct ourselves and handle ourselves is sometimes more important than what we say.

Still, it would have been a tough past twenty years without the Lord. And when it gets down to playing like I did in 1994 when I got real sick and had a health problem, those times are pretty difficult too—even being a Christian. You go from playing and finishing in the top thirty to thirty-five on the Tour every year to finishing right down at the bottom—that's a hard thing to understand and explain.

But you have to realize that the Lord's got a plan; you just don't always know what it is—although you'd just love, even once, to look to the future and see what that plan is!

Could you leave golf behind if you had to?

Oh yes. I've already made that commitment to the Lord. I had a very bad year in 1994, as bad as I've ever played out here. And here in early 1995, I'm not playing all that well either. I basically told the Lord, "If You want me to stay out here, I'd love to stay. But if You want me to do something else, I'm willing to do it too."

Playing good or even medium golf out here is fine. Playing bad golf out here isn't any fun at all.

I know that there are other avenues He might want me to travel. We're just taking it a step at a time right now, seeing if my golf will get better this year. We'll see and kind of go from there. I'm just out here on faith and waiting to see what the Lord wants me to do.

It's hard to hide playing professional golf.

It really is. I've always been one that wanted to please my peers—or at least not look bad in front of people. I think I've been too concerned about what people think of me, rather than what I should have been focusing on.

That was something else I learned over the winter of 1994-95. It's still a hard thing to change, but I learned that you don't have to please any of these people out here. The only person you really have to please is the Lord. Once you're trained in one direction, it's tough to switch that train into another direction. But at least now I've focused on that to a degree, and I understand that the only person I have to please is the Lord—*not* the people out here I play with or for.

Memorable Moment

We're doing this interview at Key Biscayne, and back in 1992 I won the tournament here—that was very memorable. I shot a 65 the last day and came from six shots behind to win.

Somebody asked me afterward, "When you get in a position like this, what do you do? And how do you keep from getting nervous?"

Well, for me—and this is something I do all of the time—after each shot I sing "How Great Thou Art." It puts the focus away from my golf and onto the Lord. I'm still nervous, there's no question about that, but it is an interesting way to release some pressure and tension and get my mind on something other than what I was doing at the time.

T i p

I think probably average players, especially with their drivers, try to play with too little loft. I think they need to add about eleven to twelve degrees, or play with a three wood, until they can get some confidence in what they're doing.

The average person slices the ball a lot. The straighter the face, the more it's going to slice. But the more loft on the club, the more it's going to have lift on it—which will eliminate some of the slice.

That's one of the things I've noticed playing with amateurs. If they'd play with more loft on their clubs, until they get a little better, I think they would be more successful.

Photograph by Sam Greenwood/PGA TOUR

Rik Massengale

RIK IS ANOTHER one of those golf-playing Massengales. After a highly successful college career at the University of Texas from 1967 to 1969, Massengale joined the PGA Tour in 1970. He hit his stride in the mid-'70s, winning the 1975 Tallahassee Open, the 1976 Sammy Davis Jr. Greater Hartford Open, and the 1977 Bob Hope Desert Classic. Too bad Dean Martin or Frank Sinatra didn't have tournaments back then as well!

Photo courtesy of
Rik Massengale

Although he still plays the PGA Tour at age forty-eight, he is currently the director of College Golf Fellowship, a Christian ministry to college golfers and coaches. Located in Flower Mound, Texas, CGF's goal is to expose college golfers and coaches to the gospel of Jesus Christ and encourage them in their spiritual growth.

When I was twelve years old, my brother Don started playing the PGA Tour. From that time forward, all of my family vacations were spent at pro tournaments watching Don compete. I was able to go into the pro's locker room and sometimes even walk inside the ropes with Don while he played. Because of this exposure to the Tour, I knew from an early age that I wanted to play pro golf.

I played other sports through high school, but I knew that golf would provide my only opportunity to play a professional sport. I was able to win some junior golf tournaments and was granted a golf scholarship to the University of Texas. My main reason for going to college was to play on the golf team, because I knew I needed the competition on the college level to prepare me for the Tour.

While in college, I really developed tunnel vision. In fact, golf became a god in my life. Everything I did was centered around golf, and every decision was determined by what would best benefit my golf future. Instead of developing a long-range plan for my future and using my college experience to prepare for it, I saw college simply as an opportunity to gain the competitive edge I needed for pro golf.

Because achieving at golf was so important to me, everything else in my life was affected by the way I played. On the golf course I would get mad and curse and throw clubs when I hit bad shots or missed easy putts. I knew that this type of attitude and behavior kept me from playing as well as I could, but I just didn't have the self-control that I needed to respond correctly.

I also had problems off the course. My identity was totally tied up in being a golfer. I was fine as long as I was around golfers and people who knew of my golfing abilities. But if I was around people who didn't know of my achievements, I became very insecure. To overcome this feeling of inadequacy, I started drinking. The only way I could socialize was to drink enough to lose my inhibitions. Because of my drinking antics, I was known as a "wild man" at fraternity parties, but the fact was that I was too insecure to be there any other way.

During my time in college, I had some good success and won some golf tournaments, including the Southwest Conference Championship and Western Amateur. The success further fueled my desire to play the Tour, and in 1969 I turned pro and entered the Tour Qualifying School.

The biggest disappointment in my life came when I failed to qualify for the Tour on my first attempt. At that time there were no other pro tournaments in which I could play, and I had to wait an entire year for my next chance to qualify. I worked at a golf course and had a lot of time to practice. Fortunately, I was able to qualify in 1970.

My first couple of years on the Tour were not as successful as I had hoped, but I accepted the fact that it would probably take a couple of years to adjust, so I persevered. However, by my fourth year on Tour my self-worth was at an all-time low. I felt fine if I played well, but I was miserable if I played poorly. And I played poorly a lot more than I played well! I became so unhappy that I decided I was going to quit the Tour.

I was also having a lot of marriage problems—which were directly related to my golf career, because I was unable to leave my golf problems at the golf course. I was often preoccupied and concerned with golf, which made me unable to meet the needs of my family.

In the spring of 1974, my wife decided to file for divorce. But before we went through with the divorce, we had a talk together, and we went to one of the Tour Bible studies. I had grown up in a church, but because my church experience lacked relevance, I quit going when I started college. However, I had some questions and thought some of the pros might have some answers.

The Reverend Billy Graham, who was playing in the pro-am of the Kemper Open that year, was the speaker at the Bible study. He made a statement that Christianity was not a religion, it is a personal relationship with Jesus Christ. That really hit me because I didn't know what that meant. I had never heard that before. I went to that meeting thinking that I was a Christian because I attended church for a lot of years.

The next week a friend of mine gave me a Campus Crusade booklet that explained how a person becomes a Christian. From it I realized that I was not a Christian because I had never made any kind of commitment to Christ. I just thought it was "try hard, do good, and maybe you'll make it to heaven."

But with the help of just these few verses, I realized that Christ had paid the penalty for my sin and that I just needed to receive that gift of salvation from Him:

- *For all have sinned and fall short of the glory of God* (Rom. 3:23). I had to admit that I had sinned and rebelled against God's laws and standards.
- *For the wages of sin is death, but the gift of God is eternal life in Christ Jesus our Lord* (Rom. 6:23). I had to acknowledge that the penalty for sin was separation from God for eternity. I realized for the first time that I stood before God condemned, and I had no idea what to do about it.
- *But God demonstrates His own love toward us, in that while we were still sinners, Christ died for us* (Rom. 5:8). Even though I had sinned and

deserved to be separated from God, Jesus Christ came and died on the cross for me. I deserved death, but Jesus became my substitute.

- *But as many as received Him, to them He gave the right to become children of God, to those who believe in His name* (John 1:12). It was not enough to know the facts about Jesus Christ, but I had to personally receive Him as my Savior.

In June of 1974 I acknowledged my sin and received Jesus Christ into my life. That was the greatest decision I have ever made. My wife made that commitment at the same time.

I didn't experience an overnight change, but over the next six to eight months I realized that God was making significant changes in my life.

Over the next few months my wife and I started seeing our relationship growing closer, only because our main priority was getting to know Christ better by reading the Scriptures together and praying together. As we started growing closer to God, we started seeing that our marriage and our relationship as a couple were improving.

In 1994, we celebrated twenty-five years of marriage, and I know that without Christ we never would have made it five years. Also, God gave me a great victory over my emotions on the golf course, gave me much more patience, peace, and self-control than I had ever had before. Golf became an enjoyable career from that point on, even though there were good years and bad years. It is never fun to play poorly, but after receiving Christ, at least my whole life is not dictated by the way I played on the course!

Memorable Moment

Well, winning the Bob Hope Desert Classic is probably the highlight—not just winning—but that whole week was probably the peak of my golf career. I never played that way again. I became a Christian in 1974, I won the Tallahassee Open in 1975, the Sammy Davis Greater Hartford Open in 1976, and in 1977 I started out leading the Bob Hope, and I won it going away from the first day.

Going into the last round, I knew I was close to the tournament record. I had a thirty-foot putt on the last hole, and I made it to shoot twenty-three under par for the week, breaking Arnold Palmer's fifteen-year-old record. The record has been broken a few times since then, but at the time, that was a pretty big highlight for me.

That was probably the most prestigious tournament that I've won, maybe because of all the media coverage that it gets on TV. Plus, that was the best I ever played. Back then it was a five-round tournament, and I only made three bogeys the whole week. My long game was good, my short game was good, everything went well that whole week.

Tip

Putting has always been my strength. My ball-hitting ability has been up and down, but I have consistently been a good putter, and I think that it is basically for two reasons.

Mechanically, the problem that I see most people having is that—if they're a right-handed putter—their left-hand form breaks down going through the ball and the right hand passes the left.

The thing that I have done, which I think allows me to putt well for a long period of time, is that I started trying to putt with my left wrist stiff. I grew up putting real "wristy," following the example of Arnold Palmer and Billy Casper, who were great putters when I was learning golf. That is a very inconsistent way to putt.

The trend over the years has really gone from "wristy" putting to very stiff-wristed putting—arm and shoulder putting. When I made that change in 1974, going from a wrist putter to an arm and

Photo courtesy of Rik Massengale

shoulder putter, that's when I became consistent. Before that, I had good days, but I also had very bad days.

I would encourage anyone to stand and look in the mirror and take a practice stroke and see if they can see their left wrist bending at all as they go through the putt. If they do, they are going to have some inconsistent rounds on the putting green. For most people, it is a very difficult thing because they are right-handed, and your right hand is where you actually feel the distance—you actually hit the ball with your right hand. If you can keep your left hand moving the whole time through, and not let your right hand ever catch up, that seems to be the thing that helps.

The drill I suggest to help reinforce this is to putt with one hand. This will give you the feel of what it is like to almost drive the putter through, rather than "flip it."

The second tip is one I received when I was still an amateur and I played in a pro-am with Ray Floyd. We were on the course and he asked me where I looked when I putted. I told him that I looked at the ball. He told me that I wasn't looking at the right place.

Ray said, "You don't want to just glare down at the ball, you want to look at the very back of the ball where the putter is going to hit. If you will do that, you'll get to where you can hit the putt solidly every time."

Just like when someone is playing pool. They look at the very back of the cue ball, the part of the cue ball they are going to hit with their stick. They look at an exact point.

I started doing that when I was in college, and people would tell me, "You sure stay down on the ball well." The reason for this is that I look very intently at the back of the ball, and I actually see the putter hit the ball every time I stroke it. The stroke is finished before I look up to see where the ball is going.

If you can hit the ball solidly every time, you have a much better chance for the ball to be on line. If your eyes move, a lot of times your stroke and the direction of your stroke move.

Here's a good drill to help you do this: Hit putts from three feet, and don't look up until you know that the ball has hit the hole or already gone past the hole. Don't watch the ball roll at all. Instead, just stroke the ball, watch the putter hit the ball, and stay down until you hear the cup.

This is very difficult to do because everyone is so anxious to find out if they made the putt. If you can just discipline yourself to watch the only thing that you can control—because you've lost control once the ball has left the putter—that should help you putt.

Dick Mast

DICK MAST IS one of the true gentlemen of the PGA Tour. Handsome, soft-spoken, articulate, he's played virtually every tour—with twenty-five victories on the mini-tours alone.

And while he's had a roller-coaster career, Mast is always near the top in putting accuracy. He had his best year in 1993, winning $210,125.

Photo courtesy of PGA TOUR

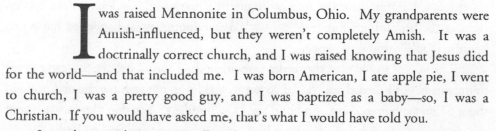

I was raised Mennonite in Columbus, Ohio. My grandparents were Amish-influenced, but they weren't completely Amish. It was a doctrinally correct church, and I was raised knowing that Jesus died for the world—and that included me. I was born American, I ate apple pie, I went to church, I was a pretty good guy, and I was baptized as a baby—so, I was a Christian. If you would have asked me, that's what I would have told you.

I was born with a strong will and very competitive—competition was in my genes. My family had a strong sports background. My dad was a coach, my grandfather was a coach, my uncles were coaches—we were always around sports.

I was a head-on type of person: A + B = C. My dad used to say, "But what if you don't make it in golf, what if . . ." I'd cut him off; I wouldn't even let him finish. "Make it? I'll make it!" But I was a workaholic. I was out of balance.

It wasn't until after *not* reaching my goals through golf in 1975 on the Tour, when another Christian golfer, Richard Crawford, shared his faith with me that a light came on. God revealed to me that I had an intellectual faith and that I did not have a heart-faith. I had never transferred my trust and put it in Christ, and so I asked Him in that night.

I didn't understand a lot of the things that I do now: doctrine, virgin birth, all of that stuff. But what was important was that you could have held a gun to my head the next morning, and I would have not denied Christ. So it was a very emotional step for everybody.

But I still had a lot of burdens in my mind: bad sponsors, I couldn't break 75 any more, and I was losing my card. All I ever wanted to do was play golf—and suddenly I couldn't play golf. Golf was controlling my life.

And so God humbled me. And that's how I got saved. That was what finally broke me. I would get up every day after playing poorly the day before—I'm an eternal optimist; I still am and I have to keep that in check—and I'd say, "Today's going to be the day!" And I kept getting knocked out, like Mohammed Ali was jumping in there to knock me out every day.

Pretty soon, I couldn't get up.

So God humbled me.

I'd had some success. I'd reached my goals a step at a time. Actually, when I started out, I almost won the first tournament I played in! So I had some success right at the beginning. But from a practical standpoint, what happened happened because God allowed it to happen.

The worse I would play, the harder I would work. I played well the first eight to ten tournaments, but I needed rest. So I'd go home, and I'd go out with my dad and play and shoot 67 on the home course. And he'd say, "Get out there! You don't know when your time is coming!" I needed rest, but I just kept playing, working, and finally I broke.

And that's the best thing that could have happened; it was the best thing that *ever* happened to me. My problems didn't go right away, but somehow I knew things were going to work out.

Matthew 11:29-30 says, "Take My yoke upon you and learn from Me, for I am gentle and lowly in heart, and you will find rest for your souls. For My yoke is easy and My burden is light." That verse really meant a lot to me at that time. My salvation experience was like a big weight had been lifted off my shoulders.

What part does the Tour Bible study play in your spiritual life?

The Bible study is great, but you really need to be plugged into a local church at home, because it is not enough out here on the Tour. It is while you're out here, but it's not enough overall. You've got to have a pastor, and you've got to have a local body that you belong to. Some guys consider this a church out here—I don't consider it enough.

Some guys are saved out here, so Larry Moody is basically their pastor.

I was trained on the mini-tours and their Bible studies, and there is a little more camaraderie because you're there every week. During my first three years as a Christian, I wasn't churched. The churches I was in before I was saved were very lukewarm. The first church I got into was a Southern Baptist church in Orlando, and I said, "Wow, look at this!"

Actually, that wasn't the first one. The first was Grace Community in Arizona. My wife, Roberta, and I thought, "There is no church like this! We've got to move out here. This is the only church in the world like this." And of course, as we grew in the Lord, we found that there were churches like that all over the world.

But the first one we got into, and where we got doctrinally trained, was a Southern Baptist, and we're Southern Baptist now. There's no perfect denomination, but we've received some necessary training in evangelism and discipleship, which I am thankful for.

The Lord took me off the Tour for five years, and I got that training that I wouldn't have had otherwise. And so it has helped me in encouraging other guys who continued to stay out here and never got that. I can see things from a different perspective.

Memorable Moment

One of the highlights of my career—and a lot of people aren't aware of this—is that I hold the record for the lowest four rounds ever shot and recorded at a PGA-run event; I did it at the Tour school in Sarasota, Florida. One time in 1985 when I was trying to get back on the Tour, I shot thirty-two under par. The lowest, to that point, was on a par seventy-one by Mike Souchak—mine was on a par seventy-two. His total was a 259, while I shot a 256 on a par-seventy-two, 6,700-yard golf course.

When they interviewed me afterward, they asked me why I played so well. I said, "I didn't want to come back out if it wasn't the Lord's will! So I had a lot of people praying for me—I guess they just overprayed!"

I shot a twenty-seven-under par two weeks before that in the Dakotas tour on a much easier golf course, but that day I was working on visualizing, picturing what I wanted, staying within the system, staying slow, imaging—all those good things you need to do.

It's like art. An artist draws a picture in his mind and looks at you, and in seconds he's drawn your picture. You say, "How'd you do that?" And the artist says, "I just traced it," because in his mind he can see it right there on the canvas. It's the same in golf. It's artistic.

Tip

Putting is my best stat. I tell amateurs the same thing I tell good players: The closer you get to the hole, the more important it is to visualize and to feel what you're doing in picturing the line.

There's a lot to putting really. For instance, you need to take the lay of the land and the contour of the green into consideration.

It helps in the southern part of the hemisphere, like Bermuda, to be able to "read" grain, because it generally goes west.

However, up north, where you have bent grass, it's not as grainy, and you can just read contour. So there you can rely totally on what you see. If it's left edge, it's going to be left edge.

So first of all, you've got to be able to program the computer. Say you have a level putt, and the greens are grainy, and west is to your right-hand side. The putt,

Photograph by Pete Fontaine/PGA TOUR

even though it is a level putt, will tend to go toward the west, because the grain runs that direction—just like a carpet. It will affect the line of the putt—and the speed. So you need to learn how to read greens like that.

I'm a real believer in putting drills because they help your visuals. I have two drills I use—and don't tell anybody this. I don't want my secrets to get out!

In the first drill, I use a ten-foot board to rest the heel of my putter on. I line it up on the left edge of the cup, and I put the heel of the putter on it so that the putter is perpendicular to the board, or square. I stroke right on the board. I put a ball down so that the ball's target line will run right into the middle of the cup—if you line the board up at the left edge.

I use that to make sure that I'm making a perfect stroke—if there is such a thing—a square stroke, as perfect as you're going to get. I keep the face square to the hole at all times, and I stroke like that.

This helps you line up your visuals, and it helps your perception. You're actually aiming where you think you are, which is one of the most important things in putting—aiming the putter where you want the ball to go. The closer you get to the hole, the more important it is to aim.

I'll also work on rhythm and my eye control. I'll look up and down the line of my putt. After you've putted there for, say, fifteen minutes, there will be a very faint line created where the ball rolled on the grass, like a faint chalk line. I look up and down that line, up and down that line, over and over and over.

If you do that for a month, say, thirty minutes a day, then you'll develop your perception. Wherever you think you're aiming it, it will help you to see a line when you go out to play.

The second thing is I'm a spot putter, and that also helps with this board idea, getting your eye alignment correct. Spot putting is where you have a breaking putt. Say it breaks two cups to the left. I generally pick a point that's approximately halfway to the hole. With a twenty-foot putt, I pick a point halfway between myself and the hole.

To practice, I'll put a couple of coins down. One coin where I'm going to hit the putt, and one coin halfway there—representing a spike mark or a discoloration or whatever object I pick on the golf course. Then I'll roll the ball just over the coin or just to the right of the coin.

If it misses, try to go a foot by the hole. You'd be surprised—you can come within one-sixteenth of an inch of that same spot, and if the speed is different, it will miss the whole cup. So what the coin-spotting drill does is develop your touch for the proper speed, and it shows you how important it is to have proper speed. You can hit nearly perfect putts, but if the speed isn't consistent, they're not going to break the same.

So these little aids really enhance your visuals and feel, especially if you go to a surface where one green is slower one week than the next. You can get the coins out and get your pace down.

Putting is much like bowling—you're trying to bring the target to you when you spot bowl. Only here, you're spot putting.

Larry Mize

IT IS ONE of the defining moments in professional golf—and it is the single moment that will always be associated with Larry Mize, despite what he may yet do in his already impressive career. After finishing tied in regulation with Greg Norman and Seve Ballesteros in the 1987 Masters, Mize hit the "impossible" shot—a 140-foot chip from the second extra hole—to win. His joyous, unrehearsed reaction is one of the sport's most vivid, enduring images.

Photo courtesy of PGA TOUR

But there's a lot more to Larry Mize than the Masters. In 1993 he had a career year, winning nearly $725,000 and two Tour events. He slipped a little in '94, while recovering from knee surgery and a decision to spend more time with his family each year. Still, the handsome, rail-thin Georgia native finished third in the Masters and fifth at the Nestle Open.

I came from a Christian family that was pretty active. As I grew older, we went to church Sunday morning and Sunday night. My dad was a deacon in the church, so we were fairly active. But I got away from that as I grew older.

Growing up in Augusta, golf was my dream. That's what I always wanted to do. It became more important than anything. As I got into my teen years, I guess I didn't go to church as much. I'd still go some Sundays, and I still believed, but it was more an intellectual belief. I didn't have Christ in my heart; I had Him in my head. He was second to golf—unfortunately.

That continued as I played golf. I was fortunate to get to play golf at Georgia Tech. And I was fortunate to get on the PGA Tour after three tries at Tour School. Then I married a wonderful girl from Columbus, where we live now. Everything was great on the Tour. I just always thought I'd go out there and be famous and make a lot of money. I won the Memphis Classic in 1983 when I was twenty-four. Then I continued to play really well. I didn't win any tournaments the next couple of years, but I played super.

The event in my life that God used to get my attention was the birth of my first child in 1986.

When I went in the delivery room—like a lot of fathers do these days—and witnessed the miracle of birth, what an experience it was for me! Just being in the delivery room was unbelievable. And to see the miracle, to see my first child be born, I can't tell you how emotional it was.

Later, in the hospital room, when I was holding David, God was letting me know: "Hey! Golf's important—it's how you make a living, and you need to work hard at it—but the most important thing is getting your life right with Jesus Christ and giving Him charge of your life."

I realized, at that moment, it was time to get Jesus in my heart rather than in my head.

Prior to that moment, I believed in God. I believed in Jesus. But I didn't do anything about it. The best way to explain it is to say that it was an intellectual belief. That day it became a heartfelt belief. That day I began trusting in God and trusting Jesus Christ with my life.

All of sudden, instead of wanting to play golf for me and to glorify myself in golf, I had to play golf for Him. I had to win tournaments to give Him the glory and let people know what's really important.

One of my greatest thrills in golf was winning the Masters and one of the neat things about that was the fact that it gave me the opportunity to share my faith and say, "Hey! Christians aren't these little complacent, wimpy people. Christians are competitive, and I'm competitive. I'm a winner in this world, and I'm very successful—but I still have that personal relationship with Jesus Christ. And that relationship is the most important thing to me. Living my life for Him and pleasing Him is the most important thing."

One of my favorite Scriptures is John 12:42-43, where it talks about how the Pharisees believed in Him, but they weren't professing Him because they were afraid of being put out of the synagogue. In verse 43 it says, "for they loved the praise of men more than the praise of God."

That verse really hit me hard for the first time in 1990 at one of our Larry Moody-led Bible studies on Wednesday nights. We were working through the Book of John that year, and I realized that I was trying to please people. Instead, my number one goal should be to please God. Matthew 6:33 says, "But seek first the kingdom of God and His righteousness, and all these things shall be added to you."

I still fall short, but I still keep working forward to live my life in Him and glorify Him—whether it is on the golf course or at home with my family or whatever I'm doing.

Is it hard for a Christian to talk about God to the media? They always seem to back off.

I try to keep my piece short and simple because it is their time. I'm not about to cram anything down anybody's throat. But I want to give the credit and the glory where it belongs—to God, for what He's done for me, for the life He's given me through Christ.

I can't do anything to earn my way to heaven; I can't do anything to earn my good grace with God—it's all His free gift. I'm just very grateful for that, and I work hard to keep things in perspective.

Out on the professional golf tour—or anywhere, but definitely out here—it's easy to get things out of perspective. After a while, your ego starts to get a little big, and you need a little humbling. I pray often for God to humble me, because I need to be humbled a great deal—too much of the time!

Sure, I get down at times, but I don't get down as much as I used to, thanks to God. Things don't always go like we want them to in life, but the great thing is that God is always there with us. And we have that peace and joy that the Bible says "surpasses knowledge."

Another favorite verse of mine is Philippians 3:13-14, where Paul is trying to understand the power of Christ's resurrection and he can't. He says:

Brethren, I do not count myself to have apprehended; but one thing I do, forgetting those things which are behind and reaching forward to those things which are ahead, I press toward the goal for the prize of the upward call of God in Christ Jesus.

I think about that a lot. I've got to keep going forward, confessing my sins to God, and living for Him in the present.

I'm looking forward to the future when I'm called home, but I'm living for Him while I'm here.

There's nothing to compare to it. I'm such a happy, more joyful person now. I'm so much more peaceful and content than I was before, because I understand things better. Not everything, but I do understand life better. I think I'm doing what God wants me to do, and it gives me a great opportunity to share my faith. I think I've got the best of all worlds: I get to share the love of God, and I get to play golf for a living! It doesn't get any better than that!

Without Christ, the golf tour is always: "What have you done for me lately?" It's easy to get beat up out here. It's a great way to make a living, but it is also tough at times. Sure, everything has its good and bad sides. But I've got way too much to be thankful for. I've got a wonderful family, three great boys, a wonderful wife, and a God who loves me no matter what. Gee! I don't deserve it.

Memorable Moment

As far as golf goes, one of the favorite memories has to be the Masters victory. And I have some great memories from 1993 when I won twice during the PGA tournament year and finished with a win in a tournament in Jamaica, so I ended up with three victories in a year—and that doesn't happen very often. So that was a lot of fun, and those tournaments are great memories.

But the Masters will always be special.

Those are the golf memories, but the life memories are even more special, particularly the births of all of my boys. David's was special because God used that event to get my life turned around. But I love all three of my boys, and all of their births were awesome. Thank God I was there for all of them. I would consider those moments some of the greatest times in my life.

I will tell you another thing, just being able to be with those boys—that's the great thing about this job. I'm able to pick and choose when I play. And when I'm home, I'm able to drive on field trips and do a lot of things with the kids.

Actually, my times with my family are just great times for me, because I get to see a lot of things a lot of people aren't fortunate enough to see. I think I get more time with my family than I would if I had a nine-to-five job.

I miss them when I'm gone, but I'm home about half the year, which gives me about twenty-six weeks that I'm home, and I can give them a lot of attention then. I can get involved in what they're doing. And that's great.

So really, I've got some special moments from day to day, just spending time with my family. Letting my boys know that I'm there, that I'm with them—and that I love my wife, Bonnie—I think those are some of the most important things I could do for my children. I feel like I've got a ton of great moments.

I'm spoiled rotten. And I love it!

Tip

I think the strongest part of my game is my short game. I am a straight hitter, and I keep the ball in play, but still, I think the strongest part is that I have an excellent short game. I've got a good chipper and putter. Some of that, I think, is that I'm blessed with a good touch.

But I also put a lot of time in on it. I work very hard on my short game. One of my goals from the past couple of years is that I like to spend at least 50 percent of my practice time on my short game—which includes bunker work, all the chipping, and all the putting.

Now for amateurs, it's a lot

Photograph by Stan Badz/PGA TOUR

more fun, generally speaking, to go out and hit balls a long way. But if the amateurs would just give this a try, they might see a difference in their game. Go to the putting green and practice your chipping. Set up a little friendly competition with your amateur buddies.

The time you spend out there will pay off much more—in my opinion—than the time you spend on the driving range. Because that's where you score, and that's where you learn. You learn how to hit different shots around the green. Playing in pro-ams, that's where I see the amateurs throw all of their shots away.

In the short game, there are so many different ways you can do it too. I like to keep my hands real soft; I like to chip very much like I putt. But the main thing is trying to hit different shots.

One of the things I like to do—and I think amateurs can do this too—is when I come out of a bunker or chip around the green with a "lofty" club, I try to see how high and how soft I can hit it by opening the blade a little bit and trying to slide under it. And that gets your hands really soft. So now, all of a sudden, you're hitting everything soft, and you can start being more aggressive because you're not hitting the shots that take off.

So a great way to practice is to see how high and how soft you can hit some shots. Just open the blade and let the club do the work; don't let your hands do it. See how high and how soft you can hit it. That alone will do wonders for your short game.

As far as putting goes, I like to work on a lot of putts from ten feet and under and then on the thirty- to forty-footers, because I think you need to work on both sides. First work on your speed on the long putts from thirty to forty feet away. And if you've got a big green, practice on the sixty-footers, because you'll get those sometimes.

Then work on ten-feet-and-under putts, because that's where you can really work on the fundamentals of your stroke. And that will do wonders for your putting. The time that you spend there will pay off, and I think you'll enjoy the game better. Good putting takes pressure off your long game because if you think (or know) that you'll get your ball up and down, you're not as tense over your shot. You're not thinking, *Oh no! I don't want to miss a green.*

So my feeling is: Momentum comes from the short game. And when my short game's good, that's when I'm playing well.

Barb Mucha

IF BARB MUCHA attempts something, you can be pretty sure she's going to master it. In college she received honorable mention All-American honors while winning both the Illinois State and Ohio State Invitationals. She won six times on the Futures Tour. She qualified for the LPGA Tour in 1986 and in 1990 won the Boston Five Classic. In 1992 she won the Oldsmobile Classic. Then in 1994 she handily won the State Farm Rail Classic. And she's done all of this despite a number of serious injuries.

Photo courtesy of LPGA TOUR

But if her LPGA career ended tomorrow, don't worry about Barb Mucha—she could compete tomorrow on a women's professional bowling tour as well!

In the end, Barb Mucha is known as both a tough competitor and one of the more thoughtful, spiritually aware players on the Tour—a rare combination indeed.

I was raised in a church environment; we went to church all the time. My parents were involved in the same church for thirty to forty years, and my brother and his wife are Christians. My brother and sister and I are close, and we're getting closer every year. I was never really forced to go to church—it was just part of everyday life.

My parents are great; they supported me growing up and throughout my whole career. I was busy in sports and a lot of other activities while growing up. I never twiddled my thumbs and thought, *Now what am I going to do today?* I was always a very active child, and I had a great childhood growing up.

God got His hand on me even while I was young, probably somewhere in my early teens. I can still remember lying awake at night thinking about death. Not many kids that age think or worry about death. It's not a part of their conversation.

I couldn't accept the fact that once you die, that's it, life is ended. So thinking about death initially got me thinking more abstractly, thinking of eternity, thinking about what's after life here on earth. It bothered me to think that after we die that there might not be anything to look forward to, that there might not be anything else beyond what we see here in the present. So, in the beginning, I think I was more afraid of what happens after we die. Not necessarily what's going to happen to *me,* but what's going to happen in a general sense.

But even at that age, I think that God was planting a seed in my heart. I don't think I really committed myself to the Lord at that point. It was just the first step of the process. I believe that it had a lot to do with my seeking after the Lord, getting closer to Him, and seeking fellowship with other Christians.

Still, I always read the Bible, and I enjoyed going to church and hearing the sermons. So it was never like: "I don't want to hear that stuff!"

I think I just grew in the Lord over the years. My brother and his wife had a big part in it. They never pressured me or sat down and talked to me, saying, "Do you believe in Jesus Christ?" It was just a matter of people coming into my life, planting seeds along the way.

Elsewhere, there were people praying for me. Eventually, when I went off to college at Michigan State, I went to FCA meetings and started getting involved.

I finally trusted the Lord on December 16, 1984. It was just a matter of everything coming together. I'm so thankful that it happened then, because I graduated that year. I was going off on the mini-tours to play and getting my career going. It was my first time traveling alone and experiencing life without parents and without college teammates or friends. I think that accepting the Lord that year was all a part of His plan. It helped me know that this was going to be a new start—not only of a new career, but a new start with Him.

I discovered, as everyone else has, that life is not easy. It has its great moments and it has its down moments and crying times. If I were without my faith out here on the Tour, I could really get caught up in the fame and the money and the performance. You still get caught up in that, even being a Christian, because it is such a worldly based, performance-oriented sport.

But my faith has not only helped me grow as a person out here, it has helped me reach out and go beyond myself and take my eyes off of myself. It has helped me say, "Okay, God's given me this talent. He's blessed me just by letting me be out here. So how can I bless others with what I've been given? How can I turn it around and try to balance that with my time and my efforts for charity and sharing who I am?"

So many people look at the scoreboard or look in the paper, and all they see is a number. They know us by what we shoot. I've got more of a life than just playing golf. This happens to be what I do by way of a job.

And the more I can get involved outside of Tour activities, the more it helps me! It helps me stretch my faith and my personality; it helps me to get a better idea of who I am. Who am I really—as a person? Not as a golfer—that's my job, that's my occupation. But who am I as a person? What am I made of? What are my characteristics? How does God fit into the mold of my life?

Where does God fit into the priorities of your life?

Well, He's very important to me. I'm seeing, as I'm out here more and more, God's faithfulness. He continues to be even more faithful, year after year. And I'm realizing that if I don't put God first, not only will my golf game suffer, but all areas of my life will suffer.

When I first started playing out here, I definitely ingrained myself in golf. I practiced constantly so I could make it to the top and be accepted out here.

But now I could leave golf behind and probably be content doing something else, whatever that may be.

I know that my relationship with the Lord is definitely moving up a notch, and that has allowed me to be more involved in what He wants me to do. I'm not afraid to take risks now outside the golf arena. I'm not afraid to get interviewed, go to FCA camps, or do television and radio shows and talk about my faith, because *that's who I am*. I mean, if Christ really is in me, *that's who I am*. That's who He is making me to be. I believe that every day He is conforming each one of us more and more into His image. And that should be our goal—to be more like Him every day in everything we do.

People know who the Christians are out here. And the more I open up about who I am and what I'm struggling with and the things that are going on in my life, the more I find that others are also struggling in the same areas out here. They're struggling with the performance, with the money, with how people think about them, with relationships, and all that kind of stuff.

So my faith has allowed me to just be myself, and consequently people have started trusting me. If they're going through a tough time, I hope they feel they could come and talk to me or come and talk with some of the other Christians out here.

I know some people have different views about the Christians on the Tour: that we're cliquish, that we're the "God Squad." But when people are going through a tough time, where do they turn? They turn to God.

In the end, it's not a matter of how many people we can win for Christ out here; it's just letting God's Spirit and His light shine through us and letting us be who we are in Jesus. That's what's going to draw others. If they're looking at all, they're going to be drawn to that.

When all of this is over, I hope I will have made a difference in one or two people's lives—hopefully more than that. When it is all said and done, people will say, "Yeah, Barb, she won a few tournaments, but more importantly, she walked her life as Christ would have walked."

Memorable Moment

Laurie Brower and I got to know each other on the mini-tours. One night she called me at 1:00 A.M., and we talked for two or three hours. She just picked my brain: "What do you think about this? How about this?" All of these questions about religion. I'd always thought she was a Christian, but she wasn't. She had fooled a lot of people.

Later, I was playing in a tournament sometime in 1991, and she called back. She said, "Well, Barb, I just wanted to let you know that it happened," and I knew exactly what she was talking about. She said, "I've asked the Lord to come into my life." I got so excited! To this day, I know exactly where I was, what time it was when she called, everything! What a thrill!

I hope I had something to do with that. I think I did. I think talking to her and being willing to be her friend and not judging her helped bring her to the Lord.

I'm really not one to evangelize. I try to let my life show it. I do more listening. I don't push it down anybody's throat.

When I became a Christian, my brother was so excited. I never saw him cry very much, but he broke down in tears that day.

I felt the same way about Laurie. I thought, *This is awesome—that you finally know that there really is a God out there, Laurie!*

So I would say Laurie's profession of faith was definitely a highlight for me. Now, from a performance standpoint, I'll always remember the State Farm Rail Classic over Labor Day weekend 1994. I had really come to a point in my career where I was not doing very well. I was missing cuts. At the same time, I was really dealing with some spiritual issues in my life, and I think God was tugging at my heart. I was ready to quit for the year, pack it up, and just get my life straightened out. I wasn't even going to play that tournament.

Before the tournament, I got on my knees and said, "All right. I mean business. Let's get this thing worked out in my life, let's go on, and I want to get to know You like I know I should know You." Then I went out and won it! I hadn't played that well in five years. It truly was a miracle.

Not a lot of people knew I was having such a tough time spiritually, doubting myself, wondering if God is who He said He was—I guess we all go through times like that. And yet, He blessed me with a win. That's what amazes me.

I think God gets so overjoyed when He sees His children come back to Him with repentant hearts, wanting Him to be first in their lives. He wants to bless His people.

Winning was just a by-product of that whole experience. I think the winning made me *not* look at the winning, because I knew that it was a miracle that I won. But it was even more of a miracle that God would even continue to walk faithfully with me after how I'd been for the previous two months! That really strengthened my faith and turned my commitment to Him around.

People saw the State Farm Rail Classic as a win for me. I saw it as so much more than a win in my life. I saw a win with Jesus.

Tip

Something I'm trying to work more with is using my visualization techniques and trying to see a shot before I hit it. That might be hard for a lot of amateurs to do, but it's like any other sport in which a ball and a target are involved. If you can see the ball going into the hole and react to what you see, things happen.

A lot of times, I don't swing at the ball very well, but I can kind of get around that by first trying to get my mind into a good frame and then allowing my body to react according to what I see. I try to get away from the mechanical part of it and get back to the feel of it.

I recently asked somebody, "How many golf balls have we hit in our careers? Millions! Literally millions." So it's not that I don't know how to hit the golf ball. I know. But I need to work on getting my mind in the right zone and allowing my senses— my sight, my sound, my touch— to feel the shot and see the shot and let my body react to what my mind is seeing.

If you shoot a foul shot, you're not going to be conscious of how you're dribbling the ball and how you're going to release it. No, you're going to be focused on the target. And I'd say that that's a good key, because a lot of amateur players—even a lot of pros—get so wrapped up in the swing aspect or the ball as-

Photo courtesy of LPGA TOUR

pect. *That's not your goal.* Your goal is to hit it into that hole over there. Shoot that ball into that target.

You need to allow your body to react to what you see and incorporate that into your swing and your routine and your playing. If not, you get so wrapped up in hitting that little golf ball, you forget *where* you need to hit it. And then, before you know it, you're hitting it everywhere. Then you get frustrated.

So give your mind a break! You've already spent all that time hitting golf balls on the range and practicing. Now let your mind get focused on where you want the ball to end up.

That's what's working for me now—and every day I'm learning more about it. Everybody out here can play. The ones who stay mentally positive and who can see themselves winning are the ones who are going to be successful. Those are the golfers who are going to play the best golf year after year.

Larry Nelson

FOR THIS SOUTHERN gentleman, golf came just as naturally as his gentle Georgia drawl. Larry Nelson never played a round of golf until he returned from overseas military service. The first time he ever played, he broke 100. After a couple of years in junior college, he turned professional in 1971. By 1974 he had already finished in the top 100 in earnings.

Photo courtesy of PGA TOUR

Since then, Nelson has won ten tournaments: the Jackie Gleason-Inverrary Classic (1979), the Western Open (1979), The Atlanta Classic (1980), the Greater Greensboro Open (1981), the PGA Championship (1981), the U.S. Open (1983), the Walt Disney World Golf Classic (1984), the PGA Championship (1987), the Walt Disney World/Oldsmobile Classic (1987), and the Georgia Pacific-Atlanta Classic (1988).

Along the way, Nelson's also played on three Ryder Cup teams (1979, 1981, and 1987), served as a Player Director of the PGA Tour Policy Board, won three major tournaments in Japan, and designed a few golf courses of his own.

But he isn't through yet. In 1994 he nearly won the Doral-Ryder Open—proving there's still plenty of golf yet in Larry Nelson's sweet, picture-perfect swing!

I came from a church family; I've always gone to church. I was in church every Sunday morning and night and every Wednesday night. I went to every service the church had, but that's all it was—church. I heard everything but didn't take anything in.

It wasn't until one day in 1975 when my wife, Gayle, came home that anything changed. She'd heard Cindy Massengale, Rik Massengale's wife, at a tea some of the Christian wives hosted for the non-Christian wives. A couple days after she heard Cindy, Gayle accepted Christ. I'd known my wife since she was two years old, and there was nobody I knew who was a better person than she was as far as being religious. So when she told me she'd accepted Christ as her personal Savior because of the sin in her life, I started questioning my position.

The year before, I'd heard Billy Graham speak in Charlotte. He'd said, "If you want to know what your relationship with the Lord should be or how to know if you have a proper relationship with Him, read the books of John and Romans."

Now, a year later, I was in a car wreck in northern California on Interstate 5. I got caught in a storm and was hit by a truck, so I couldn't play the next week. I ended up in a hotel room in San Diego. There was a little book titled *Love* in that hotel room which was *The Living Bible* New Testament.

That night I remembered what Billy Graham had said a year earlier, to read John and Romans. Verse after verse spoke to me. I found Romans 3:23, which says, "Yes, all have sinned; all fall short of God's glorious ideal." Then Romans 5:8, which says, "But God showed his great love for us by sending Christ to die for us while we were still sinners." And then I found Romans 11:27: "At that time I will take away their sins, just as I promised."

So in that San Diego hotel room, one night in 1975, I asked Jesus Christ to come into my life. As a result of my wife's coming to know Christ a few weeks before in February, I asked Christ to come into my life as well.

Since then it has been good. Of course, the road has been rocky. Well, maybe not rocky—undulating, perhaps. That's true in any Christian walk. It is going to have its ups and downs, its failures and successes. Probably no truthful person, whether the failures are in their spirit, mind, or body, will deny that. No matter how spiritual you are, if your mind is not right, it is going to be very, very difficult.

An example would be that sometimes you have to work out emotional problems before you can actually be what the Lord wants you to be. For me, I think it is probably more that type of thing than anything else over the past twenty-something years I've been a Christian.

And I would hesitate to trust anyone who says they haven't had any problems!

Right now we go to Eastside Baptist Church in East Marietta, Georgia. We're not members there, but that's where we're going. Our children, Drew and Josh, really enjoy it.

It is different now on the Tour from when I first became a Christian. The first group of guys that led the Bible study when I came out—Kermit Zarley, Rik Massengale, Wally Armstrong—all eventually left the Tour. Eventually, the Tour Bible study dwindled to just three of us: Don Pooley, Morris Hatalsky, and me. So we met for breakfast in a hotel room in Tucson one year to decide whether or not we were going to end this thing or what we were going to do, because it was ridiculous for the three of us alone to keep it going.

So we prayed about it. We finally decided we needed to be specific. We said, "We need to pray for someone to come out who is in their late thirties or early forties, married with children. Someone who could come out for free and actually lead this thing!" This was essential, because we felt like we really needed someone like this if this Bible study was going to survive. So we decided we would pray for this person to come out on the Tour.

Larry Moody was the result of that prayer. To have someone who was in a ministry and who could afford to come out—of course, we've tried to support the Moodys since—*and* who was that age, was married, had children, and who could still come out as much as he does, it was definitely an answer to prayer. And now at that same Bible study, there are some stops on the Tour where thirty to forty people will attend.

Memorable Moment

Probably my favorite memory comes from the point I was ready to quit the Tour completely, because I was tired of playing. I simply wasn't getting anything out of it. So, at that point, my wife, Gayle, and I again decided to pray about it specifically. We went to our upstairs bedroom and prayed together. We asked whether I should continue to play—because I really wanted to do what the Lord wanted us to do.

We prayed for two things: We prayed for our children and my future.

We got an immediate answer. For our children, the answer was, *Don't worry about them—they're going to be okay.* They weren't in any trouble or anything. We've just always prayed for them. It was very specific.

The answer to the other request, the one that asked whether or not I was to stay on the Tour, was just as clear as it could be: *You stay out there.*

It was—and still is—a struggle. But I committed to go ahead and work on my game. And after failure after failure, I won the PGA Championship in 1987. It was in a play-off with Lanny Wadkins at Palm Beach Gardens. I think it was the most rewarding thing that has ever happened to me. I thought I was going to win a tournament before that one. Nothing. But by winning the PGA Championship in 1987, I'm exempt until 1997—when I'm fifty years old and eligible for the Senior Tour!

Tip

All over the world, I have people ask me what is the most important thing in the golf swing. Well, even though the golf swing is made up of a lot of different body parts, different movements on different planes and stuff, to me the most important thing is the right leg.

The angle that the right leg creates with the ground during the "address position" needs to be maintained throughout the swing. The right knee can go straight back, but your right leg cannot move from side to side. It can't go away from the ball or toward the ball on the backswing; it has to stay at that same angle.

If you'll do this, it will

Photograph by Sam Greenwood/PGA TOUR

eliminate your head movement, it will eliminate swaying, and it will get your weight in the right position where it's supposed to be. There's never been a great player who hasn't done all of that.

So if a golfer will work on their right leg, they'll improve their score, no matter what they do anywhere else. That is a given.

David Ogrin

DESPITE A CAREER that's seen him go from fifty-ninth on the money list to Q School in a single year, David Ogrin remains one of the Tour's most colorful, quotable players. With his sharp wit and sneaky-funny quips, he's as popular on the Tour Bible study as he is completing a foursome at the GTE Byron Nelson.

Photo courtesy of PGA TOUR

Ogrin was a legendary midwestern amateur, winning a host of tournaments before turning pro. On the PGA he's finished second three times (losing two heartbreaking play-offs) and won a couple of unofficial events, the 1989 Chrysler Team Championship with Ted Schulz and the 1987 Deposit Guarantee Golf Classic.

The PGA Tour's ultimate Chicago Cubs fan (his fourth child is named Clark Addison—two streets that adjoin Wrigley Field), Ogrin made a great pennant run at the end of 1994, finishing with just an eyelash less than $200,000. He opened 1995 strongly as well, carding a twelve-under-par fifth-place tie at the Buick Invitational.

I think where the turnaround came for me was on a bus ride back from a college tournament in Guadalajara, Mexico. I hadn't had a particularly good day, and I was going through a mental checklist:

1. Do I practice enough? "Yes," I said to myself.
2. Do I study enough? "Yes."
3. Am I in shape? "Yes."

Then, out of nowhere, a "little voice" spoke to me and said, "What about Jesus?"

Suddenly it dawned on me. I'm one of the fellows on this team who goes to church with some regularity. I'm someone whose father cares about me, who urges me to be in church each week. I'm someone who's supposed to be a Christian.

I'd been praying sincere prayers. I had no question about Jesus Christ, the Trinity, and the Bible. But my faith was "head" faith. An intellectual faith rather than a heartfelt faith.

I realized on that bus ride that being a Christian involved a personal relationship with Christ. It became crystal clear that I either had to start believing in Jesus Christ and the prayers that I prayed—or discard them. I decided right then and there that a flip-flop must happen in my checklist. Jesus could be no place but first.

Sitting there by myself, I silently began praying. Suddenly, something awesome happened. I had a new, wonderful sensation that God was there really listening to my prayers. I felt as if my belief had dropped from my head to my heart.

I later attended a conference in Chicago with twenty-five other collegiate golfers and most of the PGA Tour Bible study group. There I learned about the power of Jesus Christ and the Holy Spirit. I found out that following Jesus Christ boils down to getting with the Spirit and getting into His Word. I also realized that if I did that, the path for my life would be drawn for me by the Lord.

A few years later, I was playing at the Honda Inverrary Classic in Ft. Lauderdale. As I was meandering down one of the fairways on the back nine, I started talking to the Lord. And it occurred to me how much had changed between college and my first years on the PGA Tour.

I compared my actions when I used to get angry with the way I just talk with Him when I get angry now. And I also compared how I talk to Him when I'm happy.

And that day, I had another talk with God. He asked me the questions this time:

"Why are you out here, Dave?"

"To do all to the glory of God," I said.

"Okay," He said.

And I walked along some more and said, "Okay, now let's do it."

And I've been trying to do it ever since.

Memorable Moment

Memories are plentiful, of course, now that I'm on my twentieth year on the Tour—if you count my college career. So there are a lot of memories, but it's hard to look past the Texas Open in San Antonio in 1994 when I shot a 26 for nine holes during the pro-am. Even today that's still like, "Whoa! Twenty-six!" Nobody's hardly ever heard of a 26! Some of the guys started calling me "Mr. 26," which is fine, I guess.

During the round, I knew it was going on—like a pitcher in baseball with a no-hitter. It was a really, really cool experience because I've done a lot of things in recent years to improve my golf game.

I once had a dentist, Dr. Humberto Berger, challenge me. He said, "You're a professional in golf just like I'm a professional in dentistry, David. But in order for you to improve, you've got to have continuing education. What have you done to continue your education?"

I thought, "Whoa! Now *that's* an interesting concept."

So I did some things. I hired Dr. James K. Suttie at Pine Needles, who is my swing coach, and I hired Dave Pelz, who is my short-game guru, and I hired Chuck Hogan, who is my sports psychologist-type guru, even though you're not supposed to call him a sports psychologist.

Then for two hours one Wednesday morning in October of 1994, all of the education I'd put together worked in this magnificent symphony of birdie shots and wonderful thoughts. It was so easy, and yet I knew what I was doing. And it didn't surprise me tremendously when I made a hole in one on the ninth hole!

I've done something now that is really special.

There are so many factors that went into it, I'm just thankful that I had the chance to experience that. It was tremendous.

Plus, the golf "magic" was with me. Magic can mean a lot of different things to different people, but when you play sports, one of the things that makes sports sports and not accounting is that the ball will bounce in varied ways. If you're in accounting and you bounce a 5 in the wrong column, you're in big trouble—and it doesn't bounce back. In golf, you hit the ball, you put it up in God's air, where He can do whatever He wants with it, and it comes down and hits on a green mowed by a human being.

Every time I hit a shot during my 26, each bounce the ball took during the nine holes made each shot better. On top of that—part of the magic, again—every time I hit a shot, it stopped just right and at such a distance that I knew I had a club for hitting the shot exactly that distance. During those nine holes, all the intangibles, every little detail you can think of, was in my favor. Therefore, the stroke magic, the golfing magic, was with me.

And that includes the ninth hole. It's a 155-yard shot, which is a perfect half seven iron for me. I've hit the shot hundreds of times in practice—155 yards! Actually, I usually hit it 150 and it rolls five.

So I hit the shot, and I'm already seven under par for the nine, so I'm already going to post a phenomenal score. I hit the seven iron solidly, it's a swing, it's in the air, and I say, "Go in!" I call it! The ball's in the air, and goes straight in the hole! It hits probably a foot left of the hole and breaks right into the hole.

When I got up to the green, I was amazed like everybody else. My ball had hit on the cup of the green where it had been mown around the edge a couple of times. My ball hit right on the seam, which helped kick it a little right.

Here's the thing: when 29 happens or 27 happens or especially when a 26 happens, everything is so perfectly crystal clear. There is no deliberation, no hesitation, no anguish, no fear, no doubt, no nothing. Everything is crystal clear. The ball is in the air, and I can see the bounce before it happens! It was a capstone for an incredible nine holes.

Tip

The strength of my game right now is straight driving. Not long driving, but straight driving. If you'll look at the straight driving statistics, you won't see a whole lot of players who aren't also successful on the money list!

The big key, I think, in straight driving is tooling. One of them is mechanical and the other is equipment.

The equipment part is the tough one, because you have to get a driver that fits you, not just lie and loft, but shaft-wise as well. That will be an immeasurable help for your accuracy.

The tip I would give the amateurs who are looking for a driver that fits them, especially in graphite, is to pay no attention to the label on the shaft. And if they can't quite find one that fits, try a softer shaft.

The mechanical tip is that, at impact, you want to develop a golf swing that has no angles. You don't want your hands way in front of the ball, or your knees really bent and twisted, or your shoulders tilted backward—or the club coming to the ball in a severe inside-out or outside-in angle either. It's better to develop a swing that is going straight down the line—with no angles. This is actually easier to do than finding a club that fits.

I know, especially for the better players, they're always reaching for more power, and so all the tips that go to power are the antithesis of straight. That's because to get power you've got to create more angles and release them later in a shorter period of time. All the power tips are the opposite of straight tips.

So, at a certain point, you're going to hit the ball as far as you're ever going to hit it. And once you recognize that point, you've got to start developing a swing so that you'll hit it straighter and straighter and straighter.

What I would say to the amateur, as a general principle, is this: All the power tips in moderation will help straighten out your tee shots.

A great drill to help an amateur learn to hit the ball straight is to take a fairly long 2 x 4 or 2 x 6

Photograph by Pete Fontaine/PGA TOUR

foot-long board and put it on the ground so that the board is pointing at your target. And then tee the ball off, right next to the board, with about a half-inch clearance for the toe of your driver and the board.

And then as you're hitting the ball, swing your club next to the board. Don't hit the board. If you go inside out, you'll go across the ball and clunk the board. If you're slicing it, you'll come outside in and hit the board before you hit the ball. So keep your club on this side of the board, without hitting the board, and you'll hit the ball solid and straight.

Don Pooley

IT'S STILL IN the early stages, but the golf world is witnessing one of the great all-time comeback stories in Don Pooley. And it couldn't happen to a nicer, more respected guy.

Pooley returned to the PGA Tour in late 1994 after four years of surgery and recuperation—including neck disc surgery in October 1993—to finish a strong third in the Texas Open. By then, even the other golfers were cheering Pooley's charge.

Interestingly enough, despite his many debilitating ail-ments, the tall, distinguished Pooley has managed to retain

Photo courtesy of PGA TOUR

his playing privileges throughout most of the 1990s. And while his numbers in recent years haven't matched the $268,274 he earned in 1986 or the $450,005 he took home in 1987, he's still played some pretty fair golf along the way.

Despite winning the 1980 B.C. Open and the 1987 Memorial Tournament, Pooley is probably best known for his dramatic million-dollar hole in one at the 1987 Bay Hill Classic—although many people don't know that Arnold Palmer's Children's Hospital also received $500,000 because of that once-in-a-lifetime shot.

As a young boy, my parents took me to church, but I didn't like it at all. When I was about to be confirmed in the church, I told them I wasn't going to get up there and recite all of these things I hadn't memorized. I wasn't sure I believed them anyway, but I knew I hadn't memorized them and I sure wasn't going to embarrass myself. The night before they let me off the hook and I didn't have to do it. After that I didn't go back to church very much. I played sports on Sunday and things like that.

In high school there was a group called Young Life that not only talked about spiritual things but had fun too. That had never been my experience before in a church setting! So during my sophomore year I went to a Young Life retreat up in the mountains of southern California, because I knew I'd have a good time. On Sunday they had a church service. I said, "I'm not going to go to that—I didn't come up here for a church service!" The people I came with said, "Well, this is the whole reason for the trip!" I laughed and said, "Yeah. Right."

But I went anyway and heard the gospel message. I accepted Jesus Christ into my life that morning. That was a long time ago.

My relationship with Christ has progressed over the years. One of the key turning points for me was in 1976. I had graduated from college, had a girlfriend I was about to marry, had just gotten my Tour card, and everything was as good as it could be—or so I thought.

But I played badly the entire year of 1976 and ended up losing my card. At the end of that year, I prayed that the Lord's will would be done, be it in golf or whatever else. I had lost my card, and I didn't know what I was going to do at that point.

So my wife, Margaret, and I prayed about it, and we decided that I would go back through Qualifying School one more time. That way we would know if golf was in God's plan for my life or not.

Q School that year was in Brownsville, Texas, and it was miserably cold. We had miserable weather. It was sleeting and snowing and raining, and the wind was blowing thirty miles per hour. They were the toughest conditions I've ever played in. And here it was the biggest tournament of my life. A career or no career in golf was on the line.

I got off to a good start in the tournament and was the low round on the first day. But as the weather got worse, my scores got higher. Going into the last round, I looked at the board and it looked like I needed a 73 to qualify. I was tied for the last qualifying spot.

At the last hole I needed a fifteen-footer for a birdie and that 73. The putt rolled up to the hole, but stopped on the lip. I tapped it in for a 74, then I went to check the board. It looked like I wasn't going to make it.

We were staying in a room close to the golf course, so Margaret and I went back to the room, got down on our knees, and thanked God for the tournament anyway, even though it looked like golf wasn't going to be part of my life. And we thanked God that He did have a plan. We said that we were going to wait to see what that plan was going to be.

I went back to the scoreboard to check it for the last time—and somehow I'd qualified for the last spot! We were excited—and surprised. We got back out on tour, and 1995 was my twentieth year out here.

Today nobody's more surprised than me, because I was never a great junior player, I was never a great college player, and I never had a lot of success growing up, but I've had a lot of success on the Tour. I've won tournaments and won a lot of money, made a million-dollar hole in one, and even won the Vardon Trophy for the low scoring average one year.

The last few years have been a struggle, but He's there regardless of how well I play. That's a given. My relationship with Christ is a given.

During the last few years I've had back problems. I didn't play at all in 1994 until October—the previous three years I played about half the time because of my back. I had two back surgeries in 1993 and '94.

It was difficult, but a couple weeks after coming back in 1994, I finished third at the Texas Open in San Antonio. So it doesn't look like it is over yet.

So many players mentioned you in connection with their conversion experience. Is that something you just fell into, or is it something you've worked towards?

I would think it is all designed by the Lord. This was none of my doing here.

Morris Hatalsky and I first met when we were about thirteen years old. He grew up in San Diego, and I grew up in Riverside, California. We played together in a junior tournament in Los Angeles, and we happened to stay at the same member's house. So I met Morris that day after the first round. He was a superstar junior, and I was a nothing junior. He asked what I shot that day, and I think I had a 92. I asked what he shot and he said 74. And I went, "74!" I never shot a 74 in my life!

And here he shoots one in this big tournament. He said, "A 92?" Then he turned, left, and didn't talk to me again!

So I didn't like Morris Hatalsky very much. We played many more tournaments together, and I didn't like him any better. I just didn't like his attitude.

Finally one day, five young American golfers were selected to go on a South African tour. Morris and I were two of them, and I immediately thought, *Oh great! I'm spending two months with Morris Hatalsky. Now that's going to be a lot of fun.* But we became best friends on that trip and have been best friends ever since.

We had a lot of discussions once we both got on the Tour, even though Morris is from a Jewish background. I love talking about my faith to someone who wants to hear about it. I don't go pushing myself on anybody, but I'm always willing to discuss spiritual things.

I think your walk speaks loudly, and that's my goal every day when I'm out on the Tour: to walk the talk and not bring Christ down in the process—like it is so easy to do. That's one of my goals.

Memorable Moment

The happiest I've ever been in a tournament was when I finished fourth in 1977 at the Quad Cities Open. I won enough money to keep my card for the next year for the first time. I was driving the Tour at that time, and Margaret and I had about an eight-hour drive through Pennsylvania afterwards, and we were just rejoicing the whole way across. It was just the biggest thrill of my life.

Another great memory was winning my first tournament, the B.C. Open in 1980. It was a huge thrill. I played with Brad Bryant and Lee Trevino in the last round.

Seven years later, winning the Memorial Tournament was another big event for me.

And I remember everything about that million-dollar hole-in-one miracle in 1987 at the Bay Hill Classic. Donnie Hammond, Andy North, and I were playing, and I hit last. I was joking with them on the way to the tee, saying, "This is our big chance to make a million dollars. Ha ha."

The hole was 193 yards away, and I hit a four iron. There was a little crosswind, so I tried to cut it in, and it went perfect, right on the pin. It just kind of held the line all the way down. All the while, I'm thinking, *This is going to be fun to see how close it gets.* You never think it is going to go in.

Then, wham, it hit the flag stick two feet up and knocked it crazy, and everybody was screaming. I couldn't see a thing after the ball hit the stick because it dropped right in. I never saw the ball.

Tip

The key in any short-game shot is not breaking down with your left wrist. The left wrist—for a right-handed player—is in the straight position, and there can be some break going back, but going through it must be firm. No breaking of the wrist going through. Whether you're chipping the ball or putting the ball, you've got to keep that left wrist firm.

You just swing the club. It's an arm swing. Focus on making your arms swing past the ball, keeping your hands in front of the club.

In the beginning, I trained myself to do that, but now it comes naturally. But with putting, it is so easy to have just a little bit of a break. You get focused on the putter head a little bit and the putter head goes past your hands. You've got to keep your hands ahead of the putter head. That keeps you from breaking down.

There are actually a couple of keys in putting. Another is that you want to keep your grip pressure constant in the stroke. You've got to maintain the same grip pressure. A lot of people tighten their grip as they stroke, and it's easy to lose your feel that way.

Photograph by Stan Badz/PGA TOUR

So maintain your grip pressure while you stroke, and other than that, it's just lining it up and stroking it down the line.

Don't make it too complicated.

That's putting.

Larry Rinker

LARRY RINKER COMES from one of the premiere golf-playing families in the history of the sport. Brother Lee just joined the PGA, while sister Laurie and sister-in-law Kellii play the LPGA. A consistent Tour performer, Rinker was a dominant college golfer at the University of Florida, and before joining the PGA, he once won six mini-tour tournaments in a single year. He's also an accomplished singer, guitarist, and songwriter.

Photo courtesy of PGA TOUR

I came from a Southern Baptist tradition, and I was seven when I made a decision for Jesus. I remember it was the Fourth of July. My father was the Sunday school superintendent of First Baptist, Stuart, Florida. We went to church every Sunday. My mother sang in the choir. I was the second of three brothers, with a sister who is the youngest in the family. As we got older, my mother began teaching Sunday school as well. I sang in the choir and played music and all that stuff. I still play the guitar.

It has been a pretty rocky journey since then. Growing up in the church, going to Sunday school every week, you have some questions when you go out into the real world, when you start going to college, when you get out on your own—questions that were maybe not answered when you were growing up. Questions like: "Why are unbelieving Jews going to hell?" or "Why are all those people who never heard Christ's name going to hell?" I had a good friend who was Jewish, and I found out how much they are looked down upon and ostracized from their families for becoming Christians. These things bothered me.

I never stopped believing, but my attitude was, "I know what I need for salvation, and I treat other people the right way, so I'll just go ahead and live my life."

When I went to college, I went to church about once a semester. I always attended when I was home, but in college I didn't. I got away from going to church, I got away from reading my Bible, and I got away from my walk. Finally, I was not going at all. In time, I did a lot of things I'm ashamed to admit—a lot of things I wouldn't want people to know that I did.

The turning point for me came when I met my wife, Jan. She was Methodist. When we met it was, "Okay, now we need to get married in a church." Being raised Southern Baptist, it just seemed normal to get married in the Baptist church where I lived—First Baptist of Winter Park, Florida. So we went in and met with the pastor, we attended the church a few times, and I can remember feeling a little uncomfortable each time.

We eventually joined the church—but we joined mainly so we could save a hundred dollars, since church members got a discount for using the church!

But I think my wife and I started growing from that point. Because when we joined, we began a progression that today makes me feel very comfortable in my faith and very happy for where we've come. I have to thank my wife for that, because she has helped give me the discipline to break some of the bad habits that I had and continue to have. Jan's been great.

When we married, we were about equal in our faith. But you're a lot more accountable to someone as a husband than as a boyfriend. And I had to measure up.

The interesting thing to me was that before then I had never read the Bible straight through. Oh, I was pretty good with the sword drills in Sunday school, and I knew all of the stories. But one day, I finally said, "I'm going to read it." So I read the New Testament first, then I read the Old Testament. I grew so much during that whole time frame. It took me about two years to do it, but during that time, God was talking to me, and my faith just continued to grow.

I read other books, including _More Than a Carpenter_ by Josh McDowell and some others by Charles Swindoll. And, being somewhat of a philosophical person, it seemed to me that the factual, archaeological, scientific information that was available to support the Christian faith was overwhelming. It was _déjà vu_ for me, because I'd already read so many of the old favorite Bible stories. It became addicting. I wanted to read more; I wanted to learn more. I was thinking, *Wow! I want to know this history better.* And now, as an adult, I had a whole different perspective than I had as a teenager.

So I continued to grow in the faith, and I eventually began to write Christian songs. I'd written a few songs before that, but the best songs I've done have been Christian oriented. It is all inspired, so it is not really from me. I hope one day to do a Christian album or an album that has some Christian songs on it.

It has been a great walk since my wife and I got married in 1987—those years have been very good.

The Bible study we have out here on the Tour has helped as well. Larry Moody is great; he's there for anybody on the Tour who wants to talk to him about anything, and he's got the right approach to it. I've learned a lot from him.

For instance, I've learned that nobody's perfect, and I think that at times we, as Christians, are critical of the ways other people worship. I don't think that's right. I've learned a lot about grace and about how we need to treat each other with grace rather than have a holier-than-thou attitude.

Larry has told us that there are guys on the Tour who are Christians that you would never see at the Bible study—and that's fine too. Some guys are going to be more private about it. Then you see a guy like Paul Azinger, who was very private with his faith, and yet with what he went through with the cancer, it has opened him up to where he wants to share it now.

We all go to God when we have problems, and we see our country go to God when the country has problems. When we're not having problems, maybe we don't go to Him very much. But when we're down and out, He's always right there.

Memorable Moment

I'll never forget in 1982 playing in the last group in the U.S. Open at Pebble Beach on Saturday and finishing fifteenth—which got me into the Master's for the first time and back into the U.S. Open. It was at the end of my first year on the Tour, and I had not played well. I don't think I had finished in the top twenty-five or thirty in any tournament up to that point, so that was a peak. It put me on another plateau; it got me over the hump to where I felt like I belonged on the PGA Tour. That was very meaningful.

In 1985, when I had my best year, I was thirtieth, and my sister Laurie and I won the JCPenney Mixed Teams—that was another high point. My younger brother caddied for Laurie, and my parents were there, so that was something I'll never forget. It was a celebration for our family. Laurie has gone on to do well on the LPGA, and my brother Lee just got his card. My dad was the one who was responsible for our playing golf, and for him to be there and see us beat Curtis Strange and Nancy Lopez was a special moment.

T i p

The strongest part of my game has been the putting and short game. By short game I mean 140 yards and in. I led the Tour in putting in 1990. The thing about putting and the short game is that they're both tied in with the art of scoring. In the art of scoring, you can have a guy who hits the ball well, and you can have a guy who can put the ball on the green, but there is something else about getting that little white ball in that four-inch hole. There are guys that just have a way of getting it in. Maybe they "will" it in, maybe they have a magic, but they get it in the hole—and that's called the art of scoring.

There's not one top player in the world today who is not a master at the art of scoring, because nobody hits every green, and nobody hits every fairway, but they find a way to get the ball into the hole.

A lot of us are guilty of overworking our swing mechanics, our technique, and everything

Photograph by Sam Greenwood/PGA TOUR

else, but what it really comes down to is this: There's the ball, and you're trying to get it from here to the hole.

That's what separates the men from the boys out here. You've got guys who can hit it well, and you've got guys who can putt it well, and then you've got guys who can make the number, and that's where it's all at.

And when I'm playing well, I can do that.

So I believe it is all mental. You have to have a positive outlook. When you stand over a five-foot putt, you've got to believe you're going to make it. If you're feeling unsure and don't feel like you're going to make it, that's going to decrease your chances of making that putt.

And it is something you can work on. You work on trying to control your conscious mind; you work on trying to free it up. Sports psychologists work with athletes in all sports, and the one thing they've found is that all top athletes in all sports are not thinking too consciously while they're making their shots in golf, or walking across the balance beam, or whatever they do.

Sports psychologists refer to the left brain and the right brain. The left brain is your analytical side, and the right brain is your feeling and artistic side. You use your left brain to figure out what you're going to do, and you use your right brain to hit it. There're a lot of sports psychologists out here, and that's what they work on with these guys. They talk to them about it, and they work on controlling emotions— and some days you're going to have better control over your emotions than others.

Most guys who win tournaments will say, "Out of the four days, I had maybe two great days and two mediocre days." Very rarely is someone on four days in a row.

So it's something we work on. I work with Dick Coop, who also works with Payne Stewart and Corey Pavin and a lot of other guys. We work on controlling the conscious mind. If you have a bad thought, Coop says, "Let it out the back door. Don't let it stay in the house." Sometimes you can't control the thoughts that come in your mind, and you think, *Gee whiz—that isn't me.* But you can control how much attention you give to those thoughts.

Jack Nicklaus is the all-time master of the mental part of the golf game. He always seemed to know what he needed to do to win. And he was able to do it, to rise to that situation or occasion.

And that's what you strive for.

Laurie Rinker-Graham

GROWING UP IN the fiercely competitive Rinker household, Laurie held her own with golf-playing brothers Larry and Lee—now both on the PGA Tour. She qualified for the LPGA Tour while still attending the University of Florida, but not before she was a two-time collegiate All-American. She won the USGA Girls Championship in 1980 and the 1982 Doherty Challenge Cup. Rinker-Graham was also honored as "Golf Digest's Junior of the Year" in 1980.

Photo courtesy of PGA TOUR

On the pro circuit, Rinker-Graham has been nearly as successful, twice placing in the top 12 in total earnings. She's won two LPGA Tour victories (1981 Boston Five Classic and the 1986 LPGA Corning Classic) and two unofficial events (1984 JLPGA Bridgestone Ladies Open and the 1985 JCPenney Classic).

She married Rob Graham on January 5, 1991.

My parents are Baptist, and I was raised in a Baptist church as long as I can remember—I'm sure since I was born. My parents were very active in the church.

I don't remember exactly how old I was when I came to know Jesus. I didn't have one of those lightning bolt experiences. I was about eight years old.

I think, growing up in a church and all, I knew all about Jesus and all of the Bible stories. But I remember the sermon Dad preached the night I went forward. He related it to baseball. I remember him saying something like, "In order to hit a home run—to get to heaven—you have to accept Jesus. There is no other way to do that." Being so sports oriented, that saying hit home with me, so that's when it happened.

Years later, at this point, it is still a daily battle.

My faith is definitely important to my game. I became a Christian at a young age, but I didn't necessarily rely on my faith from a young age. That's something I've done more in the past five years.

I was very successful when I went out on the Tour—right from the very beginning, for at least the first six years. But the last five or so have been more of a struggle.

Still, it is almost easier, from a human perspective, when things aren't as good, because then you rely on your faith more and you trust more. Just in the last few years I've come to realize that things happen for a reason. I've also realized that I don't necessarily have to be on top to be a good witness.

From a young age, I played competitive golf and grew up thinking, *Winning is everything.* You have to win. You *must* win. And I based my whole self-worth on how well I played golf.

Finally I realized, in the grand scheme of things, it really doesn't matter.

As of January 1995, I have been married four years, and until I got married, golf was it. That was my whole basis for living and self-worth. After that, I realized that there's a lot more there. Just because you win a golf tournament, you're not any better than the person who finished dead last. It's a hard thing to get a grip on, but once I saw that through God's eyes, I finally knew that winning a golf tournament is pretty insignificant. That's an especially important lesson in our society, where we love the winners and hate the losers.

Could you live without the game now?

I don't know. It's kind of neat now; it's become fun again, because it doesn't mean as much to me anymore. If I miss the cut, miss the cut, win, miss the cut—whatever happens, I know that I'm still a good person and that it doesn't really matter and that my husband doesn't love me any less.

I think I could probably give it up and go do something else—because I do have a different perspective right now than I had before.

My husband, Rob, is a Christian, and we met, interestingly enough, in the same Baptist church my parents met in, in Stuart, Florida.

I'm not one of the most faithful ones, but I attend the Bible studies on the Tour more than half the time. On the Tour, it becomes your church, and it is a good support group. Cris Stevens is wonderful.

Larry and Lee tell me that there are a lot of egos involved on the PGA Tour. But overall, here on the LPGA Tour, I think we're a little more friendly, maybe a little more supportive of each other.

As a veteran, do you think the younger players are thirsting for the Spirit?

I'm definitely in the veteran class, and yes, there's always a handful of newcomers who is thirsting. The ones who are really thirsting for the Spirit are often the ones who are struggling early. It's tough out here.

But it's also fun, particularly when you play with the players you know. Some of them you know from amateur days or college days. Very few people come out here and just don't know anybody. Sure, it's kind of cliquish out here. For example, the foreign players kind of hang out together, and the Christians often spend time together. That's the way life is in general.

But even while my golf game has been a struggle the past few years, overall, my life has been going well. In the last few years I've looked back and said, "God, if you want me to continue, I'll do it. If you want me to play like this, I'll continue to do it. If not, please show me something else." And nothing else has come along, so I just figure this is where I'm supposed to be.

Has the LPGA Tour given you the platform to witness?

Yes, but mostly at the FCA camps. Some of the girls out here, friends who are not Christians or who I'm not sure about, I feel comfortable talking to a little bit. Out on the Tour, I think it is more of a witness by example thing.

I think one of our biggest witnesses is how we behave on the course—and it is something I struggled with early on because I have a hot temper. Back then my face showed how I was playing. That's one thing I've worked on a lot. Just being different makes a statement. Someone might think, *Gosh, she used to have a temper— and now look at her. She's handling that pretty well. I wonder what the difference is?*

That's where you can make a difference.

Memorable Moment

I think winning the JCPenney Classic with my brother Larry in 1985 is my favorite memory. That was very special. I've had some other victories, but it is kind of neat when you can do it with your brother! The year we won it, we beat Curtis Strange and Nancy Lopez—when they were both Player of the Year! That was pretty neat. Plus one of my brothers was caddying for me, and my parents were there. We led from the first round and had a two-stroke lead going into the last round.

Tip

My tip to amateurs is on putting. It's pretty simple, but I think most people don't do it.

Putting is basically all feel. And in order to have a good feel, you have to have a light grip. I think what a lot of people do is that they either start off with a real tight grip and stroke it that way, or they increase their grip pressure throughout their stroke.

My tip is to start off with a light grip and keep it constant through the stroke. That way you'll have more of a smooth, fluid stroke.

I'd suggest that the amateur start off with a light grip—but not so light that the putter will fall out of your hands! When you putt, concentrate on having the same grip pressure and maintaining the same grip pressure back and through.

Photo courtesy of Long Photography

Loren Roberts

LOREN ROBERTS—dubbed "The Boss of Moss" by fellow golfers because of his putting skills—broke through with a vengeance in 1994. One of a record six members of the Millionaires Club in 1994, Roberts nabbed his first Tour victory, the Nestle Invitational, in dramatic fashion. He enjoyed it so much he won it again a year later in March 1995!

Photo courtesy of PGA TOUR

But before you can have a career year, you've got to endure the famine years as well. Roberts was forced to requalify through Q School in 1980, 1982, 1983, 1986, and 1987 before finally becoming a force to be reckoned with in 1989.

A former club pro (he won the 1979 Foot-Joy National Assistant Pro Championship), Roberts's gradual rise to the top of his profession has come through dogged persistence and a well-deserved reputation as one of the hardest working pros on the PGA Tour. As a result, he led the Tour in both putting and fourth-round scoring average in 1994. Just another overnight sensation—thirteen years in the making!

My parents gave me a lot of love and support. As far as growing up in a Christian home, there wasn't a born-again situation in my house, but I did grow up in a very moral home. My parents were nominally Christian because they did—and still do—the right things. They paid their taxes, they didn't murder, and they didn't cheat on their spouse. That, to them, was a Christian home. That was the type of situation I was in.

I grew up Presbyterian, and I went to church. I enjoyed going to church. I did all of the Westminster Fellowship things in the church, and in high school I enjoyed doing all of the youth group activities. I had a great time with the youth group. I would say I believed, at least I had that head knowledge.

Even today, when I give my testimony, I usually start talking about head knowledge. I didn't have a problem with it, nor did I suffer with it like some people do. There are teachings in the Bible some people simply cannot accept, especially when they hear about Jonah or Abraham offering his son as a sacrifice—all of those kinds of things. They have trouble with them. But I didn't.

Back then, I had the knowledge, but I didn't know how to apply it. I really wasn't worried about those sorts of things at the time—I just didn't think about it. A personal relationship with Christ wasn't something that was important in my life. But being in church *was* socially important—I really enjoyed that. I had fun.

I didn't start playing golf full time until I was about sixteen or seventeen years old. In fact, it was my sophomore summer in high school when I started playing. I played on my school golf team during my junior and senior years. So I started late, but I eventually became a club professional. I never actually thought about playing the tour competitively. I tell people that it just kind of happened.

Somehow, I qualified for the PGA Tour in 1981, but I didn't have a very good year and lost my card. I came home, got married in 1982, and sat out the Tour that year. I finished up my PGA Class A requirements, came back out, and again qualified for the Tour in the fall of 1982. I came back out for the 1983 season and have played ever since.

But 1983 was just another horrible year, golf-wise. I was struggling. I didn't play well. I didn't swing well. I think I only made about four cuts that whole year.

During that year, though, I went to the Bible study a couple of times at Wally Armstrong's prompting. I met the guys who were involved and liked them: Morris Hatalsky, Larry Nelson—there weren't a whole lot of guys back then. I don't think Rik Massengale was even playing at that particular time, or he might have been only playing a limited schedule, because he was struggling with back problems.

I missed the cut at Milwaukee and came back home. I was so frustrated! That's the only point in my life to which I can look back and say, "Well, that's when I decided that I needed to make some changes in my life."

The main change was getting into a right relationship with God. I was beginning to realize that even though the gospel had been presented to me a couple times when I'd gone to the Bible studies, and even though I had all of this head knowledge, I didn't have the heart knowledge. At least, that's the way I describe it. I needed to apply that head knowledge to my heart to have a personal relationship with Christ.

And at that moment I finally knew what I had to do.

I wish I had some sort of great testimony—a roadside conversion like Saul—but I didn't. But that night I looked at my life and said, "I need to change some things in my life in order to get right with God and have a personal relationship with Jesus Christ." And that's exactly what happened.

From then on, obviously, it has been a growing process.

In 1993 Larry Moody baptized me in the swimming pool at the Polynesian Resort at Disney World. It was supposed to be at the lake, but the lake was closed, so we had to use the swimming pool. I was baptized with Larry's oldest daughter—which meant an awful lot to me. We've had a bond between us ever since.

Larry Moody's Search Ministries has been a real key in my spiritual life. Besides the organizational end of Search Ministries and the wealth of caring, meaningful messages Larry presents when he comes out with us, Wednesday-night Bible study is basically our church—because we're all hoping and praying that we're still playing on Sunday. Larry provides the leadership. I think he is rock solid in the presentations he makes, because he is always presenting the gospel.

We're always trying to reach the other professionals through the Bible study. We want them to be able to come, hear the gospel message, and have it affect their lives. I don't think any of us is interested in a Bible study where a lot of us may understand what's being discussed, but someone new may feel left out in the cold. I think Larry is very good about just presenting the gospel message in a persuasive, informative way, so that any nonbelievers who come do not feel that they're intimidated or that they're left out of the discussion. That's one of the strong points of the study. And I think that's why he's been able to reach some of the guys out here on Tour.

Bernhard Langer got to know the Lord when he was brought to a Bible study by Bobby Clampett. Larry Moody and Bernhard have become close friends, and look what Bernhard has meant to the faith, as far as giving his testimony and starting a Bible study on the European Tour—which is really a tough market to crack.

The Bible study also brings all of the guys together. We're all trying to beat each other's brains out there the rest of the week. We're all trying to win. But there's a common thread to our faith that allows us to be competitive, while also allowing us to say, "We're good friends." It enables us to compete—but it also enables us to root for each other when we're having a good tournament.

October is the time of the year when nerves get raw and guys on the bubble start getting worried about facing the prospect of going back to Qualifying School. It's a tough time. But because of the Bible study, guys who have had great years are honestly interested in what some of the other guys who are struggling are going through, and they give them all the support they can. And that's great.

With Jesus, you have the perfect teammate and the perfect coach—one who will call the perfect play every time. Whether it works out or not at that particular moment, it's always going to end up being the right call down the road!

Memorable Moment

I made my pronouncement of faith in 1983. I needed to get my life back in shape and to get my priorities straight—that's when I started my personal relationship with God. But it wasn't until 1993, after I'd been praying about it for some time, that I got to the point where I needed to make a public profession of faith. So that's when I decided I needed to be baptized. That was a personal commitment for me to be better, to work harder at my faith. It was a real motivational thing for me as well.

That process finally got me to the point where I was really able to finally turn things over to the Lord in a tough situation—like the Nestle Invitational at Bay Hill in 1994. I didn't birdie the sixteenth hole when I had a chance to win the tournament. The weekend before, I would have thought, *Well, you've blown it. Now you haven't got a chance.*

But instead I thought, *Anything can happen these last two holes.* Then I knocked it onto the green on the seventeenth hole. I was about fifty feet away, and I figured I needed to birdie one of the last two holes to have a chance. I hit a fifty-foot putt about six feet past the hole.

And as I stood over the putt, I whispered a quick prayer, "Lord, please give me the strength to do the best I can. But also help me deal with the emotion. Please help me accept whatever happens and go on from here. I want to do my best, but let me accept whatever happens."

And I knocked it in the hole.

I went on and parred the last hole and won the tournament—my first. I think that was the first time in my life that I was prepared, that I was able to say I would accept the outcome.

The next time was at the U.S. Open, when I had a very similar situation. I had a putt on the last hole to win. How many kids are on the putting green dreaming: *This is a four-and-a-half-foot putt to win the U.S. Open.* That's every young golfer's dream. And I had it. I had that situation on the last hole.

But I didn't make the putt.

Things didn't go the same as they had done the week of the Bay Hill. But the fact that I was able to turn it over to the Lord and accept it made the fact that I lost the tournament a whole lot more palatable.

A lot of people expected me to be devastated over that loss. But now I'm very upbeat about it, even though it's looked at as something that defines a golfer's career. To have that chance and not do it, that's very hard for most people.

But I know that God has the ultimate plan—the best plan for my life. Obviously, I can't float through life and let it all happen. I have to try my hardest, and I also have to give thanks to Him for giving me this talent. And I have to accept whatever happens, because I know in the end, as long as I'm giving 100 percent and trying my hardest, that's the right thing.

Tip

The main thing I see—and I see a lot of it playing in pro-ams—deals with putting. Putting is my best stat, especially in 1994, when I led the putting category.

What I see is a lot of amateurs having trouble with speed. I think the speed of the ball, the speed of the putt, is everything in putting. I can be on the perfect line, but if the ball is the wrong speed, it's not going to go in. A ball does not have to be on the right line, but if it is somewhere in the area of being the right speed, it might still catch the edge and go into the hole.

Consequently, I try to gear everything to speed. If you were to put an amateur twenty-five feet away from the hole on the green, he or she would end up no more than two feet off the line either way—even on their worst putt. But I *have* seen people be ten feet long and twelve feet short from twenty-five feet—and that's terrible.

As a result, you should practice working on your speed. The best way I've found to control the speed of my putts is that I never hit *at* the putt—I hit *through* it. If you were to put a yardstick on the green and put the ball in the middle of it, whatever distance your backstroke was—say twelve inches—the swing would need to take the same on the follow-through—twelve inches.

That makes you develop a stroke where you never ever hit *at* the ball with a short backstroke and long follow-through or a longstroke back and a short follow-through. *That's* what you want to avoid. You want the same distance back and through. That promotes a good, flowing putting stroke—a putting stroke where you never, ever hit *at* the ball.

Think of your putter as a big pendulum and the ball as just something that gets in the way of the putter head. As a result, the ball always comes off the putter head with the same hit and same speed.

Photograph by Sam Greenwood/PGA TOUR

Ted Schulz

TED SCHULZ IS the kind of lighthearted, easygoing guy you love to have around whether it's as part of a foursome at the Bob Hope Desert Classic or a philosophical discussion on the book of Deuteronomy in the Tour Bible study.

Along the way, he's gone from running a driving range at Bermuda Dunes in 1984 to winning more than a half a million dollars on the Tour in 1991. The winner of the 1989 Southern Open and the 1991 Nissan Los Angeles Open is also something of a legend in Kentucky golf circles, having won numerous amateur and professional tournaments in his home state.

Photo courtesy of PGA TOUR

I grew up Catholic. My parents believe in the Bible, they believe in going to church, and they never miss a Sunday, so they have a faith there.

But for me, golf was the most important thing in my life. Even when I was growing up in Louisville, my dream was to be a professional athlete. I used to work in my father's small old grocery store in downtown Louisville. I was a stock boy, working long hours in the store and delivering groceries. My dad encouraged me to find a sport I could play well enough so that I would not have to work in the store for the rest of my life. This sounded great to me because I didn't like to work in the store.

I tried baseball first, but I wasn't good enough to pursue it as a career. I remember crying every time I struck out!

Next I took up golf. It all seemed so natural. Three times I attempted to qualify for the PGA Tour, and I made it in 1987. My main goal in life was reached. Or so I thought.

But when my wife, Diane, and I made the Tour in 1987, we had a hard year—kind of like 1994. When golf was going well, we were in a great mood, and when it wasn't, we weren't. And it wasn't going well at all that year. It was really a downer. When I got to the Tour, it was a lot harder than I thought. I just didn't do very well. And once you get out here and lose your card, it's harder still.

But during that year, Diane started going to some of the women's Bible studies. And one day when she came back, I saw a big difference in her. Our marriage wasn't doing so great, so I wondered what was going on.

She said, "Why don't we start going to some of the studies in the evenings?" I said okay. I didn't really want to go, but I said, "Why not?"

Back then, I thought I knew all about it. I knew about Christ. I thought I was a believer—and I did believe it all. I always had a fear of God, and I always wanted to do what was right. I had felt that way ever since I was little. There never was a moral reason why; it was more a fear of getting caught, of punishment. I still battle with that, even to this day, because that is so ingrained in me.

Diane and I became Christians at the B.C. Open Bible study in 1987. We announced to the group that evening that we were going to commit our lives to Christ. We really didn't know what we were doing—at least I didn't know—but we eventually knew as we learned more about it. My faith strengthened as I began reading the Bible and about the evidence supporting the Bible.

I lost my card that year, and we went to Asia. Diane and I took our Bibles with us. It was a very slow growth process. The next year, though, I got back on the Tour, and we started going to the Bible studies and started growing in the Lord.

We'd looked all that year in Louisville for a church before we found one. It's a great church. Since then, it has been a process of just trying to grow in the Lord. I've had some ups and downs, played some good golf, and in 1994 played some poor golf and struggled.

But along the way, we adopted two children, and being a Christian has made these adoptions easier. I never would have considered adoption before. Not that adoption is a "Christian thing"—it's not. But Christianity changes the way you view things.

But it is still hard to apply Christianity in your life. Even now I go through doubts—not really doubting God—but when things don't go so hot, you begin to doubt God's plan for a while. It doesn't last for long.

Then you realize you need more of an eternal viewpoint than a temporal one. I think that's what gets us through more than anything—realizing that this world isn't all there is out there. We're not in the land of the living going someday into the land of the dying. It's the other way around. So that keeps us going.

It's frustrating when you don't have any security in your job—but that's when you need to rely on Him more. If I played great all of the time, I wouldn't have to rely on Him.

It's not like I'm hurting financially. I'm not. It's more that this is what I want to do with my life. I want to play the Tour and be a witness out here, whether it is speaking at a dinner or breakfast, or giving out a little card with my testimony on it.

I've learned to keep some of those cards in my pocket at all times, because someone can ask for an autograph anywhere—and I can't give them a card if I don't have it, which makes me feel bad. I give them to my pro-am partners and to people who ask for my autograph in the mail—I put a card in with my autograph and send it back to them. I'm not sure how much good it does, but I think if it even helps one guy, then it has been worth it.

I really think God has called us to be out here and spread the good news.

Memorable Moment

Winning the Nissan L.A. Open in 1991 was huge for my career in that I was having another hard year. I'd missed the first four cuts. I was hitting really well, but I was putting badly. What happened that day is kind of a personal thing, and I don't really want to go into details. But it was a faith thing, and God responded. It was really neat. So I had a lot of peace out there that day.

The same thing happened in 1993. I was having a hard year going into the Greater Milwaukee Open and had to have a very good tournament to keep my card. I always try to keep my testimony cards with me, as I've said, and during the final round I'd placed them in my bag, because I keep my glove in one pocket and the yards book in the other. But this day, for some reason, I'd left one in my pocket.

It was the fourteenth or fifteenth hole, and I was scorching it—I was five or six under for the front nine. But I started getting a little nervous. I reached in my pocket for the yards book and pulled out that single testimony card instead. And it was like it was saying to me, "What's the most important thing in your life?"

As I looked at that card, I read again where I said that golf isn't the most important thing to me. I asked myself, "Well, is it or isn't it?" And at that moment I realized, "It's not—there are lots of things that are more important." Just remembering that helped me get through that event.

Not that the nerves ever completely went away, it was more of a feeling of *It's okay if I don't win. If I don't play well, it's still okay.*

I didn't win; I lost the play-off and finished second. But I did keep my card for the following year. Sure, if I'd won, I wouldn't have gone through what I did in '94. But as David Ogrin told me at the Texas Open in 1994, "It doesn't really matter if you make it or miss it. You know that either way it is what God wants. He can use you either way."

You have a tendency to tie your successes with your self-worth. I'm still fighting through the thought that, *If I'm a good Christian, I'll play good golf.* It doesn't work that way, but at the same time, if you're not playing well, you think *What have I done?* You examine your life to see what you're doing wrong.

It's a process; the whole thing's a process. It's not going to end until you die—then you're going to be with the Lord.

Tip

I've always stayed pretty consistent out of the trap. My trap shooting has always gotten me fairly close to the hole.

First of all, it is important to be a good bunker player, because then you don't have to fear the bunkers when you're shooting for the greens. Fear in your swing is what causes errant shots. It happens if you're afraid of hitting it over there or over here. So if you work on your sand game, and you can get out of bunker, you know you're going to get up and down most of the time. Then you won't be afraid to hit that shot at the pin if it's tucked near a trap. Being a good bunker player helps other parts of your game.

The most important thing for an amateur to remember is that the sand is what moves the ball out of the bunker. How hard you hit the sand and the amount of sand you take is what is going to place the ball where you want to hit it. Again, it is a feel thing; you have to get in there and feel what you're doing.

You never want to hit the ball. A lot of players who try to chip it out hit the ball first. That's not what you want to do. You want to explode through the ball. It's always an explosion shot of some sort.

You need to use a good sand wedge, and the way you hold the wedge in there, as far as how much you open it up or close it down, is going to determine the type of shot that you hit.

So you're always trying to scoop a certain amount of sand out of there—which is the explosion, the blast. The impact of the sand is what moves the ball.

That's the most important thing for an amateur to remember: you want to hit *behind* the ball. It's a feel thing. You don't try to aim at a spot or anything—you're just feeling it. It's more of a "spank"—you're spanking the sand. So if you have a real short shot, you're going to open the blade more and spank under the ball more so you get a little less sand and the ball doesn't go as far. If you want to hit it farther, the blade is going to be closer to square—maybe just a little bit open—and you're going to dig more and spank a little more sand. More sand knocks the ball farther. That's basically the way you play bunker shots.

The other consideration is the texture of the sand, and you've got to feel that with your feet. You've got to get in there with your feet and feel how loose it is or how dense it is. If it is wet, that's also going to call for an adjustment in how hard you hit it.

Photograph by Pete Fontaine/PGA TOUR

Scott Simpson

THIS DEVOTED AND loving family man has quietly become one of the most successful—and feared—players on the PGA Tour. Through 1994, he'd earned more than $4 million in prize money and taken home six trophies: the 1980 Western Open, the 1984 Manufacturers Hanover Westchester Classic, the 1987 Greater Greensboro Open, the 1987 U.S. Open, the 1989 BellSouth Atlanta Classic, and the 1993 GTE Byron Nelson.

But then, Simpson has always been a successful golfer. He was the winner of the 1976 and 1977 NCAA Championships while at USC, the 1976 Porter Cup, the 1975 and

Photo courtesy of PGA TOUR

1977 PAC-8 Championships, the California and San Diego junior titles, as well as the 1979 and 1981 Hawaiian State Opens. He's also won various unofficial tournaments both in the U.S. and in Japan.

It seems that Simpson is at his best in the U.S. Open, where he has challenged for the cup virtually every year, including 1991, when he narrowly lost a play-off to Payne Stewart.

Simpson shows no signs of letting up either—opening 1995 with an eighteen-under-par sixteenth-place tie at the Bob Hope and a twelve-under-par tie for fourth at the Nissan in Los Angeles.

I came from a very good, very moral family. My mom and dad were elementary school teachers in San Diego. I went to Sunday school a few times when I was a little kid, church a couple times more, and that was it. When I was ten, I started playing golf. My dad was a great amateur golfer in

San Diego—one of the best in the state. Playing golf was, for us, much more important than going to church on Sundays, so we didn't go to church any more after I took it up.

I don't remember talking about religion while growing up. We were raised to do well in school, and I was always a good student. By the time I was in high school, I had intellectually blown off Christianity—I didn't believe any of it. In my mind, at least, I thought Jesus was probably a pretty good teacher, but there were just too many rules and regulations that I didn't want to follow. I was a pretty dedicated agnostic at the time. I was very skeptical.

But in high school—my senior year—I met my wife-to-be, Cheryl, and she was a Christian. She'd grown up going to Sunday school, and her parents were Christians, but she didn't have a great knowledge of the Bible—she just knew that Jesus was the Son of God and that you had to put your trust in Him to be saved. A simple faith.

Fortunately for me, she didn't know anything about the problems of being unequally yoked—Christians marrying non-Christians. I did my best to show her the error of her ways when it came to religion, but I was too interested in Cheryl to let that stand in my way. We hit it off so well that eventually we just didn't talk about religion. I definitely didn't believe any of it. I loved my rock and roll. I was a political liberal—bordering on radical. And I always loved to play golf.

I'd been playing golf steadily since I was ten. I was good enough to win the state Junior title, was second in the U.S. Junior, and got a scholarship to USC. I never did drugs, heavy drinking, or anything like that, because I wanted to do well in golf and do well in school. I went out with Cheryl, and that was about all. I really wanted to be as good as I could be in golf, because I loved playing, I loved the competition, and I had that drive.

I was fortunate enough to win the NCAAs my junior and senior years, and that gave me enough confidence to give it a try as a pro. That had always been my dream, but I was realistic enough to know most don't make it. Most of the kids who dream about being a golfer never even get a chance to play the PGA. Or any pro sport, for that matter.

Still, I was one of the lucky ones. I made the Tour.

That's when I met Morris Hatalsky. He's a fiery guy, a tremendous competitor. But if you had to pick a most-liked guy on Tour, Morris is one of the picks. Everybody loves him.

Morris also grew up in San Diego. He's about three years older than I am, so we rarely played against each other. But I obviously knew who he was.

When I got on the Tour, he was already out here. And, for some reason, maybe because Morris has a heart for evangelism and seeing people come to Christ, we got together. I used to argue with him all of the time. We'd argue about social issues and religion and everything, because I was sure that Christianity was wrong. I thought there was a better chance of Buddhism being right, or some Eastern religion, than Christianity. Morris enjoyed a friendly debate as much as I did, so we argued all the time.

In the end, it was one-on-one evangelism, person to person, that made the difference. I could argue with Morris, but at the same time I could see him live his life, and I could trust that he was telling me the truth.

Finally, in 1980, he persuaded me to come to a Bible study. He remembers this too. The talk that night was on Psalm 23: "The Lord is my shepherd." We talked about that for the entire hour of the study, what it meant to be a shepherd, what it meant to be a sheep. They said that sheep can't take care of themselves without someone to watch over them. They said that God is the Great Shepherd and that we are His sheep.

I got out of there and turned to Morris and said, "You mean your whole goal in life is to be a sheep? Not me, buddy! I don't want to be a sheep, Morris!" It was a while before he asked me to go again!

In 1981 they asked me to come to an open discussion group led by Larry Moody, who was deciding whether to come on the Tour and lead the Bible study. There had been a Bible study led by other players. It was a small thing, only three to five players attending, and they'd finally reached a point where, if they were ever going to see the Bible study grow, they needed someone to come out who could lead them, who could teach on topics—as opposed to guest speakers all the time.

Larry Moody had the time and he'd previously worked with the Baltimore Colts. It was a fortunate set of circumstances that brought him here—fortunate for me at least.

The open discussion group was where we could come and ask any question on God or life. There wasn't anything pushed down my throat. All Larry did was give biblical answers. It was totally nonjudgmental. This really appealed to my intellectual nature. Whenever he came out, I tried to think up questions to stump him because I wanted to prove him wrong. I didn't want my kids growing up going to church and having that stuff forced down their throats. I wanted them to make up their own minds.

One night I finally challenged Larry. I asked him about the hypocrites in the church—the people claiming to be Christians and not acting that way—and how they really turned me off. He simply challenged me to find out if Christianity is true or not. "There are hypocrites in any religion, whether you believe in something or not," he said.

"In fact," he added, "that's not as important as whether or not you believe in the truth. You can believe that you can fly off the Empire State Building. You can totally believe it, but you're still going to jump off and go splat! Your belief is only as good as the truth of what you believe in."

That really challenged me to search and find out the truth. So I started reading books. I started reading the Bible for the first time ever. And Josh McDowell really appealed to me because he went through the same kind of search, trying to prove it wrong. The more evidence you look at, the more it proves Jesus—and who He claims to be.

It was a gradual process for me. I think it was the intellectual part of me that first became sure it was true.

Meanwhile, my golf was going fine, and my marriage was going well. Our first child was born in October 1984, so my wife was pregnant at the time.

It finally happened while I was coming home from the Memorial Tournament that year. I was flying home, reading Josh McDowell's *More Than a Carpenter*, where he talks about praying for the first time and accepting Christ into his life.

And, at that moment, I couldn't argue with it anymore. There was too much proof that Jesus was God and that He did come and die for our sins. So I prayed on the plane—the same prayer I read in the book because I didn't know how to pray. I'd never prayed before. I didn't believe there was a God before. Now I did.

I showed up the next week at the Bible study with a Bible, and Larry Moody said, "Whoa!" I'd been to previous studies, mostly because I'd developed a friendship with Larry, and that friendship, I felt, was not contingent on my becoming a

Christian. I knew that even if I never became a Christian, we'd still be friends. That meant a lot to me. That friendship gave him the platform to share the truth with me. It was the same with Morris. That was 1984.

Cheryl was really happy when I made the decision, although she was probably wondering, *What's this going to do to this guy?* I think overall she was happy with my decision.

After that, I had one of my best years ever in 1984. I get asked all of the time, "Does being a Christian make you a better golfer?" I don't think in any way that God makes my ball go into the hole. But what He does do—when He promises us an eternal life and an abundant life—is promise us a better life here if we follow His commandments.

He also gives me the ability to keep things in perspective and have the right attitude. So, in that respect, being a Christian has made my life better. And my golf better. It gives me a reason to do my best and a reason to be content in the good times and the bad times. And there will be definite ups and downs in golf—for everybody. It's been a great time.

Memorable Moment

The two moments I best remember, I don't know how to rate. Everybody figures one would certainly be winning the U.S. Open in 1987. That was memorable because it was the greatest event I could ever hope to win. If I could pick one major—for Larry Mize it would be the Masters—it would be the U.S. Open. We've both been fortunate that we've won the tournaments we would pick as the most important. To beat Tom Watson at the Olympic Club was pretty special.

But what I remember equally well was the Bible study before that U.S. Open win, when Larry asked the question, "What is your contentment?" Larry's thesis was that if your contentment comes from Jesus Christ, then it doesn't come from winning or losing or where you are on the money list.

I went from a frustrated golfer at Westchester to a golfer who really had peace and contentment—and one who, in some ways, really baffled the press. They asked me afterward about what was going through my mind as I approached the last hole. I told them that I really had peace and joy that week and that I thought that had enabled me to do my best and to win. Then they asked me, "You'd never won a major, Scott. Why did you seem so relaxed out there while you won?" So I shared why I was relaxed, why I did feel contentment.

That win was special, especially because my dad was laid up with a bad back, and he was watching at home on Father's Day, awaiting back surgery in a couple weeks. That was really special. That was definitely one of the top two.

The other would have to be in 1993, when I won the Byron Nelson. I hadn't played very well and hadn't won since 1989, even though I'd lost the play-off at the U.S. Open in 1991 to Payne Stewart.

At the Byron Nelson, I had a lead of four shots, then I made a bogey and it went to three, made a bogey and it went to two, made another, and it went to one. And at the last hole, I was staring at another bogey! After a hundred-foot bunker shot, I had a twelve-foot putt for par, and if I made that shot, I would win the tournament. If I missed, it would go into a four-way play-off. And I didn't like my chances in a play-off after finishing with four bogeys!

The thrill of hitting that putt, the last putt of the tournament, and hitting it right where I wanted it to go, and watching it break off the right edge right into the hole, it was the most thrilling moment I've had on the Tour. That was really special.

It was even more special since I was winning Byron Nelson's tournament. If I have one hero in golf, he'd be the one. He's come to our Bible studies and shared just how important his faith is to him. He's said how great everything has worked out in his life, how he has more friends than anybody he's ever known, and how it is only because he's tried his best to do what the Bible has told him to do. It is that simple. He's had his failures and his successes, but he's always had that goal in mind: to follow the Book!

And the neat thing about Byron Nelson is that you don't see many guys who are in their eighties with so much joy in their lives. Byron's so thankful for the good things, and he still has such a real expectation of even better things.

So often we see people get older, and they're bitter about things that didn't happen right or things they would change. Byron isn't that way at all. That's what's so attractive about him, I think. I'd love to be like that—if I get the chance to live eighty years! To really live it out and really finish the race. He's sprinting to the finish line.

Those are my two highlights, and they beat any lowlights I might have had through the years.

Tip

I think the best thing about my game is consistency. I'm not really flashy in any area, but I hit the ball consistently. I'm not a real long hitter, and I'm not the straightest driver, but I think I'm long enough and I'm pretty straight—which is why I've done well in the U.S. Open. And I think I have a good short game. Not the best of all time, but a good one.

I believe that consistency is both mental and physical. Mentally you just try to stay at an even keel. You look at the great players in history and the majority of them stay emotionally calm through the ups and downs, and I think that helps them to be consistent. That's true from Bobby Jones to Byron Nelson to Ben Hogan—all the way to Jack Nicklaus and Tom Watson.

I think it is a discipline, to learn how to concentrate on each shot and let go in between. Letting go means: Just mentally relax. Talk or walk around or something like that.

You practice to get all the mechanics down, then you do it.

Golf is different from a reactionary sport like basketball or tennis, where you have to clear your mind a little more to let things happen. Golf is more like shooting a free throw than charging with a basketball, because you have all that time to think about each shot.

What you need to do is quiet your mind and go through your routine.

For me, one of the big keys is to have a routine. For me, it is taking two waggles, stepping out, looking at the target, taking a practice swing, then two more

Photograph by Pete Fontaine/PGA TOUR

waggles, then look at the target one more time, and then I go. I don't vary the routine. If I can't get a routine I'm comfortable with, one that I can use on the practice tee, then I won't be able to hit the same shots in competition.

Anything you change messes you up, tightens you up. You need to keep the same grip pressure, the same everything. That's the purpose of practicing.

Paul Stankowski

WHEN PAUL STANKOWSKI finds his groove, he really finds it! The boyish, energetic Stankowski ended 1994 with a sizzling fifth-place tie at the Las Vegas Invitational. The $54,750 in prize money boosted him to 106th on the money list—and back for 1995. Nineteen ninety-five started off nearly as well: He challenged briefly at the Bob Hope Classic before finishing with an eighteen-under-par 342 and eighth-place tie (with two of his longtime idols, Scott Simpson and Larry Mize).

Photo courtesy of PGA TOUR

Stankowski was a three-time All-American at the University of Texas at El Paso and won the Western Athletic Conference championship in 1990.

I grew up with a Catholic background. I was an altar boy at St. Anthony's Church, went to a Catholic school for first through eighth grades, and went to church every Sunday and holiday—but that was about it. I didn't know anything about a personal relationship with Jesus Christ.

My brother accepted the Lord in high school. I remember him doing a lot of Bible studies, reading the Bible a lot, making a bunch of notes, and all that kind of stuff. He's four years older than I am. And my sister, Teresa, as well. I remember she had a boyfriend who was a Christian, and they always prayed together. But I didn't know what it was all about.

Tom went to Arizona State; he was a senior when I was a freshman at the University of Texas at El Paso. He shared with me, off and on. I always told him,

"I'm not ready for that. I'm in college. I want to party and have fun. And I can't give that up yet." I liked hanging with my teammates and all of that fun stuff.

But Tom was patient. He shared with me Phillipians 1:6: "being confident of this very thing, that He who has begun a good work in you will complete it until the day of Jesus Christ." That stuck with me, though I really didn't know what it meant, and yet it was becoming more clear as time went on.

College Golf Fellowship was an organization that had banquets at certain college tournaments, and I went sometimes. My freshman year at the NCAA, Scott Simpson shared his testimony at North Ranch. They sent cards around, and I checked off that I wanted to know more about furthering my relationship with Jesus Christ, so they sent me a Bible. That was that stage.

But I kept living the college party life. A friend of mine, John Sosa, went to the University of Texas at Austin. He gave me some contemporary Christian tapes: Michael W. Smith, Russ Taff, and others. They were pretty neat, and I'd stay up listening to them. On March 9, 1990, I accepted the Lord. It was from all the things my brother was telling me, the things I was hearing from College Golf Fellowship, the Bible studies I attended while I was in college, and the words of a friend of mine from Oklahoma State, Kevin Wentworth, who would lead the Bible studies. I went to some of those, and I eventually accepted the Lord. I can't remember where I was, but I'll never forget the date.

Meanwhile, I lived with the golf team—about ten of us—in a big golf house near UTEP. For about a week I was reading my Bible, I was listening to my music, and I was praying nightly—but I didn't have any fellowship. While I was reading and listening to my music, I'd hear the guys downstairs partying and playing cards. I could hear the beer cans opening up.

After about a week, I put the Bible away, put the tapes aside, and went back to living that life. From there, I pretty much went deeper into sin: drugs, drinking more often, everything.

Then in December of 1990, I turned twenty-one, and we went out on my birthday. Some of my teammates and I did some things we shouldn't have done. After it was over, we got into a fight among ourselves. It was a bad night altogether!

On our way home, a teammate and I were messing with this car in front of us: swerving around, flashing our brights on him. Finally I went around him, and the guy started chasing me through the dark streets of El Paso. At one point, I zoomed through a yellow light and screeched through a left turn. There was a cop there—and he pulled us over. I was wasted—and I still had my golf clubs in the back of my car.

One of the rules we had at UTEP was that if you ever got a ticket for drunk driving, you were immediately off the team. Basically, my life, my college life, my golf life, would have been gone if this policeman had given me a ticket.

I panicked. I claimed a guy was chasing me, which was the truth—I just didn't tell the policeman *why* he was chasing me. The policeman never saw the car following me; I guess the guy had pulled off when he saw the cop. Somehow I talked my way out of it. The officer let us go.

The next day, I began thinking, *This is not good.* We had a big team meeting, and some of my teammates wanted to kick us off the team for the stuff we'd done the previous night and for the fight afterwards—they were tired of it. I was tired of it.

As time marched on, January and February, I kept looking forward to my brother Tom's wedding in March. He was a Christian, and his Christian friends were going to be there. I was going to get to hang out with some Christian people. I couldn't wait! It was like a fire was burning inside of me, like God was knocking at my door, or knocking at my head, saying, "Hello! Let Me in; let Me take charge here!"

Finally, on March 9, 1991, Tom got married. At the wedding, we got in a little circle around Tom, and we started praying for him. When it was my turn to pray, I lost it. I lost it all. Here was a guy who'd basically led me to the Lord. He'd planted all of those seeds, and he'd helped water them, and God made them grow—if it wasn't for Tom, I might not be a Christian today.

That day I rededicated my life, and that night I went to a party. I didn't drink, but I was still there, so I was torn. I drank water, and when I saw the parents of a friend of mine at the party, I stayed and talked with them.

I went back to college the next day and went right back out to the bars. I went with some teammates to a couple of restaurants with bars and got smashed by noon! By 3:00 P.M. I was wasted again and talking about some of us going to a country nightclub in El Paso.

I went to the golf house for a couple of hours and tried to sober up. When the guys called and said, "Are you ready to go?" I said, "No, I'm not going to go."

On the eighteenth of March I quit drinking—which I thought would be a hard thing to do—but I haven't had a drink since.

The other things in my life, which I thought would be the easiest things to leave, are still creeping around in there. So Satan still has a foothold, and he's trying to knock on my door, and he's keeping those poison darts coming my way.

Still, I call March 9, 1991, my rededication time, and it took about a week and a half to get settled down. I found a church to go to. I discovered the Fellowship of Christian Athletes at UTEP, I started going to their meetings on Tuesday nights, and I met some great people and had some real fellowship. Since then, I've had so much Christian fellowship in El Paso, it's scary! Everywhere I turn, there are Christians! I go to a prayer breakfast every Thursday morning at my church that has a real mix of age groups. I've come a long way, but I have a long way to go.

I got out of college in 1991, turned pro, played the Golden State Tour, and tried to get my eligibility card that fall. I missed getting my card, but I got to the second stage. I missed getting into the final by a couple of shots. I was kind of disappointed. I never had a doubt in my mind that I'd get on the Tour that year. It was like, "This is it! I'm going!" It was just a matter of going through these stages—and I didn't get it.

I played the Golden State Tour again in 1992, full time. I played well, won my first tournament, and started dating my wife-to-be, Regina.

We'd met in May of 1991, two months after I'd rededicated my life. She's a wonderful Christian girl. It took a while to get that relationship off the ground, partly because I left that summer to go play golf. It was hard being away, because we'd just met, and I left for two months. We grew closer, and I moved back to El Paso.

I continued to play the mini-tours. At the San Juan Open, in Farmington, New Mexico, she caddied for me, and I won! It was my first win as a pro—it was pretty neat. A few months later, she caddied for me again at the New Mexico Open, and I won again! Boy, was my regular caddie bummed!

We kept dating and ended up getting engaged in May 1992. On the one-year anniversary of our first date, I asked her to marry me, and she said yes.

I didn't try Q School in 1993 because we set a date of January 9, 1993, and I didn't want to be a newlywed and go back the next week and go on tour. I figured, "Let's go play the mini-tours again, let Regina get used to the travel—which you never do, anyway—and just have some fun and get to know each other." It worked out well, we had some fun, and I had some success on the Golden State Tour—though I didn't win any big ones. But I played solid golf, and I had a good time with Regina and learning all about her.

We tried Q School again the next time I was eligible and got through it. I got my card, and the rest of that December I was on cloud nine. I had my birthday during Q School finals week, and getting to go out on Tour was a good birthday present! We then went to Hawaii and had our one-year anniversary in Hawaii.

So 1994 was a total blessing.

Memorable Moment

Two moments: In Hawaii, first tournament of the year of 1994. I missed the cut by a shot at the United Airlines Hawaiian Open—a four-footer on the last hole. I was sitting there dejected. We went to dinner that night, and suddenly I realized, *This is the first tournament of twenty-five I'm going to play this year! It's not a big deal!* Immediately, God said, "This was just one little thing. Keep on going."

I missed the next couple of cuts, but I played well at the Bob Hope Classic.

The best week I had was the week of the Federal Express Classic in Memphis. I flew out to Memphis early. It was the week of the FCA Golf Camp, in Olive Branch, Mississippi, just two miles south of Memphis. I talked to Tim Kilmer and told him I'd love to go and help out. I started helping out on Sunday, got to meet the kids, and had a good week. I did some clinics for them and shared my testimony for the first time. I was nervous, but it went well. And Regina was there, so it was a good week. We got to see some pretty strong kids.

I was a little frustrated as the week went on because I didn't see any spiritual growth. It was as if they weren't excited to be there for the Lord—it was just another golf camp to some of them. But the very last night of the week they had an open mike, and the first kid up there was strong, bold, to the point—it was awesome! This kid was on fire! It was so cool.

I went on to play well that week. I had my best tournament of the year, tied for eighth, until the Las Vegas Invitational, where I tied for fifth. I wasn't expecting it in Memphis though. I hadn't spent too much time on the golf course because I was helping out with the kids through Wednesday night—and He rewarded me for the work I did with the kids. So I was richly blessed, not only by the tournament, but by seeing and hearing those kids.

My heart goes out to high school kids today—they're struggling. The peer pressure is unbelievable. I think you've got to reach kids before they get to college. If you can get a kid, reach him, and tell him about Jesus *before* he gets to college so he can accept that truth and live it in college, life will be so much better—and easier. I'm so thankful to have accepted Christ in college. I got to live my last three months in college walking for the Lord.

Tip

Bunker play is my strongest point. I was a horrible bunker player in high school and college—I was pathetic.

So I practiced it a lot with my brother during my first couple years as a pro. We'd go practice, and my brother would stand far away from the hole and hit the highest bunker shots in the world. Mine would always come out low and then scoot. His were high and soft. So I worked with him a lot. I had no clue what he was doing. So he showed me. He told me to step into his stance, and I kind of got a feel for it.

And then I was watching Fred Couples in person and on TV, and nine times out of ten,

Photograph by Pete Fontaine/PGA TOUR

his hand would come off the club and he'd do it one-handed—but he hit great bunker shots.

So I put the two together: standing farther away like Tom and trying to mimic what Freddie looked like hitting bunker shots. And one day I found the magic. It was amazing. Now I think it is the best part of my game; I feel I can make every bunker shot I hit. The confidence is there.

I now tell golfers to open up their bodies, open up their stances, and open the blade. If you can point the blade at the hole, or your target, or where you want to land the ball, then you open your body to that. Look at your feet line, and put your club down so it is aiming on that line, then open up your body. I basically take the club up and outside, drop it down behind the ball, and accelerate—and try to knock the sand out of the bunker.

For an amateur who doesn't hit bunker shots well, aim two inches behind the ball, and try to knock the sand out of the bunker in a descending blow—not swinging up. Swing down at it. If you do that, your ball will come up and out. And that's basically how I've learned.

If you knock the sand out of the bunker, you're not worrying about the ball—you're swinging down and through the ball, not up at the ball. As long as you're going down, two inches behind the ball, the ball will pop up. That's what all that club loft is for.

I grew up aiming straight at the hole, digging down, and I just couldn't hit good bunker shots. So now I open up my body—probably aiming thirty feet left of the pin—and I point the face of the club at the target, take it straight up, and drop it down. You're almost cutting across the ball. You've got to stay with it—crop it a little bit.

And you've got to accelerate through the ball to get it out. Otherwise you're going to hit it fat, and the ball's not going to go very far, and that's not good. It's got to go far.

It's a simple process—it's just not easy. Just like everything in golf.

Suzanne Peta Strudwick

SUZANNE STRUDWICK MAY only be in her first few years on the LPGA Tour, but she was a regular English lion on the Continent. As an amateur, she placed fourth on the 1982 European Junior Championship and finished sixteenth that same year in the English Ladies Open. Joining the WPG European Tour shortly thereafter, she won both the 1989 French Open and the 1991 AGF Paris Open. A year later, she qualified for the U.S. Women's Open and finished a very impressive sixteenth.

Photo courtesy of LPGA TOUR

In her first two full years on the LPGA, Strudwick's already made a name for herself. In 1993 she earned the LPGA's Rookie of the Year award for a season that included a fifth-place tie in the Jamie Farr Toledo Open and a tenth-place tie at the Standard Register PING. In 1994, besides increasing her earnings significantly, she finished with a tie for third at the State Farm Rail Classic and a ninth-place tie at the Weetabix Women's British Open.

The resident of Stafford, England, began playing golf when she was only eleven. In the U.S. she's become extremely active with the Habitat for Humanity program.

I certainly wasn't raised in a born-again, personal-relationship-with-the-Lord type of environment—but I definitely was given an awareness that there was a God. My family and I went to church in England, where the church is, unfortunately, part of the state. The Church of England is built on the lines of the Catholic Church, and is very strict, and everything is done exactly the same. So as a child, it was very boring and not something to look forward to.

It wasn't until much later, when I turned pro, that I realized that you could actually have a personal relationship with the Lord.

How did that come about?

I met an American professional golfer, Meredith Marshall. She teaches in Orlando now, and she works with lots of pros. She's a wonderful lady. I was very young and very impressionable when I turned pro; I was just seventeen. She basically took me under her wing.

We first met when she came and lived at my parents' house, and I traveled with her in England. She had a sponsor's card and I didn't have anything—but she didn't know her way around England. I drove and directed while she was there, and she stayed at the house and ultimately directed *me* to the Lord. So it worked out really well.

She witnessed to you while you traveled?

Yes, with tapes and her own witnessing, as well as the Bible she brought me. She really let me see that you could have a personal relationship with Jesus Christ. Before then, Jesus was always some sort of something that happened in history. I was never really told that He is still alive and that He can live inside you.

Is Cris Stevens's Bible study a positive experience for you?

Oh yes, very much so. That's the thing that gets us going. The fact that we play on Sundays means we never get to church, and we're never really home enough to build relationships within a church. Consequently, we just never form a home group, a home body. So Cris's fellowship on the LPGA Tour *is* our church. The other players become more than competitors, more than just compatriots out here—they become friends in Christ. It's worth staying out here for. Otherwise it would be very difficult.

This wasn't always the case when I played abroad. After about five years, I moved away from the Lord and became very disillusioned because we didn't have a solid fellowship on the European Tour. I played the European Tour for ten years before coming to America. Meredith had left the Tour and gone home, so the backbone of the fellowship was gone. It wasn't long before it basically collapsed.

When that happened, I eventually went back to the friends I had before. I started getting into going out at night, that sort of stuff. I was twenty-three or twenty-four and felt as though I could do anything. I eventually realized that I'd placed the foundation of my faith on Meredith and on her teaching. When she left, I saw that my own structure and my own faith weren't solid at all. It wasn't until I came over to the U.S. Tour that I came all of the way back.

I was pretty much in the wilderness for about four years.

And it was that hard wilderness, where you know that there's something better, but you don't know how to get there.

In the meantime, I tried everything. I went through a big New Age thing, trying to find what I was missing in my faith.

Finally, I decided that I wanted to come over here and get my card. Strangely enough, it was one of the easiest things that I've ever done. I'd been told that the U.S. Tour Qualifying School was one of the most difficult things you'd ever do in your life. But it wasn't; it was very easy. I won the prequalifying tournament by seven shots and finished fifteenth to get my all-exempt card.

At first it felt very easy, but the following year I realized for the very first time why—it was because the Lord was bringing me to a place where I could really get a solid foundation in my faith and start again. I feel very strongly that He brought me over here to get me away from my old life, to start completely fresh, to start a new career.

I wasn't trying to escape or run away from the old things, but I needed to be able to close that chapter in my life and open up a new chapter with the Lord. I needed to start anew and really build the foundation of the Christian faith in my heart, and I feel like I'm doing that. I haven't done it—I'm doing it.

I think my first speaking engagement, when I was in the U.S. in 1993, was probably one of the biggest breakthroughs for me, because I finally had to make an announcement that I was a Christian. I'd never really had to do that before. I'd never totally admitted it to my friends or anyone else. So saying to Cris, "Yes, I will do that engagement. I will speak at that church," had a big effect on me. I was very nervous, but it was definitely moving, even though it was the first time they had asked for a Christian golfer to come speak at this particular church.

I told them my story, of how I wasn't that committed, how I was basically in the wilderness, and how my foundation wasn't solid until I had a personal relationship with Christ. When it was over, they seemed to have really enjoyed it, and they asked for another player to come back again in 1994. They told Cris that it had gone very well, and a lot of people who were not totally committed did commit themselves that night.

Being on the Tour gives you a platform to reach people, which makes it, perhaps, a little bit easier, because people are automatically going to listen to what you have to say. It also means that we're reaching a bigger audience, so if we make a mistake or if we're a little bit insecure, we're going to hit more people with something that they might not want to hear otherwise.

I try and act like I should on the Tour. I try to let my own personality come out, to be a friendly and approachable person. I try and let that come out when speaking to people. Or when somebody wants to come up and talk, I try and do that too.

When I'm being interviewed, I definitely let the reporter know that I am a Christian. If they write it, then that means that more people are going to say, "Oh, so she's a Christian." Naturally, that has a good side and a bad side to it. The good side is that I'm reaching people, and they might be pleasantly surprised. But it might bring up the negative side, which is, "Well, how could she be a Christian and throw that club?" or "I heard her say this!" or "She didn't sign my son's autograph—how can she call herself a Christian?"

I believe that once you step out of the locker room, you have to be totally aware that you are a Christian, that you have a responsibility, that you're an ambassador for Christ. That must be in the forefront of your mind at all times.

What changes have you seen since your faith has become such an important part of your life?

For one thing, I've realized that if you're the least bit shy, it really comes out on the Tour. Even not having somebody to go out to dinner with each night is tough. Maybe you go out three nights a week. Well, that leaves the other four nights alone.

A lot of the young players can't afford hotel room service, but a lot of other girls hide in that safety net. They stay in a sixty- to seventy-dollars-a-night hotel so they can just order room service every night. But if you can't afford that, you're staying at the Red Roof Inn and having to get take-out or something and go back to the room—and there's nothing there.

That's when everything closes in on you. So my goal for next year is to reach out a little bit more to some of the friends that I've made up here who aren't Christians, but still need a friend. Not necessarily to witness to them, but just be a friend.

Memorable Moment

Definitely the State Farm Rail Classic in 1994—that was a big week. I finished tied for third. Going into that week, I was in a position where I was 110th on the money list—and the cut was going to be at 90th, so I was in danger of losing my card and having to go back to the Tour School. I had five more tournaments to go, and I just really had a tough middle part of the season. I started the season really well, but I played terribly.

And perhaps because of that bad streak, I'd been very angry with God, and that anger came out on the golf course. Here I was in a situation where I was going to lose my card.

But going into the State Farm, He brought me to a different place. The week before the tournament, I said, "I'm going to totally trust You, whatever happens." So I totally put my trust in Him. I decided that, if I wasn't going to be happy, I was going to fake trying to be happy out there! I just tried to relax and really enjoy myself on the golf course.

I was very nervous on the last day, but at the same time, I was also very calm. I had a deep inner peace that I hadn't had for a long time, and I had a confidence I hadn't felt for a long time. I know that was definitely the Lord's doing.

When you put yourself in a position where your back's against the wall, and you totally trust in Him, that's when He works. If you do it on your own, then you're just flailing about in the dark, and you probably won't make it. If you totally trust in Him and give it to Him, then everything seems right at the end.

Tip

Knowing your own capabilities is very important. I'm not a long hitter, and the Tour definitely wants to promote the longer hitters. The group that designs the golf courses each week caters to the longer hitters. So I have to remind myself what my strong points are: While I'm not that long, I am straight. And, to go with that, I have a pretty good short game.

Knowing that part of my game and not being totally wrapped up in the fact that I don't hit it as long as many of the girls out here, I can play within myself.

My suggestion is that you should understand that, though you're not like everybody else, what you have is just as good if you'll trust it and go with it.

Know your capabilities. Trust in yourself. And work really hard. I think those are the things that can make a difference in your game.

And of those, one of the biggest things is to work very hard in everything that you do. Always give 110 percent. If you want it badly enough, that's what it is all about. Work hard and you'll achieve it.

For me, that means that on the day of a tournament I'm up at 6:00 A.M. running and stretching for a 7:00 A.M. tee-time. I practice maybe two or two and a half hours after every round. Then maybe I'll go work out. By the time I get back home, it's seven or eight o'clock. And that's seven days a week.

But if that's what it takes for you to excel, then that's what you need to do.

Mike Sullivan

AFFABLE, GENTLE-SPIRITED Mike Sullivan did what you'd expect him to do after fighting a variety of serious back and neck injuries over the past four seasons—he went out and won the 1994 B.C. Open. And, in the process, enjoyed his best year ever with nearly $300,000 in prize money.

Photo courtesy of PGA TOUR

Still, it has been a roller-coaster ride of a career for Sullivan, who "briefly" attended the University of Florida and says he "survived" rooming with Andy Bean. He turned pro at age twenty, won the 1980 Southern Open and the 1989 Independent Insurance Agent Open—and suffered through a number of lean years in between. But somehow his winnings on the PGA Tour have now climbed above $2 million. And, along the way, he's gained more than a few friends on and off the greens for his unflappable good nature.

I was raised Baptist. I've got an aunt, my mom's sister, who was a Baptist missionary in Nigeria for, gosh, a long time. Both sets of grandparents were Baptists. My mom led me to the Lord when I was about five or six. I remember getting down on my knees and asking Jesus into my heart.

I grew up in the church until I was in high school, then I picked up golf. When I started working on the weekends on the golf course, I kind of got out of the church scene. I went to college, and it was more of the same. I didn't do anything bad, but I certainly wasn't growing spiritually. I met my wife-to-be, Sandy, at college and quit school after a year and a quarter. After we got married, I started playing on the mini-tours.

In time, I started going to church with Sandy. We both felt like it was important. We soon found we weren't getting much out of the church we were going to. We felt like we weren't learning anything about the Bible. Instead, they told some nice stories about people doing good things.

After I qualified for the tour and played a year or two, I talked to Don Pooley and told him how frustrated I was. He said, "You ought to come to the Bible study." At the time, I had this perception of the Bible study as being real charismatic. I'd heard some people had been put on the spot—and it wasn't anything I'd feel real comfortable doing. I wasn't willing to go and get put on the spot. But finally I went anyway.

That was about the time Larry Moody started coming and doing the study. Larry gave the Bible study a lot more credibility, and, for the first time, there was some consistency in the teaching. It wasn't just individual people sharing. I've always been pretty private and kind of close to the vest with everything, so I felt really uncomfortable about possibly getting into a situation where I'd have to share some of my feelings and things that were close to my heart. It's just hard for me to do.

But not long after I started going to the Bible study, I decided I'd been drifting a long time and it was time to get some direction back, so my wife and I started attending a lot more regularly. We felt like our church was the Tour Bible study, because that's where we were most of the time. We still went to church most of the time when we were home, but I'd fall asleep a lot.

Finally, my wife's sister's husband, who was raised Baptist and had been going to the same church we'd been going to, decided, "It's time to move. My kids are getting close to high school age, and I want to get them in a good youth program." So he switched to a Baptist church. My wife's sister was baptized in the church. We went for the baptism and listened to the sermon that night and really enjoyed the preaching. Afterward, Sandy and I said, "We ought to start coming here."

So we started attending and went for five years: Sunday mornings, Sunday nights, and Wednesday nights. When Rebecca, our daughter, decided she wanted to be a candidate for baptism, we went forward with her and finally joined the church as well.

In the meantime, Larry had baptized my wife in Orlando at the Disney Open. There have been several baptisms down there over the years, including Loren Roberts.

I knew that it was by faith, not by works, that you're saved. Yet at the same time I was always thinking, *Okay, I got mad out there, I banged a club, I wasn't a very good example, I wasn't a good witness today.* And that would eat at me all the time. I was trying, basically, to do it on my own.

My faith really took a major step several years ago when I was hurt. It caused me to think, *I don't quite have control of this situation.* Then one afternoon in the summer of 1993, I sneezed, and that was it. I had missed all winter, had gotten better, was playing okay, and was starting to feel better about my game. But I sneezed, and when I tried to raise back up after sneezing, I couldn't stand up. I was out another four months. I didn't have disability insurance for my back because I'd had back problems before and couldn't get coverage.

So there we were: no income, no disability, no nothing. Fortunately we had some money for retirement we were able to draw from.

It was my wife's faith that helped strengthen my faith during that time. She kept saying, "I've been praying about it, and I just feel like the Lord's going to take care of us." This was a drastic departure from everything I'd known in the past. Before I'd think, "We need some money? Why, I'll go out and play better."

But now, I couldn't even walk around. It was a tough time for me. I spent a lot of time praying, and I spent a lot of time reading. And I finally said, "Well, I worked out all I was supposed to work out. I did all of the stretching and all the other stuff I was supposed to do. And I still couldn't keep myself well. God, if you want me to play golf again, I'll play. If You want me to do something else, then I'll have faith that You'll show me what else to do."

After that, I had a real peace. I thought that the rest of the summer of 1993 would be a long, miserable time. But, as it turned out, all of our needs were met. As for Sandy and me, our marriage grew stronger than ever. With Rebecca, our daughter, we became a much closer family. We realized you don't have to have money to enjoy doing things. I felt like my faith was tremendously strengthened, because I had to sit back and trust that God was actually going to do what He said He was going to do and take care of us.

And I realized—finally—trying on your own to be good won't cut it. You can try all you want to, and you're never going to measure up. You do the best you can, you fail, you ask for forgiveness, repent, and then go on. It was a big year for me in that respect, because of all the things that had been stumbling blocks and obstacles in the past. It just shattered them all.

Same goes for 1994. I was playing on a medical exemption, which it looked like I might not get for a while because of some circumstances. But I got the exemption at the last minute, so it has been a free ride ever since—almost. Winning the B.C. Open was an affirmation that this is what God wanted us to do.

Memorable Moment

There is a sad but funny memory in my past. It took place in 1990, before the New Orleans Open. That year, the winds reached thirty-five miles an hour at times. Still, I played pretty well—until the fifteenth hole. The fifteenth hole is a par five, and the wind was kind of into us, left to right, and there was water around us on all sides, with an island green. I thought, *I don't want to miss it right, but I've got plenty of room left.* So I hit my drive way left. So far left, in fact, that I didn't know where it was at first.

I found the ball in a sidehill lie, so I decided to hit a hook into the wind. I hit it, and it went pretty good, but once it got up into the wind, it started going left. It drifted down and trickled down the side of the island, but I didn't see it splash.

I got to the island, and the ball was about two inches—at most—from the boards that separate and support the green in the water. I thought I could take my sand wedge and sort of lift it straight up by chopping straight down behind it and squirting the ball out onto the green.

All the while I was thinking, *If I make a bogey here, I'll settle for a bogey.* So I asked my caddie if he thought I could do it. He's a pretty good player, so he looked at the lie and said, "Yeah, you can do that." I took the sand wedge and took a couple of practice swings.

Now, while all this was happening, although I didn't know it, the NBC-TV cameras were taping the action.

I swung, but the club hit the boards behind the ball and bounced over the ball.

I missed it completely and had to take a shot. I thought, *Well, I have to be more steep this time.* I tried it again and the exact same thing happened!

Then I had a temper tantrum and turned the club upside down, and I thought, *I'm going to hit this ball in the water!* So I hit it, it hit the boards—again—and bounced a foot away from the boards, where I finally had a shot.

Finally, I hit it toward the hole and—being a relatively new course—it hit a seam in the sod. Once the ball hit that seam, it bounced up over my head and splashed into the water behind me! So I had to take a drop, and I ended up with an 11 on the hole.

And the whole time the cameras were grinding.

That entire sequence ended up on several blooper tapes and has been seen by millions. It was a CNN "Play of the Day." Johnny Miller had it on *The Today Show.* I think it was on *Late Night with David Letterman.* And, of course, it was on the year-end CNN and ESPN shows. It's even on the PGA computers at each tournament under "Memorable Shots." Well, it certainly was that!

Tip

I'd like to talk about something that's like a lob shot. It's a shot out of the rough around the green—a shot you use to get up over a bunker quickly. The way I try to hit it, so that the ball comes out pretty much consistently each time, it becomes a dead-handed shot. *No* hands.

I try and think of it as if the wedge and your arm are forming a triangle—it's now an arm and shoulder shot. Since you don't

Photograph by Sam Greenwood/PGA TOUR

cock your hands, you don't have to recock, so you never really increase the speed of the club, except with your shoulders. It's like a pendulum. You can actually move your big muscles fast, and swing relatively hard, yet the clubhead never gets a whole lot of speed to it. No wrists either.

You can either keep the club square, if you want to get it up fast and land soft, or you can open the club way up. It's whatever height and distance you want. It's easier to reproduce that swing under pressure if you're not using your hands.

If you do this, even on hard pan, you can do it out of the bunker. It's not as good out of the bunker as it is off grass, but typically you'll get a pin that's cut close to you, with the ball down in the rough. Instead of quickly setting the club with your hands and popping down on it and not knowing for sure if your clubhead speed is the same with every swing, this way you can almost feel it every time.

Jim Colbert told me about this swing a long time ago. He told me, "If you get under the gun, you can hit hard and—if you're in between clubs—instead of taking a longer club and trying to swing easy, you take a short club and try and hit it harder."

It's the same kind of thing. You can hit it hard and the ball comes out soft, with no spin on it. As a result, it usually just hits and rolls itself out.

Nancy Taylor

NANCY TAYLOR IS that rare individual who is both perky and thoughtful, someone with insight and depth—and yet is great fun to be around.

Her amateur golfing days are filled with highlights. She won the 1982 Public Links Championship and was the runner-up the following year. She was a semifinalist in the 1983 Trans-National and a quarterfinalist in the 1983 U.S. Amateur. That same year she finished second in the Women's South Atlantic Championship.

Photo courtesy of LPGA TOUR

In 1985, Taylor competed on the Women's Florida Golf Tour. A couple victories on that tour were the impetus she needed to join the LPGA in 1986.

Taylor's best year to date was 1987. She finished second at the Jamie Farr Toledo Classic en route to earning $33,787 for the year.

My father was career military. He spent thirty-three years in the Air Force, and we moved twenty-four times. We went to church when we were younger, but once we were teenagers, we were allowed to decide if we wanted to go. As a result, I didn't become a Christian until after college.

I think my faith was something that came together because of my good Christian friends in college. I went to the FCA meetings at the college tournaments—but I was caught up in doing the normal college things. God was on my mind, but I went on living a normal college life. I think it was my move to Tampa, where others reached out to me, that made the difference.

I moved from Arizona back to Florida to start playing on the mini-tours. A friend of mine who also plays on the Tour, Joan Delk, invited me to go to her church, so I went. That was in July 1984. The Evangelism Explosion program was going on at her church, and they came out and visited me at my house afterward. I was out washing my car one day, and these three people showed up and started asking me all these really profound questions. It took me by surprise.

But one of the questions they asked was, "If you were to die tonight, do you know for sure that you would go to heaven?" I kept looking at the hood of the car—you're never ready for that kind of question! Finally I said, "I'm not really sure." All my life I'd been a pretty decent person. I had mostly done good things. But I wasn't *sure.*

He said, "Well, you think about it. We'll come back tomorrow if you'd like."

So when they came back, the man who was asking the questions asked me the same question again. I said I didn't think I was ready to make that kind of commitment—it just seemed like a huge commitment to me. But they then patiently explained the gospel message to me—and I gave my life to the Lord that very night!

Everything was so new and so confusing; I wasn't really sure at first, but slowly the Lord started to get a hold on me.

Since then, my faith has had a dramatic impact on my career. Now I can't imagine being out here without knowing Christ. It really makes you take a step back and look and see where the non-Christians are coming from. It gives you a burden for them when you try to imagine life without Christ on the Tour.

Before I became a Christian, golf was everything in my life. My life was living and dying on golf. Golf was my god. Golf is still a priority in my life, but God is obviously the highest priority now.

Being out on the Tour gives me an opportunity that is very much of a challenge, because we're in a world that's within the real reality. Everything is thrown at you, including all kinds of temptations. It's a constant battle to be a servant and to keep your eyes on Christ out here, because you're given or offered so many things.

Is it easy to speak about your faith while on the Tour?

I think God has helped me develop that. I think everybody initially has a fear of that, but He helps you with that as you grow.

It's difficult anywhere to sit down and witness, but I definitely do when people ask me questions about my faith. What's helped me is reading the Word every day. Absolutely. No question. That's the most important thing; it has made the biggest difference in the world in my life. It is something I really try to have the discipline to do.

Is there someone who has been a particular influence on your personal faith journey?

Joan Delk is one. Cris Stevens probably has been that to a number of players out here. Barb Knudson is another.

Have you found the Bible studies helpful?

I think so—they're helpful regardless of where you are. They help you keep perspective, keep you focused on your real objective, and remind you why you're out here.

Being a Christian helps you prioritize things; it puts things in perspective. Sometimes you get a little away from the Lord when you get frustrated from not playing well. Or maybe you've gone through a few weeks in a bit of a slump. So I think it is a definite priority to keep your eyes on the Lord.

Memorable Moment

There have been times when I've been with players, and I've been aware that they're having hard times. Once it was very interesting because it was in the middle of a party. I was talking with someone, my faith came up, and suddenly the man I was talking to opened up about his struggles—everything came tumbling out. I was so surprised!

But later I was able to do some serious follow-up to our conversation, and it was a much more heartfelt approach to things. I was able to offer some passages from the Word as well as some encouragement that God could do something in his life. That was probably one of the biggest things I can remember happening to me, even bigger than winning any tournament.

Tip

Probably the biggest things I see that amateurs need to work on are the basics: posture, grip, and alignment. Golf changes from week to week. You feel different every day. Some days, you feel the hole looks eight inches wide instead of four inches, and you just know where you're going to hit it.

So I think that over a period of time, your setup and alignment and those things can slightly change. Things change if you're playing in windy conditions, for instance. So I continually suggest that golfers go back and work on their grip, posture, and alignment.

These facets of your game are repeatable, and you know what they're supposed to look like. So, if the weather's bad, you can work on them inside with a mirror or using a video camera. Either way, you need to watch what you've done so you'll know what's correct and what's right. If you work inside with a mirror, you can get the best picture and feel—then you can take all of that out to the driving range.

Of course, some people have a lesson or two and take that "feel" back on the golf course and end up overexaggerating it.

In the end, working with a mirror or a video camera, you can tie the correct feel to the correct picture. Even the people who live up north in the snow will have no excuse not to practice if they'll use this method!

Photograph by Sandi Higgs/LPGA TOUR

Doug Tewell

THE AVERAGE FAN in the gallery may not know his name, but you can bet that the average PGA touring pro does. Since his amateur days in Oklahoma (where he won both the 1966 Oklahoma State Junior and Scholastic titles), Doug Tewell has quietly carved a niche for himself as a steady, dangerous player.

Since 1976 Tewell has won nearly $2.5 million dollars, in part due to his well-deserved reputation as one of the games straightest drivers. His four PGA Tour victories include the 1980 Sea Pines Heritage Classic, the 1980 IVB-Philadelphia Classic, the 1986 Los Angeles Open, and the 1987 Pensacola Open.

Photo courtesy of PGA TOUR

In 1994 Tewell bounced back from shoulder troubles for a eight-place tie at the Motorola Western Open and a seventh-place tie in the Walt Disney World/Oldsmobile Classic.

I grew up in a Southern Baptist Christian home. I attended University Heights Baptist Church in Stillwater, Oklahoma—as early as I can remember, we went there. I was married by a Baptist preacher, and my wife, Pam, and I are currently members of a Southern Baptist Church.

As a youngster, around the age of nine or ten, I made a public profession of faith, although I probably didn't realize what I had done until I was somewhere around the age of thirteen. I feel like sometimes when you're nine or ten you make a public profession because you look up there and think *I ought to do this because my best friend is up there doing it.* You don't really do it for the right reasons—you do it because of peer pressure. It wasn't until I was about thirteen that I knew the reasons why I had done it—so I did it again, but in my own way.

I was married at an early age—nineteen—and I married my high school sweetheart, whom I also attended Sunday school with. I remember our pastor talking to us and saying, "How many times can you rededicate your life to Jesus Christ?" I think that was probably my third time! Pastors must want to hear it again, especially before you get married.

But Pam and I made that commitment to each other, and we've been married twenty-seven years now in 1995. I honestly believe that our marriage couldn't have survived without our relationships with Christ. This is a very volatile business, and like a lot of professional sports, there's a lot of temptation out there. If God hadn't been my foundation, I probably would have faltered many times. Not that I haven't, but He is so forgiving. I don't want to keep asking Him for forgiveness every year. Fortunately, I haven't had to do that.

At one time, I would have said that it is harder being a Christian on this Tour than in regular life, especially without really understanding how God works. What I've had to understand since then is that He often sets us up to fail, because we learn a lot more from our failures than we learn from our successes.

The great thing about having a personal relationship with Christ is that it builds. It never really goes away. You may not build on it for a while, but it stays there—solid as a rock. You just keep putting a little more clay on it each time, and it gets larger and larger.

I think now, at age forty-five, I'm really starting to grow more. I don't feel like I've been the spiritual leader in my family, which I really should have been. I think that my wife has been more of the spiritual leader. She has had to stay very dedicated through her wives' Bible studies and things, because I think our wives tend to get pushed off into the shadows of a pro career. So we try to involve ourselves more in the things of the faith. We try to spend more of our time with Christian friends than non-Christian friends, although we have a lot of non-Christian friends.

I've never been comfortable with being an evangelist, so to speak, but I'm finding myself getting more comfortable with sharing my joy with the people around me. For instance, people often say, "I can't believe you've been on the Tour for so long. How do you do it?" I tell them, "I believe that God has a plan for me, and I just leave it in His hands every year."

Of course, I sure wish He'd quit making it so hard! If He wants me to stay out here, I wish He'd let me know by about April every year instead of running it out to August or September! Then again, maybe that's His way of keeping my eyes open.

I think probably the most satisfying thing to me about this life is that my two kids have grown up to be Christians. My son, who was nineteen in 1994, has the most marvelous disposition and love for Jesus.

My daughter grew up a little bit more rebellious, but now she's active in a church in Dallas. Not that that's the answer—just to get up and go to church on Sunday mornings—but you've got to make the first step. I'm so thrilled, and I give my wife all the credit.

I'll say this—and I've said it over and over—I married absolutely as well as I could. My wife is wonderful. God had it in my plan early, I guess, because I found a sweetheart. I think you need a wife with a strong backbone when on the Tour, because I'll tell you what: We don't treat them well at times. I'll admit that right out. I don't abuse my wife, of course—I never would. But I think I abuse her in the sense of the stress I probably impart to her from what I do. I have to apologize a lot—and immediately—"Honey, I'm sorry I bit your head off because I'm unhappy with the way things are going on the golf course." And I love her very much. She's a dandy.

Still, along the way, God's had to call me down a few times. I used to have a temper on the golf course, and my mouth—well, I said a few expressions that would have made sailors blush. I'm never happy with myself when I do that. I recently read *The Screwtape Letters,* and I'm finally learning a little about how the devil works! Larry Moody gave me that book, and I later told him, "That's the hardest reading I've ever done in my life."

Do you find the younger players receptive to this message?

I find that we have to go to them. There are a couple of players right now we're working on, because I see them struggling, and I think, *If they'd just open up their hearts a little bit, that struggle would get somewhat easier.* I'm not guaranteeing that if you say, "Oh, I'm going to go to the Bible study and accept Jesus" that you're going to play better golf. That's never a guarantee. But I'll tell you what—you'll have a greater peace about you. I have such a great peace now that whatever I'm going to do, it's in the Master's plan. That's what He wants me to accomplish. And I'm happy with that.

On the other hand, I do speak to kids all the time. I recently spoke to a bunch of junior golfers in Houston, and I said, "I don't care how long your hair is. And I don't really care if you've got an earring. But what I do care about is that you have Jesus Christ right here in front of you. And if He is right here in front of you, then that's really my concern for your life. If you were my son or daughter, we'd have to have a little 'do-better talk' about that earring! But you're not. You're a child of God, and He's looking after you. And if you'll put Him in your life, then okay, I guess you can do what you want to as far as your looks!"

I try not to judge people by their looks, even though we are so ingrained to do that. It's hard not to sometimes. Likewise, I try not to judge other people about what I think they're doing right or wrong, even within my church.

When I'm home I get together a lot with my Sunday school class. They have a weekly Bible study, which I'm never home for. It doesn't matter—they stay in touch; they're a great encouragement for us. You never realize, as an athlete, how people put you up on this pedestal. The greatest compliment to me is to go somewhere and have people come up and say, "Thank you for being here. It just means so much to see someone who goes out and plays for millions of dollars and does whatever he wants to in life take the time to stop and say, 'Hey we're really all the same—in One Person's eyes.'"

Memorable Moment

I think the most exciting moment for me happened when I was about three years into my career and struggling. I was at the B.C. Open with Rik and Cindy Massengale. Rik, as you may know, has the college golf ministry. Rik was on top of the world then: he'd won the Bob Hope Desert Classic, and Chrysler was his sponsor. He even drove this great big Imperial. I remember we were sitting in that Imperial one evening in a hotel parking lot, and I was almost in tears over the way my life and my golf career were going. When you are out here, your life is totally controlled by how well you're doing on the Tour.

Rik really had a great talk with me. It has been so long it is hard to recall the specifics, but he reiterated over and over: "You've just got to let God guide you. If you'll let Him guide you, then you're going to do the right thing. Some of the things may not look right, but at least when you get through with something, you're going to have that peace about yourself. And that's all you can ask."

Whether you win or lose, if you walk off and say, "You know, Lord, I did everything I could today. I just didn't quite have it"—then you're on the right path. And Rik made sure I was.

I recently saw *Forrest Gump*, and at one point he says, "Some days you just don't have enough rocks." Well, some days, you really don't have enough rocks. That's the way I feel now after a bad round. I'm upset, but I did the best I could, and I'll get over it in about five minutes. It doesn't take long.

Anyway, I went on and played pretty well the rest of the tournament, and the next year I finished third at that same event. I double bogeyed the final hole to lose!

I've always said, "Sometimes you have to get so far down that the only way to look is up." And you have to look up to the right Man.

Tip

I led the Tour in driving accuracy in 1992 and 1993 and finished tied for third in 1994, so I've always prided myself on being able to drive the ball straight.

Photograph by Pete Fontaine/PGA TOUR

I think it is because I have a very compact swing; I don't have a swing that has a lot of movements.

I'm also very target oriented. When I walk up to look at a hole, I try to decide where I'm going to drive the ball in the fairway, and I try to set up on the tee box accordingly. A lot of people tend to walk up and go to the middle of the tee box and hit their tee shot. But if you realize that you've got a tee box that's as much as fifteen yards wide, by starting on the right side, you can make the fairway bigger, depending on the type of shots you're trying to hit.

So you should always gauge that if you hook the ball, you probably want to tee up on the left side, because it gives you a bigger target. If you fade it, you want to tee up on the right side because that makes your target area that much bigger.

Also, I don't try to overpower the ball. My swing is not a real easy one, but it is not a hard one either.

Then I just try to do the same thing every time.

I really concentrate while driving on picking out a target and focusing on that target. Then I try to walk into the shot each time. That's really the best tip I can give to any amateur golfer. You've got to look at your target, keep your eyes on the target until you get set up, and then really concentrate on trying to put the ball in a specific spot. And don't try to overpower it. I think that's what makes me a good driver.

As for my swing, I make a kind of restrictive turn. I don't get the club parallel with the ground. Instead, I try to release in the lower body and really drive through the ball, getting a lot of the power from my hands and forearms.

Stan Utley

IT'S HARD TO get Stan Utley rattled about his ups and downs on the golf course. When you've stood side by side with your neighbors lifting sodden sandbags to stop the flooding Missouri River, bad lies and dogleg threes pale by comparison. And when you've sat and hugged the kids at Rainbow House in Columbia (a safe house for children that Utley's "Go for the Gold" skins game benefits), sand traps don't seem quite so sinister anymore.

Utley's best year on the PGA Tour came in 1990, but he's dominated the NIKE Tour in the years he's played. For instance, in March 1995 he won the $36,000

Photo courtesy of PGA TOUR

Louisiana Open in Broussard by a comfortable margin. And the two-time All-American has never forgotten his Tiger roots and remains an avid supporter of Missouri athletics.

My parents were both Christians, and I grew up in the Church of Christ tradition in Thayer, a small town in southern Missouri. My mom's side of the family—she has a sister and two brothers—are all Church of Christ. Going as far back as my grandparents, there have been no divorces on that side of the family. So there's been a great example set, and that had a big influence on my life.

My upbringing in the Church of Christ is very fundamental. We were taught that not only must you accept the Lord and ask for forgiveness, but you need to be baptized as well. I feel like I understood the principles at a very early age, but I was about fifteen or sixteen before I actually made that commitment, went up, and was baptized.

I think it was a decision I'd labored with for a long time, and I don't know whether I struggled with the commitment or simply the display of faith. Certainly, in my upbringing, I understood that it wasn't just good people going to heaven—there was an acceptance there that you had to make.

It was a great day in my life, and I certainly remember the circumstances. There was a preacher doing a revival, speaking every evening for a week. A couple of us went up that night, including a friend of mine. It was a great day.

As far as pressures from being a Christian, I think I dealt with those early on—even in high school—because I never drank or did drugs. You have to make those decisions early on, because either you're going to or you're not going to. I found myself something of a loner in high school and college, because I was in a minority as far as that stand goes. But I also found myself being respected, especially in college among my golf team members. I played golf at Missouri, and they never pressured me; they always respected the fact that I made my choices and they made their choices. So I dealt with things like that early on, and they haven't been a problem since.

One of the interesting things about being out here on the PGA Tour is that I grew up in a small town and small church atmosphere, so I wasn't exposed to a variety of religions. I found out later that several Christian churches claim to be *the* church. Yet the Church of Christ people I grew up around felt like you needed to be a member of the Church of Christ in order to be saved. When you grow up with that belief, that's just something you accept.

The thing that's been enlightening on the PGA Tour has been being among strong Christians who didn't come up from the Church of Christ and yet are good Bible scholars, Christians who are stronger in their faith than I might be.

And the more I learn, the less I judge. That's kind of been my approach.

I have a church that I go to at home, one I've gone to for the last three or four years. It's a Bible church; it doesn't even have a title. And I like that! We have a great pastor who teaches from the Word, and I'm comfortable with that at this point.

I've felt very blessed being involved with the Bible study out on the Tour. I know in 1992, when I was off the Tour, I missed it. Even though they have the FCA Bible Study on the NIKE Tour, which I attended pretty regularly, Larry

Moody and David Krueger are about as strong as it gets when it comes to teaching from the Word. That's been a good influence out here.

The Tour is also interesting in that I wouldn't call it a close bunch of people. It's so businesslike, it's so ongoing, and there are so many demands on you. If you've got two or three couples you can go out to dinner with once a month— you're doing pretty well.

My wife travels with me on the Tour some, though not full-time, so we're really close and we do great—just the two of us. Out here, I can't say that there's been any big pressure put on me as a Christian, nor have I taken any harrassment at all.

Memorable Moment

Though I've only got one PGA Tour victory through 1994, it was as dramatic as it gets, from a career standpoint, because I've still yet to ever make it through Qualifying School. I've played five years on the mini-tours, and when I won the Chattanooga Classic in 1988, I was a mini-tour player playing on a sponsored exemption.

That totally changed my career path. It jumped me up two levels—almost at once! I felt prepared. I had been a consistent player on the mini-tours and felt like I was ready to come out here. But the day I won, the fashion in which I won, and the processes I went through to get to that point—to have them all happen at one moment was really special.

I'd made some big choices, as far as career goes, a year and half before that. I'd decided to go get a sports psychologist. First I went to my college coach, Richard Poe. He told me that there is a sports psychologist who is a track coach there at Missouri. I'd gone to Missouri for several years, and I never knew the track coach was also a sports psychologist!

His name is Rick McGuire and we set something up and went to work. That was in the fall of 1988. The first time I ever went into Rick's office, he made it clear that, from his standpoint as a sports psychologist, there were no quick fixes, and that his job was to make my life as comfortable as possible and to put me at ease in order for my talent to come out. Sometimes that's easy to do, and sometimes it's a hard thing. Obviously it is always changing.

He told me to go home and list my priorities in life and we'd start from there. Of course, coming from my background, that was easy. I could list my priorities from the word go. It was first, being a Christian; second, being a husband and having a family; and golf came down the list. That made his job easier because sometimes that's not the case, especially among professional athletes.

The really awesome thing is that Rick's also a Christian! And he's a strong Christian. We both go to the same church and he's very involved. We both are members of the same "care groups" at our church, where, instead of a midweek Bible study, the church is broken down into small groups. Our families are involved with the same group.

Another twist on the same topic: David Cook is also a sports psychologist at the University of Kansas, and *he's* also a Christian. So I got involved with two sports psychologists who are both very strong Christians. David is also one of the leaders in his church in Kansas.

So they told me, "Here's the way you live your life according to the Bible. These principles work!" That's a powerful place to come from!

And as I approached victory in Chattanooga, I was really strengthened from what I'd learned from those two people, particularly since I'd only met David about three weeks before the tournament! But he'd given me a mental routine that I used during that tournament and still use quite a bit.

So it all came together on that day. My wife was there, and it happened that my parents were at that tournament, and they almost never get to come to my tournaments since they both work. But my dad loves golf, and he would rather play golf and travel and watch me than work. We were among friends and family, and suddenly we won some money, and we were on the Tour! And that's definitely my most special moment on the Tour.

Since then I've had lots of ups and downs. I played pretty steadily after that for a couple of years, but then my 1992 season was horrible. I can't see getting through that the way I did without being a Christian. I believe that. It was a year that was so difficult. But through it all, my wife and I got stronger, and our marriage got stronger. I leaned on her, and she was there to hold me up. I think our faith has been strengthened through those experiences.

The NIKE Tour in 1993 was wonderful—everything went as good as could be planned. But being back on the PGA in 1994 was a struggle again. It had its ups and downs. But it was a far different struggle than in 1992, because in '92 I was extremely confused, and my golf game was very poor. In 1994 it wasn't quite like that. There were different reasons for not doing as well.

Tip

My strength has always been my short game. The clinic I like to give amateurs—and the only statistic where you'll find my name listed among the leaders in the media guide—is sand play.

The thing that amateurs don't understand about sand play is mostly the way the sand wedge was designed. It has a bigger flange on the bottom of it, and it is designed to help you get the ball out of the sand.

The thing that an amateur has to realize is that he doesn't have to enter the sand with the leading edge of the club. He needs to enter the sand back where the club peaks behind the leading edge. This is called "bounce," and you can look down and actually see that instead of there being a level slope on the sole of the club, the backside of the club is angled higher than the leading edge.

What amateurs need to understand is that they need to use that part of the club the same way they would skip a rock across water. If you throw a rock across the water, you make the back end of the rock hit the water, not the front end, and that keeps it skip-

Photograph by Sam Greenwood/PGA TOUR

ping. Amateurs need to learn how to enter the sand so that the backside of the club hits the sand first—and to apply the same principle of rock skipping to their sand shots.

If you can enter the sand two or three inches behind the ball and just go ahead and let that bounce splash the ball up out of the sand, your club won't stick in the sand. The sand moves the ball.

If you swing down, and the leading edge hits the sand first, it's going to dig and run right under the ball, and the ball is not going to come out very consistently. One time you may actually thin it up there just right, but another time it may only go four feet.

But if you can learn to use the backside of the club, you can swing very aggressively—and much harder—and the ball will just splash itself up in the air and out onto the green and land softly. We've all tossed a rock across the water, and I think that's something that may help amateurs a lot.

DeWitt Weaver

WE'VE GROWN TO expect excellence from the Weaver clan. DeWitt's father was a legendary football coach at Texas Tech, while DeWitt was a multisport letterman at SMU. As an amateur, he dominated Georgia golf before turning pro in 1964.

Photo courtesy of PGA TOUR

On the PGA Tour, Weaver was at his best in the early '70s, winning the 1971 U.S. Professional Match Play and 1972 Southern Open. In 1971, he finished in the top twenty-five in total earnings.

Weaver joined the Senior Tour in 1989 and almost immediately vaulted into the upper echelon of touring pros. He's already earned nearly two million dollars and taken home the winner's trophy at the 1991 Bank One Senior Classic. Weaver has led the circuit in eagles twice and has, in recent years, fired amazing rounds of 61 and 62 at different tournaments.

I was raised in a Christian environment, although we only went to church at Christmas and Easter. I believed in Christ, but I didn't really have a relationship with Him. I didn't really acquire that, or gain that, until I met my wife and a good friend of mine in the late '60s.

My wife, Sheri, was actually going to become a nun when I met her. She is probably the finest woman I've ever met; she did so much for me and brought me so much closer to the Lord. And while I was raised a Protestant, after meeting Sheri, I became a Catholic.

But I still really didn't have a personal relationship with Christ, and I was a selfish person. I wanted to play golf, and I wanted to do everything for myself. I was really selfish in the early stages of my career, when I was in my late twenties.

I was really struggling. I was smoking. I was drinking. I was missing qualifying cuts. I was really depressed and having a hard time. I was away from my family when I met a friend of mine out on the West Coast, Cobby Ware from Atlanta. I said, "Cobby, what do I need to do?"

And he said, "You just need to turn it over to the Lord. Give your life to Christ. You need a personal relationship with Christ. He'll lead you along. You're trying to do things on your own, you're struggling, and you're depressed. Put that responsibility on the Lord and really let Him lead you along."

I immediately understood what he meant. I had been trying to do that myself. I believed in Jesus Christ and knew that He was the Son of God and that He was going to save me, but I really didn't know to just turn my life over to Him. I was taking all of the responsibility on to myself and not giving it to the Lord. I didn't know that until that time, even though my wife was a Christian long before me. She already had a personal relationship with Christ, but I really didn't know how to get this relationship. I had to find out on my own by being at my lowest time.

Through my discussions with Cobby Ware, I began to understand what a personal relationship with Jesus Christ meant, and that gave me an opportunity to ask Christ into my life. Once I did that, it just seemed like a huge burden was lifted off me.

Cobby and Ramsey Gilchrist are now involved with our Tour Bible study group. They're the two leaders of our Tour Chapel. They come out and lead our Bible studies and Chapels and they're always there for us. They were with Bert Yancey's family in 1994 when he passed away, and they've been there when we've had problems or somebody is sick. They're wonderful people, and it really has been a great relationship to have them out on our Tour.

Isn't it difficult maintaining your Christian faith in the fishbowl life of professional golf?

I don't think it is all that tough. Some people may look at you differently. Some players look at me differently, but they knew me back when I wasn't this way.

All I want to project is love. I love my family. I love everybody out there on the Tour. If sometimes they think I am trying to gain favor by being the way I am, all I can say is that I truly love everybody on this Tour. I love the game of golf.

And mostly I love Christ for doing what He did for us. I know we're going to be with our friends and our loved ones forever and ever.

My wife travels with me, and all three of my sons and my son-in-law have caddied for me. It has been a wonderful family experience. On my PGA Tour I had to leave them and go out on my own, which was a hard, hard thing. I gave up the Tour in 1976 because of that.

Now, I don't pretend to be perfect by any means, and none of us ever will be, but I really try hard. I always ask the Lord to lead me along the way. I gave my life over to Him to guide me. And still we are tempted by the devil, and things happen that aren't really Christlike. But we're always forgiven by the Lord. And things get so much better, and we're less and less tempted, because the Lord's never going to put anything in front of you that's more than you can handle.

Memorable Moment

In 1971 I was at my daughter's house. She had a tremendous influence on me because she became a Christian at Black Rock Mountain FCA Camp back in high school, and she came back just beaming. And she's continued to beam.

Anyway, I was at her house, and up on the wall was a plaque that said, "Delight yourself also in the LORD, / And He shall give you the desires of your heart" (Ps. 37:4).

It made such an impression that, still to this day, I inscribe that on all my golf balls. I give them away to people. It has come back to me in a lot of ways.

I keep that in mind and put that on my golf balls because it always gave me an inner peace when I saw that. It always reminded me that the Lord is with me at all times, regardless of whether I'm winning, regardless of whether I'm playing well or not. It always gives me peace. And if you have that peace, you're able to play to a level of ability you wouldn't believe.

I've played with Lee Trevino in both Tours, and he's had a tremendous change of heart. He has a new family, a new set of values, and I truly believe that the man is a real Christian. And now he talks about the Lord.

It all began when we were playing together not long ago and he looked down at my golf ball where I had inscribed "Psalm 37:4" on it. Then we got into a conversation about what life is all about—as opposed to just golf.

Lee Trevino used to be entirely golf oriented. That was his whole life. All he ever did was golf, golf, golf. And now he has a family. And he truly has a pure heart, where before, golf was all there was to life. I think the man is truly at peace now, much more than he ever was.

And that quotation on those golf balls gave me an opportunity to discuss that with him.

As for the Tour, back in 1991, I finished third in Atlanta and won $50,000. Then I went up to Lexington the next week, and I played the last three holes and two holes of a play-off to beat J. C. Snead to win the tournament.

And the whole time, all I thought about was walking with the the Lord in peace. Not for His favor, but for His glory.

T i p

It's all balance in golf. Balance is a very important part of the golf swing. It's a transfer of true weight to the right side. If you'll notice, all baseball players are 100 percent on their right side, setting up, ready to hit a baseball. That is the same place a golfer has to be for his backswing. You're making a shift to your right side and actually getting behind the ball. And from that position, you're swinging up and down the line. And once you move your weight forward, you're moving everything into it, and the club will square up right at impact every single time.

Photograph by Pete Fontaine/PGA TOUR

So many golfer's balance works opposite. They sort of reverse tilt or bend forward going back, and when they come through, they appear to fall backward trying to lift the ball in the air.

A ball has to be hit down in order for it to go up, and hit up to go down. It's just like shooting a cue ball. If you hit the top of the ball, it's going to turn over and roll forward. If you hit down on it, it is going to go up. It's the same idea in golf. And it will help a person's balance to move through from the left side, hitting down while the ball goes up—staying in perfect balance.

You can put both feet together. A great example is Jim Albus. The idea is to put both feet together on the right side, standing together, and step into the ball like a batter does in baseball.

Use a batting tee occasionally, and hit some balls off it. If you can ever get to the point where you can hit it solidly off a batting tee, you'll never miss one off the ground. If you swing at a ball on a raised tee, you're going to hit underneath it every single time. If you learn to hit through it, and hit the ball solidly, you'll really improve your game.

Kermit Zarley

KERMIT ZARLEY DOESN'T look a heck of a lot older than he did when his University of Houston team won the 1962 NCAA Championships. Clean living and weightlifting are two of his secrets.

Zarley is another one of those rare individuals who has succeeded on both Tours. As a member of the PGA Tour in the '60s and '70s, he won both the 1968 Kaiser International and the 1970 Canadian Open. Before quitting the PGA, he earned three quarters of a million dollars.

When Zarley joined the Senior Circuit full-time in 1991, he hadn't played competitively since 1987. No matter. Zarley has reeled off seasons of $341,647, $414,715, and 1994's $538,274, to reclaim his rightful place among the game's elite.

Photo courtesy of PGA TOUR

I was born and reared in Seattle. I didn't come from a churchgoing family, but during my preteens my dear mother consistently got me and my two sisters off to Sunday school.

When I was thirteen, a Sunday school teacher led me to faith in Christ. Gordy was a college student and a golfer, and I liked him. He had our class memorize ten verses in the New Testament.

Up to that time, I thought that if I just tried to live a good life, surely God would accept me. But one of those ten verses had me perplexed. It said, "For by grace you have been saved through faith, and that not of yourselves; it is the gift of God, not of works, lest anyone should boast" (Eph. 2:8-9).

So one day after class, I asked Gordy about these puzzling things. He said that God would forgive us of our sins and give us eternal life if we would accept His Son, Jesus Christ.

Then Gordy reviewed the last verse we had memorized. In it, Jesus says, "Behold, I stand at the door and knock. If anyone hears My voice and opens the door, I will come in to him and dine with him, and he with Me" (Rev. 3:20).

Gordy said this meant that Jesus was standing outside the door of my life, wanting to come in and have fellowship with me. He then asked, "Would you like to accept Jesus into your life?" I said yes, and we said a prayer together.

That is when I believe Jesus came into my life and I was born again. I have always regarded that as the most important decision of my life.

We soon moved away from that church, and I no longer attended Sunday school. It wasn't until I went to college at the University of Houston that I started growing in the Christian life by getting involved with other athletes who were meeting together for Bible study and prayer.

Is it tough being a Christian on the Senior Tour?

In trying to follow Christ, I've always believed that it helps a lot to gather together with other believers for worship, prayer, fellowship, and Bible study to hear the Word of God. But in pro golf we play on Sunday, so that makes it difficult to go to church. However, we have a weekly meeting called the Senior Tour Chapel, and that serves as church for some of us.

One thing that's been kind of remarkable in professional athletics is the number of athletes who have made their profession of Jesus public. They're doing it in all of the sports, all of the time. I guess that it is part of an evangelistic movement that has been going on in our country for many years.

That's something that didn't exist when I started on the PGA Tour in 1964. You rarely saw it in professional athletics.

Other golfers credit you with starting the PGA Tour Bible study group in 1965.

Babe Hiskey and I started it, with the help of Babe's brother Jim Hiskey—and they remain two of my closest friends to this day. Jim saw what was happening in baseball with the baseball chapel, which is where organized Christian witness started in professional sports in this country in the early '60s. The Bible study group on the regular Tour has had its ups and downs, but it has continued through all of the years, and it has affected a lot of people's lives. It is attended by players and their wives and led by certain recognized players.

Babe and I are thrilled to see that what we started thirty years ago continues to thrive even more today. In addition, many of the players who attend nowadays have won major championships in pro golf, which didn't happen much in our days.

After you quit playing the Tour, what did you do?

I quit playing the regular Tour in 1982 and started the Senior Tour in late 1991. I played very little golf during that nine-year period. I conducted some private golf schools, did golf outings, did public speaking for Christian organizations, and worked with groups like Links Fellowship (formerly Golf Fellowship). And due to my strong interest in Bible study, most of the time I spent researching and writing theological books. I've had three books published: *The Gospels*, *The Gospels Interwoven,* and *Palestine Is Coming.*

Memorable Moment

My first Tour win on both the regular Tour (1968) and the Senior Tour (1994) were both at the same place—Silverado Country Club in Napa, California— twenty-six years apart. Two of my three children—Michael and Christy—have been caddying for me on the Senior Tour. They refuse to ride carts.

Christy was the bag toter at Napa when I won. On the ninth hole of the last round, I hit my ball into the edge of the water, submerged about a foot deep. When we approached the ball, I was groaning about how close it came to being a good shot and a possible eagle opportunity.

Christy blurted out, "Aw, c'mon, Dad—you can play it." I looked at the twinkle in her eye and busted out laughing. That humor seemed to ease the tension.

I then hit a great pitch shot over the water to save par and went on to beat Isao Aoki in a play-off. Moments in golf that I will treasure most are probably not winning tournaments, but experiences like that with my children.

Tip

I think the best golf tip I've ever heard is what Joe DiMaggio once told me. I had the privilege of playing golf with him in the pro-am at Doral in 1971. He had a nice, smooth swing and drove the ball super that day. I said, "Joe, what was the most important thought that you ever had when you hit a baseball?"

I waited breathlessly, expecting some gem of wisdom to come out of his mouth, perhaps some secret I had never heard of before that I might apply to golf.

Joe said, "Oh, I think it is the same thing in golf: Keep your eye on the ball."

Yeah, sure, Joe—now who hasn't ever heard of that? I thought. In my mind, I wasn't giving this great one his due respect. I'd heard that tip all my golfing life. But I soon came to realize that Joe was so right—and I'd never given the idea enough credit.

We golfers can get pretty uptight about where we're going to hit that little pellet. If we take our eyes off the ball before it is struck, that causes our body to prematurely straighten up and leave the clubface open at impact. Pros call that a blocked shot—the ball starts right of the target and slices.

I have a drill where I turn my head to the right so I'm looking at the ball more with my left eye. That helps you have a more full shoulder turn in your backswing. It also keeps your eye on the ball a little longer.

I think of how it's the same way in the Christian life. Keeping our eyes on the ball is like

Photograph by Pete Fontaine/PGA TOUR

"looking unto Jesus, the author and finisher of our faith" (Heb. 12:2). But when we take our eyes of faith off of Jesus, we don't have that solid contact with God and therefore block out our spiritual life. If we'll just keep looking at Jesus' life and words in the New Testament, we'll stay right on target.

About the Authors

Robert Darden is the author of sixteen books, including *Too Close to My Heart* (with Mary Darden); *Into the Endzone, Interviews with 25 Christians in the NFL;* and *The Option Play.* He was for ten years the gospel music editor for *Billboard* magazine and is currently the editor of *The Door* (formerly *The Wittenberg Door).* He and his wife, Mary, live in Waco, Texas, with their three children, Daniel, Rachel, and Robert Van.

P. J. Richardson is the president of Tanglewood Holdings, Inc. He is active in the Fellowship of Christian Athletes and is well-known in golfing circles. He and his wife, Billie, live in Frederick, Maryland, and have two children, Terrance and Michael.